Between Two Rivers

Ancient Mesopotamia and the Birth of History

Moudhy Al-Rashid

hodder
press

First published in Great Britain in 2025 by Hodder Press
An imprint of Hodder & Stoughton Limited
An Hachette UK company

3

A CIP catalogue record for this title is available from the British Library

Hardback ISBN 9781529392128
Trade Paperback ISBN 9781529392135
ebook ISBN 9781529392159

Typeset in Bembo MT by Hewer Text UK Ltd, Edinburgh
Printed and bound in Great Britain by Clays Ltd, Elcograf S.p.A.

Hodder & Stoughton policy is to use papers that are natural, renewable
and recyclable products and made from wood grown in sustainable forests.
The logging and manufacturing processes are expected to conform
to the environmental regulations of the country of origin.

Hodder & Stoughton Limited
Carmelite House
50 Victoria Embankment
London EC4Y 0DZ

The authorised representative in the EEA is Hachette Ireland, 8 Castlecourt Centre,
Castleknock Road, Castleknock, Dublin 15, D15 YF6A, Ireland (email: info@hbgi.ie)

www.hodderpress.co.uk

ana labbī libbīya

Contents

CONTENTS

Introduction

Mesopotamia Matters

A stepped pyramid soars almost 100 feet above the sprawling ruins of the city of Ur, which once sat at the mouth of the Euphrates River in the sandy expanse of what is now southern Iraq. The meandering waters of the river changed course millennia ago, leaving the inhabitants of Ur with no choice but to abandon the desiccated site. In what remains of this ancient city, in the shadow of the pyramid, lie the ruins of a small palace built for a princess over 2,000 years ago. For those millennia, most of Ur has remained buried; only after careful excavation did it start to reveal its many ancient secrets.

When excavators began to uncover the princess's palace in the 1920s, they found a seemingly ordinary chamber with an eroded but otherwise intact brick floor. That floor was so covered in layers of dust and ancient rubbish that the diggers initially doubted they would find a single relic of its long-gone inhabitants. But over the course of several days, they managed to clear away enough of the rubble to reveal an extraordinary collection of artefacts. To their confusion, though, each object they found was from a different era in Ur's past, rather than all of them dating to the time when the palace was built. Why would this apparently random mix of objects, with hundreds of years between them, all be together in one room? The excavators were facing an archaeological puzzle.

Every archaeological dig begins on the surface. In a previously undisturbed site, the land looks distended, like a belly pregnant with possibility. Maybe only a broken brick, jagged pottery shards, and flecks of bitumen hint at what lies below the layers of sand and soil. It is these hints, however, that show that the mound of earth, or *tell* in Arabic, is not a geological feature of the landscape. It is not a hill or some other thing that has almost always been there; beneath this unassuming mass of dirt lie multitudes of stories that time has buried.

At a dinner many years ago, a man I barely knew asked me why we had to *dig* to find archaeology. It felt a bit like he was annoyed at me personally that the field of archaeology was not easy. Why are the buildings not on the surface? Why is the stuff so deep and difficult to get to? Every question in what quickly began to feel less like a conversation and more like a cross-examination had the same frank answer: people's stuff. Wherever there are people, there is their compacted trash. A mud house gets rebuilt atop the foundations of an older crumbling one, the broken bits of the inhabitants' things get buried under the new building or over time spill into the road outside, and that road gets repaved a few inches higher than the previous road, over and over again, locking into place clues about the people who inhabited each layer. In the case of Ur, deposits reach 65 feet below the visible hints at civilisation on the surface.

Archaeologists love exactly this kind of garbage. An archaeologist 5,000 years from now sifting through my bin would find, among other things, some overzealous Amazon packaging, the discarded top of a yogurt pot, and an empty packet of dog treats. They might conclude that I had a more or less domesticated dog, was not lactose intolerant, and worshipped a deity called 'Amazon' whose iconography included a faceless smile capped by an arrow at one end (or, according to comedian Jimmy Kimmel, a stylised penis). You can learn a lot about a culture from the things its people throw away, and the layers left behind are precisely why we have to dig.

But some monuments tower so high that they remain immune to the accumulation of detritus from the lives of those long since dead. In the case of Ur, the stepped pyramid – called a ziggurat – never fully disappeared under the dirt like much of the city. Thousands of years after its first bricks were laid, it still stood, with less obvious buildings buried at its feet. The princess's palace had been built in its shadow in the sixth century BCE when the princess was alive and Ur was a flourishing city in a region known as Mesopotamia – a name that comes from the Greek meaning 'between the rivers', as the area was nestled between and around the fast-flowing River Tigris and the languorous Euphrates. The name for the region in Arabic, *bilad bein al-nahrein* – 'the land between two rivers' – also invokes the Tigris and Euphrates, highlighting the importance of these life-giving bodies of water to the many ancient civilisations that rose and fell here over millennia.

But while the palace dated to the sixth century BCE, the

collection of objects found within the room all came from wildly different eras. Excavators found a small dark stone obelisk dating to around 1400 BCE – almost a millennium before the palace was built. The stone was carved with the iconography of various deities, symbols, and mythical monsters, and it recorded a long-dead man's ownership of property in the city, like an illustrated stone title deed. Elsewhere in the room was an even older item, a cone made from clay and covered in the wedge-shaped characters of cuneiform script, the writing system used throughout ancient Mesopotamia. The inscription, written around 1900 BCE, commemorated some building work by a man named Kudur-Mabuk, who dedicated the home improvements to the gods. Dating to the same era, the excavators found several clay tablets with the telltale, messy handwriting of young kids – typical school exercises, pressed into clay. As the team continued, they also found part of a statue of a king known to have ruled around 2100 BCE, as well as the round granite head of a weapon called a mace, which appeared to pre-date both the clay cone and the statue fragment. How did these objects, with thousands of years between their original makers and their final resting place, come to be here? What circumstances could have led to such a disparate collection of objects under a single roof?[1]

It would have been like finding a sculpture of the Greek god Zeus alongside bronze Islamic coins minted by a seventh-century caliph in a castle built by Christian Crusaders in Jordan, or a Roman dagger with Celtic coins amid the remains of a medieval monastery in England. As I explained to my curious dinner companion, archaeological sites are like rainbow layer cakes, with each coloured layer representing a different time period – newest on top and oldest at the bottom. If these objects had lain undisturbed, relegated to their own timelines, they would have been buried under layers of debris far deeper than the unbroken floor of this small palace chamber in the appropriate layer of the cake. Yet, here they were, out of place and out of time, like a patchwork instead of a rainbow. The 1920s excavation team were confounded: what could it mean?

Some explanations make for less sensational headlines than others. Archaeology is imperfect, and some of the older objects found in the debris may have simply ended up there by some accident of preservation. A slab of flooring could have crumbled in just the right way to reveal something from an era buried further below, or a wall made of reused materials could have collapsed. Alternatively, the chamber could have been an organised storeroom, where artefacts found in the building's foundations or environs were collected for safekeeping. After all, ancient Mesopotamia's sixth-century BCE inhabitants already had millennia of history to contemplate.

Ancient Mesopotamia and its cities like Ur were home not to a single civilisation, but to various peoples and cultures in antiquity. The Sumerians, Babylonians, and Assyrians were among those who lived in and around these two rivers thousands of years ago, so the whole region is thickly layered with the remnants of past civilisations. When the princess's palace was built, Ur would have been, without a doubt, one of the most important of the many cities in that very long history. Continuously occupied for almost three and a half millennia, the city covers an area of at least 120 hectares (295 acres), more than twice the size of Vatican City, but at its largest might have been a sprawling 500 hectares (1,250 acres), about one and a half times the size of Central Park in New York.[2] It would have been a major cultural hub as well as a vital port on what is now the Persian, or Arabian, Gulf at a time when the coastline cut further inland than it does today.

The 1920s archaeologists were of course aware of this long history, and likely had this in mind when they eventually found a clue amid the rubble that would help make sense of the mysterious collection. A cylindrical lump of clay covered in cuneiform script, like a little drum small enough to fit in the palm of your hand, gave them the answer they needed. They were convinced that they had found the world's first ever exhibition label and, by extension, the world's first museum.

Someone recently asked me why people today should care about ancient Mesopotamia, and my brain did this helpful thing that it does when too many thoughts crowd together at once. It froze. Why should we care about the region that gave us some of the world's firsts, like writing and the wheel?

For thousands of years, the civilisations of ancient Mesopotamia shared the world's earliest known writing system, cuneiform, which gets its name in English from the Latin *cuneus*, meaning 'wedge', for its wedge-shaped characters. It's thanks to this early writing system that we know so much about the people who lived and died in this part of the world, and its inception marks a turning point in human history. Before cuneiform begins to preserve moments in the lives of people in ancient Mesopotamia, people left behind a multitude of things to give us insights into their lives and values. From the tiniest stone tools and fragments of pottery to megaliths that may have once formed the world's first temples, we can learn a lot about the inhabitants of the distant past. Writing overlays a whole new dimension onto what we can learn about them *in their own words*. It marks the beginning of written history, the transition from what has sometimes been called 'prehistory', a dated term for periods that pre-date writing, and the beginning of 'history', the point at which things begin to be written down.

To some, cuneiform marks the birth of 'history' understood in this way. Personally, I think that anything that came before us is history, written or not, but cuneiform does mark a birth of history in one important sense. Writing allowed the people of ancient Mesopotamia to begin to record their own past, to put into words a collective memory of people, places, and events. They made lists of their kings, including kings so ancient they live on only in legend, and they memorialised their wars. They left behind the first rough drafts of economic history in their unremarkable receipts, as well as self-conscious accounts of their deeds for posterity. Writing gives birth to a written record of their past, which even expands to include eras so ancient to them that no memory of them survives – a primeval past populated by deities and an earlier iteration of humanity, a Mesopotamian 'prehistory' of life between the two rivers. In this sense, the birth of cuneiform is also the birth of history.

Cuneiform preserves almost all aspects of life in ancient Mesopotamia. This wedge-shaped writing preserves historical turning points, such as some of the earliest known diplomatic correspondence (which included the famous boy-king Tutankhamun) and the death of Alexander the Great. Alongside these turning points appear traces of people's everyday lives, like advanced maths, tax evasion, a bickering couple, a midwife's presence at the birth of a baby boy, and a rollercoaster ride of a horoscope for a child born in April 263 BCE.[3] We can read a princess's letter to her sister-in-law telling her to do her home-work, or an astronomical textbook that records observations of lunar eclipses, or a lapis lazuli cylinder that immortalises the name of a Sumerian queen, as well as countless receipts for beer. This random list barely scratches an obscure square inch of the top of a sizeable iceberg. It actually beggars belief just how much we can learn about the people of ancient Mesopotamia.

From the stories and snapshots left behind in clay, we know that these ancient people were not so different from any of us. A beautiful Babylonian lullaby finds a parent desperate to comfort a crying baby:

> Little one, who dwelled in darkness,
> now you've come and seen the sun.
> Why the crying? Why the worries?
> What has made your peace undone?[4]

My daughter and I got Covid in early 2021, and I remember cradling her in the middle of the night while both our fevers raged. She was barely eighteen months old, and I sang 'Twinkle, Twinkle, Little Star' softly on repeat in her pitch-black room. She was the miracle baby I never thought I'd have, so even dark and feverish nights like this one felt like a gift with her hot cheek on my shoulder and her tiny breaths against my neck. This lullaby reminds me that we have been singing to sleepless toddlers and babies for a very long time.

A broken chunk of clay preserves part of a story about Babylonian students sitting an exam at school around the same time the princess's palace was built in Ur. I can imagine them squirming on their wooden benches with wet tablets and reed styluses in hand. Even thousands of years later, it is hard not to relate to their stress. 'Do not constantly be afraid, do not let your throat tighten,' their teacher advises. 'Your mouth should not be full of complaints, your attention should not be directed toward the door.'[5] Moments like these forever live in the little wedges pressed into clay that historians piece together to let the people of ancient Mesopotamia speak. The past may be a foreign country, but these moments don't feel far away. They don't feel like they belong to strangers.

Cuneiform is a reminder that if I can find something in common with someone who lived well over 2,000 years ago, then I can certainly find something in common with almost anyone alive today. Cuneiform is a reminder of all the big and little things that go into our shared humanity. We are more than the sum of our differences.

The earliest cuneiform tablets come from the city of Uruk, not far from Ur, and were written in roughly 3350 BCE, around the time that Stonehenge might have been built and seven centuries before the great Pyramid at Giza. At the other end of the scale, the most recent cuneiform tablet that we know of is an astronomical almanac from 79–80 CE, also found in Uruk. This sweeping span of time also gives a sense of the huge scale of history we're talking about when we consider Mesopotamia. Thanks to the durable nature of clay, hundreds upon hundreds of thousands of such tablets, covered in the tiny tetrahedrons that make up cuneiform script, have survived the millennia that separate their ancient makers from their modern readers. However, those modern readers have to do a lot of work to make sense of the stories left behind. We have to reconstruct the history of ancient Mesopotamia from eroded fragments scattered throughout multiple museums and collections. Even for those broken bits of clay that do fit together to tell something of a coherent story, large gaps remain, and countless more tablets lie beneath the unexcavated mounds of modern Iraq and Syria. It's like assembling a multi-million-piece puzzle with missing parts and no final image to work from.

Most of these tablets, broken or not, would fit comfortably in the palm of your hand, but some are as small as a thumb and others as large as a laptop. If you look closely enough – I mean, really closely – you can see the parallel grooves of a sharpened reed stylus pushed into the clay to make the impressed wedge of any cuneiform sign. Although sometimes compared to the footprints of a chicken, I think the script's geometry is beautiful and the myriad stories it tells us of those who lived and died along the banks of the Tigris and Euphrates thousands of years ago even more so.

I first learned about cuneiform as an awkward pre-teen in a history class at my elementary school in Saudi Arabia, and just over a decade later it re-entered my life quite by chance. I was in the process of applying to law schools when, on a whim, I attended a week-long course on ancient books in London. My little brother and I had to stop in London anyway en route home to the Middle East from America's East Coast, where we both lived at the time. We decided to turn our day-long layover in London into a week, so, like any normal twenty-something, I randomly signed up to an intensive course called 'The Book in the Ancient World', not expecting it to change my life.

On the first day an energetic man in a purple corduroy suit with a white beard down to his chest walked us through two rooms at the British Museum. His name was Irving Finkel, and he tapped his fingertip alarmingly hard on one glass display case in particular to point out a clay tablet that was about the size of his hand. On the little lump of dried clay was a drawing that looked to me like a circle with a bunch of triangles sticking out of it, interrupted here and there by brief lines of tiny triangle-shaped characters.

Finkel told us how he had essentially completed a clay puzzle and fixed together a fragmented part of this object to help reveal an ancient bird's-eye-view map of Babylonia and Assyria, empires that were criss-crossed by the Tigris and Euphrates rivers and encircled with a sea (the circle), surrounded by eight mythical regions (the triangles). This map, I later realised, told a long and ongoing story that begins with its maker in ancient Mesopotamia and finds new life millennia later with Hormuzd Rassam, the Mosul-born archaeologist who dug it up in 1881. The map's history eventually became intertwined with the bearded British curator standing before me, who helped piece parts of it back together. Its story and the story of Babylon get retold in every new interpretation of the schematic map of the ancient city (and there have been many interpretations).[6] Indeed, every object we looked at that day told such a tale, traceable from its inception in the ancient world to the moment it landed in a museum, whether abroad or closer to its original home.

Among the other artefacts I saw that summer morning – and have revisited since – was a foot-long clay barrel covered in neat cuneiform handwriting. Tucked in a crowded display case, that barrel-shaped clay 'document' records the rebuilding of the stepped pyramid at Ur by King Nabonidus, the last independent Babylonian king and father of the same princess who had lived in the palace where that mysterious collection of objects was found jumbled together in the 1920s. When I first saw the clay barrel that day, 3,000 miles from its original home, I did not know I would one day try to tell the story of the mismatched objects from that princess's palace at Ur, and, through them, a history of ancient Mesopotamia. I did, however, know that after just a few hours, I had fallen for cuneiform and was ready to sack off law school to read clay tablets for the rest of my life.

As well as the earliest known writing system, ancient Mesopotamia saw the birth of the world's first cities, the first historical records, some of the first large-scale agriculture and much else that went on to revolutionise societies around the world. The objects found in the princess's palace give us a unique lens onto this all-important region in human history. Each item from the mysterious collection reveals an aspect of society and culture, from early warfare to women's rights, and from the basics of early language to the foundations of science through complex communication with the gods. In each of the chapters that follow I will take one object from the collection as a way into a particular aspect of the region's history. This range of objects, each from a different era, will introduce the history of ancient Mesopotamia, and how its people understood their own history, allowing us to reflect on how we understand our own.

The idea of the museum and its place in Ur's history deserves some reflection, and Chapter 1 takes us through this ancient setting and its modern interpretation. The small clay cylinder, or 'clay drum', seen by the excavators as the world's first museum label dated to the 600s BCE, actually describes another object: a mud brick dated to 2100 BCE from the era of King Amar-Suen. This 'label' reproduces the *extremely* ancient inscription – ancient even to the clay cylinder's creator – that would have been stamped into the brick, although the brick itself was nowhere to be found in the collection. In Chapter 2, studying the supposed museum label and the long-dead language it reproduced introduces us to cuneiform as a writing system, to the languages cuneiform was used to write, and to the birth of written history. In Chapter 3, considering Amar-Suen's (now missing) brick itself takes us into the architecture of Mesopotamia's cities, the literal building blocks of social and political innovation and the symbolic power behind the humble brick. In Chapter 4, the remains of the statue of an ancient king provoke questions about the nature of leadership, both real and legendary. The school tablets found scattered throughout the palace will open a window onto education and the anxieties of student life in Chapter 5. Through the clay cone in Chapter 6, we explore how people communicated with divine forces and how they received messages from the gods in return – a constant dialogue that allowed people to build knowledge and lay the foundations of science. In examining the engraved stone obelisk in Chapter 7, we see that there's nothing new about the complex economic interplay of people, property, and profit. There, we bear witness to stories on each end of the socio-economic spectrum, from a royal crony who receives land from the king to a mother who fights for her enslaved children's freedom. In Chapter 8, the plain granite mace head that might have been older than everything else found in the princess's palace has much to tell us

about violence, warfare, and death, and how people memorialised and made sense of conflict.

Finally, in Chapter 9 we turn to the princess herself, a woman
called Ennigaldi-Nanna for whom the palace containing these
objects was built. The princess was the daughter of King
Nabonidus and she was the last in a long line of high priestesses
whose role was to serve the Babylonian moon god, Sîn.
Ennigaldi-Nanna would have wielded considerable secular and
religious power in Ur. In this chapter we will discover what
Ennigaldi-Nanna can tell us about the lives of working women
in ancient Mesopotamia, and in turn what other women can
tell us about her. Is it feasible that as well as a princess and
priestess, Ennigaldi-Nanna may have acted as a sort of curator
of this museum of ancient objects? What can we learn from her
about the nature of history itself, how and why we do history,
and how she and her forebears might have put it to use?

There is something special about beholding, and even
holding, an original object from long ago. When I first held
a cuneiform tablet, it felt like I was holding hands with the
ancient scribe who cradled the once wet clay to impress so
many cuneiform wedges – otherwise left undisturbed for
millennia before being dug up, dusted off, and studied. As
people today may value that connection with a person long
dead and their distant era, so too did the people of ancient
Mesopotamia. Whoever brought together those diverse artefacts from disparate eras had a sense of and respect for the
great age of those objects, and for the objects themselves.
What better way to connect with the past and its people than
to try to understand how they connected with their own
past? Throughout this book, we will explore not just the
history, but the *history of history* in ancient Mesopotamia.

𐎛

1

An Ancient Museum
and the History of History

Grainy greyscale photos often show C. Leonard Woolley, the lead excavator at Ur, hunched over an ancient artefact in knee-high boots and a tweed jacket against a backdrop of dusty brickwork. In the 1920s, Woolley's name was practically synonymous with Ur, where he led digs for over a decade. Almost unfailingly, photos of him preserve a look of deliberate, acute concentration; thick eyebrows bunched together above narrowed eyes as he stares into the distance or at the ground, perhaps even puzzling over the motley collection of objects he had found in the princess's palace.

'What were we to think?' wrote Woolley, in a detailed memoir of his years excavating Ur.

Here were half a dozen diverse objects found lying on an unbroken brick pavement of the sixth century B.C., yet the newest of them was seven hundred years older than the pavement and the earliest perhaps two thousand: the evidence was altogether against their having got there by accident.[1]

Among these bewildering finds was an object that Woolley called 'the key', for he believed it held the power to unlock the mystery of the collection – this was the same object excavators would later refer to as an exhibition label or museum label. This 'key' was a small cylindrical piece of clay that had been inscribed in the written dialect in use at the time the palace was built. Despite its unusual cylindrical shape, it was essentially a clay tablet – a written record of information. Its inscription described *another* object that was itself now nowhere to be found: a brick dated to around 2100 BCE (about 1,500 years before the construction of the palace) that had been covered with an inscription written in Sumerian, the earliest known written language that once dominated what is now southern Iraq.

The 'key' was in essence a record for posterity of the brick and its (re)discovery by the governor of Ur in ancient times (before it was then lost again). This is still common archaeological practice; Woolley and his team made thousands of similar records of what they found in the course of excavating Ur, millennia after the city turned to ruins. In an attempt to reprise the long-dead Sumerian language, the scribe who recorded the governor's find had also copied the brick's original inscription, but with a handful of errors. The language of the brick's inscription, after all, would have been as ancient to him as he is to us.

In Woolley's eyes, this awkward exhibition label explained the disparate collection of objects whose only common denominator was their antiquity. To him, they must have comprised a small museum – perhaps even the earliest approximation of a museum anywhere in the world. In a room so filled with debris they had initially doubted they would find anything at all, excavators had unearthed what seemed to them to have been a deliberately curated collection of local antiquities.

It might have seemed to Woolley like the only explanation, or perhaps just the most media-friendly one, but calling it a museum excludes other possibilities that are perhaps less exciting, but are equally, if not more, plausible. As centres of administration as well as the earthly home of deities, Mesopotamian temples typically had a number of storerooms for things like grain or wine. Could they have also had rooms to house older artefacts found during building works and renovations? Artefacts from earlier periods were also often reused for other purposes in later centuries. Most obviously, older bricks were typically incorporated into newer buildings, but other ancient objects also found fresh uses. Ancient statues of a Sumerian leader named Gudea were dug up and displayed in the forecourt of the palace of a much later king as *objets d'art*.

Woolley himself found evidence of something similar in the princess's palace. A small limestone relief from around 2100 BCE, carved ornately with divine icons, got reused as part of the arch of a nearby doorway that dates to her era and occupation of the building.[2] Some of the objects discovered by Woolley may have simply come from an earlier era and, through various accidents of preservation and erosion of walls or flooring, ended up on the same level. (Woolley was, however, careful to describe the brick flooring in the room as 'unbroken'.[3]) There are, in short, other ways to account for the collection of antiquities, ones that would not fare well as headlines for *The Conversation* or *Gizmodo*. 'Closet full of old stuff no one really knew what to do with uncovered in Ur' is not exactly clickbait.

So why did Woolley call it a museum? Could he have been viewing the collection through the lens of his own role as an archaeologist with an interest in the ancient world, or even as a curator at the Ashmolean Museum in Oxford? It is, after all, impossible to completely divorce one's own perspective from one's interpretation of evidence – one of many reasons why diversity in the field of history is essential. He may have similarly understood the collection in light of what he knew about Nabonidus and other kings who had shown a keen interest in history and archaeology. Could Woolley have felt pressured to give aspects of the Ur excavations a spin that would resonate with a wider population and, ultimately, secure further funding for the (often cash-strapped) dig? I think that might be too cynical. His conclusion that the collection was a museum appears in the official, academic excavation report of 1962, well after further funding was needed for the dig that shut down decades earlier, so it seems safe to discount money as his motivation for calling the collection of antiquities a museum.[4]

More likely, Woolley may have thought that the clay drum, the alleged exhibition label, was sufficient evidence to discount all other possibilities. It is undeniably an unusual object; its stumpy cylindrical shape, its content, and even the cuneiform characters it displays still give historians pause in dismissing the museum thesis altogether. Another object from the mysterious room also raises questions about deliberate curation: a fragment of the statue of an ancient ruler, King Shulgi. Although the statue is so damaged that no part of the king's likeness survives, the portion of the statue bearing an inscription appears to have been filed down to preserve only the text, as one might do in a museum as an act of curation. After pulling these objects one by one from the room, the idea of a museum may have seemed like the only feasible explanation.

It's worth bearing in mind, though, that archaeological excavations are organised chaos, so maybe the simplest if least satisfying explanation is that the objects were not found together at all. Tens, sometimes hundreds, of people scrape at the earth in squared-off ditches with trowels and tooth-brushes. Far from the booby traps and car chases of Indiana Jones, with nary a whip in sight, archaeology is gruelling work. The Ur excavations led by Woolley, a joint expedition sponsored by the British Museum in London and the University Museum in Pennsylvania (now Penn Museum), were one of the largest in the era of 'big digs' between the two world wars, and the first in the new nation-state of Iraq, which had only just been formed in 1920 in the aftermath of the fall of the Ottoman empire.[5]

The excavations at Ur, which began in 1922, took place over the course of twelve consecutive seasons with about 150–200 people on site at any given time, though this number occasionally swelled to about 300.[6] Woolley led the first eleven seasons of excavation, and Katharine Woolley, his wife, led the final field season, with Sheikh Hamoudi ibn Ibrahim as the main foreman throughout the twelve years. Other professionals at the site included architects, illustrators, and archaeologists such as Max Mallowan, husband of author Agatha Christie whose 1936 novel *Murder in Mesopotamia* features a character who is thought to be based on Katharine Woolley.[7]

Although Woolley oversaw the majority of the excavations himself, he also appointed the foreman Sheikh Hamoudi ibn Ibrahim who, together with his sons and another foreman named Khalil ibn Jadur, organised the local excavators. Unsurprisingly, one of the many challenges of archaeological excavation is the actual digging, which involves the removal of literally tons of dirt from a ruin. By Woolley's own reckoning, in the course of excavating the Royal Cemetery at Ur, for example, 'the daily output should average rather more than a cubic metre of hard soil, something above three-quarters of a ton, for every man employed'.[8] The sheer volume of earth being shifted around this delicate ruin is staggering to contemplate.

If excavations are dusty, multi-layered chaos, then post-excavation notes can display a disorder equally difficult to navigate. I discovered this myself on an archaeological survey of rock art carved onto the many faces of a limestone outcropping known as Jebel um Sanman in the desert of northwestern Saudi Arabia. Jebel um Sanman looks like a giant Bactrian camel asleep in the sand, as its two sandstone hills rise up to well over 3,000 feet at their tallest. The head of the expedition, Dr Maria Guagnin, had expected to find rock art on perhaps 100 rock faces along the small mountain's base, but we instead found as many in just the first morning.

Some images were carved into the rock hill itself, while others appeared on the hundreds of boulders that dotted its base. We assigned each panel a number and, for each one, filled out an information sheet including a sketch of the art, measurements, GPS coordinates, a brief written description of the contents, and the photo numbers generated by our cameras for all pictures taken. We worked in teams of two, and each night, when temperatures plunged to below zero, we sat on the marble floor of the unheated wedding reception hall where we also slept to enter the information into a database.

Less than one month later, Dr Guagnin called me to ask about a sheet I had filled out in the field. 'Its photo numbers go with a different sheet,' she said, 'so I just want to know if you happen to remember which photos actually go with it?' I had absolutely no idea. This was a two-week survey involving fewer than ten people and almost no digging – in other words, not a particularly complex project. But without pristine notes and matching databases, post-excavation analysis can become an obstacle course littered with inconsistent labels and unreliable memories.

The excavation notes from Ur, all of which have now been digitised, are meticulous. Detail, unfortunately, does not always translate to dependability. Each presentation of Woolley's analysis, from the notes messily scrawled onto excavation cards to his polished memoir, is an opportunity to deviate from what was originally observed and recorded. And deviate, they did. For example, Woolley gives three different findspots for the clay cone of Kudur-Mabuk across three different publications.[9] Such inconsistencies make it impossible to know exactly where the objects were found.

Excavators at Ur spent years uncovering the walled area that included the ziggurat and its surrounding buildings, including the *giparu*, which is the Akkadian name for the small palace where the museum was found and where Princess Ennigaldi-Nanna lived.[10] Among the tens of thousands of artefacts found across multiple years, can we really know for certain that this collection of objects was actually a collection at all? Given how much Woolley's museum conclusion has stuck, I think we can retain his label for now while acknowledging that other explanations also exist. The museum has become a part of how we talk about Ur, and it offers us a helpful shorthand for discussing a curious collection of objects and the insights they offer into a past that was distant even to Ennigaldi-Nanna.

At the same time, I think it's important to add that I don't think the answer to this question matters as much as Woolley and others might have thought. Even without this overarching label, the presence of this motley crew of objects – either together as a museum or separately as a range of artefacts from different periods – tells us something important: that the footprint of this place had an incredibly long history. This palace was in some ways a palimpsest for Ur's own millennia-long history of occupation, and it chronicles all the major civilisations that rose and fell in ancient Mesopotamia. The Akkadians, the Sumerians, the Babylonians, the Assyrians, and others all leave something behind in Ur, and the artefacts themselves offer a way into some really interesting themes in ancient Mesopotamia's rich history. We will continue to call it a museum but, museum or not, what matters is just how far back in time the city transported its ancient residents and can transport us today.

The sheer scale of historical time in ancient Mesopotamia can be dizzying, from its earliest Palaeolithic settlements, long before cuneiform writing was developed, to the centuries that follow Princess Ennigaldi-Nanna. But we must begin this story even further back than that in order to understand her ancient setting. Over the course of millions of years in what is now southern Iraq, the deposition of dead things deep inside the ground at the boundary between land and sea led to the formation of bitumen, a natural petroleum tar. It is so viscous that, unless heated or diluted in specific ways, it is immobile; unlike liquid crude oil, it cannot flow on its own. (The same processes that led to the formation of bitumen left vast deposits of crude oil below Iraq and neighbouring countries that have motivated such violent foreign interference in the region in modern times.) Black and thick, it bubbled up from beneath the fertile plains of ancient Mesopotamia, where the inhabitants of Ur and other nearby cities used it as an adhesive to make things like boats, baskets, and buildings. Fragments of a drainpipe from Ur show that its splintered pieces were once stuck back together with the naturally occurring tar in much the same way you might solder together pieces of pipe today. The tar fills a scar down the centre of a painted ceramic bowl, also from Ur, and on what's left of a statue from the same city, a thick layer of the dark substance connects a terracotta foot to the bottom of a terracotta leg. On a much larger scale in major building works, the water-resistant material was used to bind mud bricks together.

So ubiquitous was this sticky substance that it gave Ur its modern Arabic name *Tell al-Muqayyar*, meaning 'Mound of Pitch'. After the city was abandoned, just a century after Princess Ennigaldi-Nanna's lifetime, the ghost town of Ur lay untouched by anything other than the sand and soil that buried it to form a tell. Under the tell, whole eras lay preserved, and on its surface lay countless fragments of dried bitumen, inspiring the mound's modern name.

The mound itself preserves at least 3,500 years' worth of occupation in antiquity. Painted pottery, clay figurines, and minuscule carved seals survive from the time before written records. This era, from the late fifth to the early fourth millennium BCE (in other words, around 6,000 years ago), belonged to the Ubaid culture, which flourished in Ur for almost 1,000 years before the arrival of the Sumerians, whose civilisation would go on to dominate the region on and off until 2000 BCE. At the end of the fourth millennium BCE, about 5,000 years ago, the Sumerians developed new technologies such as irrigation agriculture – or agriculture that used irrigation techniques to overcome the vagaries of the weather – and writing to keep track of their resulting food surpluses. These developments helped settlements swell into the first cities, whose dense populations then began to stratify into social classes. A cemetery found just outside Ur yielded a treasure trove of artefacts from the lives of the early city's Sumerian elite. The gold jewellery of a queen, an elaborately carved mace head belonging to a king, and some of the oldest surviving musical instruments in the world were uncovered among the bodies.

Ur rose to prominence around 2300 BCE when Sumerian cities were conquered by King Sargon. He and his army came from a city called Akkad, the remains of which are yet to be found. Once the capital of this massive empire, the city's name appears in countless written records, from kings' accounts of their deeds to humdrum receipts. It was a social, political, and economic centre that in later periods comes to symbolise 'the world' in a sense and takes on mythical proportions. Kings continue to call themselves 'king of Sumer and Akkad' long after these political entities decline as a way of saying 'king of the world'. Despite its importance, the city's ruins remain buried, perhaps swelling below one of the many undisturbed tells in Iraq's landscape or beneath a bustling modern city, and archaeologists have no idea where to find it.

Sargon and his dynasty brought with them an entirely new culture and language, Akkadian, the earliest known Semitic language and a distant ancestor of the Arabic widely spoken in the region today. King Sargon's autobiography, recorded of course on cuneiform tablets, describes a rags to riches story of how he was born the illegitimate son of a priestess, abandoned as a baby, and left to float down the Euphrates in a basket – coated with bitumen to keep it waterproof – before rising to power in Akkad. As the new ruler of the region of Mesopotamia, he established the cult of the moon god in Ur, who was known in the Akkadian language as Sîn, but as Nanna in the language of the Sumerians (though both names were used, given that many of the people in the region were by this point bilingual, speaking both Akkadian and Sumerian).[11] In a move that would be replicated by subsequent kings for centuries, he installed his daughter, Enheduanna, in the role of high priestess in the city of Ur. The presence of the king's daughter in such a powerful symbolic and practical role helped bolster Sargon's dominance in southern Mesopotamia. Almost 2,000 years later, Ennigaldi-Nanna would find herself in the same role of high priestess to Sîn at Ur, with an equally fascinating legacy.

Sargon's empire didn't last long, however, declining about a century after its inception. In its wake came the Third

Dynasty of Ur, which saw a brief revival of the Sumerian language and culture. The dynasty's founder, King Ur-Nammu, launched construction of the huge ziggurat at Ur as part of an immense building campaign. The temple atop the ziggurat was christened the Etemenniguru, a Sumerian phrase that translates as 'House whose foundation bears a fearsome splendour'. Of the over seven million bricks used in the ziggurat's construction, many bear a stamped text in cuneiform that reads, 'Ur-Nammu, king of Ur, the one who built the temple of the god Nanna'. Building work of this scale would have been a massive logistical undertaking, requiring a well-organised administration team and specialist labourers who fashioned the bricks from mud set into wooden moulds. Some bricks were baked, but most were left to dry in the sun. One, which is on display in the British Museum, immortalises two paw prints of a dog who perhaps trudged over it in search of food while it lay in a line of other damp bricks. Dogs commonly helped their human companions in ancient Mesopotamia with hunting, healing, and even war.

Despite major accomplishments like the ziggurat's construction, the Third Dynasty of Ur only lasted a century, before two new civilisations rose to power: the Babylonians in the south and the Assyrians in the north. The ancient Assyrians would create a vast international trade network around 2000 BCE in the Old Assyrian period that prefigures the rise of their empire from c. 1360 BCE to 600 BCE, from the later Middle Assyrian into the Neo-Assyrian periods. Under King Ashurbanipal in the seventh century BCE, the Neo-Assyrian empire would become the largest the world had yet known. His royal library housed some of today's famous clay tablets, including chapters from the *Epic of Gilgamesh* that tells the story of a legendary king and his quest for immortality.

In the south, the Babylonians settled in for the long haul, though under the leadership of various dynasties who adopted their language and culture, much as the English throne remained 'English' regardless of whether it was controlled by the Normans, the Plantagenets, or the Tudors. The Old Babylonian period witnessed the first of these major dynasties, the Amorites, who came from the north-west, near modern-day Syria. Their king Hammurabi would leave behind the first complete collection of laws, engraved onto a diorite column that once cut an imposing figure in Babylon but now stands in a section of the Louvre's Richelieu Wing.

After their capital city Babylon was sacked in 1595 BCE, the Amorites fade from the upper echelons of Babylonian society to be replaced by another foreign tribe, the Kassites (who kick off the Kassite period). Little is known of their native language and origin, as they seem to have quickly assimilated into the local culture, perhaps to peacefully assume power, which they retained for over 400 years. After that, a new Babylonian dynasty rises to power in 626 BCE in what we call the Neo-Babylonian period, meaning Princess Ennigaldi-Nanna was a 'Neo-Babylonian' in our understanding.[12] This last era of independent Babylonian rule lasted until the princess's father, King Nabonidus, was defeated by Cyrus the Great's Persian army in 539 BCE.

The once mighty Ur was abandoned just a century later when the languid but life-giving Euphrates wandered too far off course to allow for irrigation and the desert reasserted itself. Its fate might serve as an ancient reminder that humanity relies on just the right climate for its survival. A Sumerian poem known as the *Lament for Sumer and Ur*, written long before the city was finally abandoned, grieves a much earlier collapse of the city following a military defeat in the final days of the Third Dynasty of Ur around 2000 BCE. It is a work of literature, not history – a work of art in response to history – but to me, it captures what the end of a city's life might feel like to its population. The poem describes a cataclysm so terrifying even the dead get chased away, their corpses floating in the Euphrates. 'The dark time was roasted by hailstones and flames,' reads one section, 'the bright time was wiped out by a shadow.' Line after line describe utter devastation and death with every possible metaphor for destruction. People lay smashed like clay pots, cattle cut down like date palms, and date palms torn out of the ground like grass. Not even fear remained. 'How long until we are finished off by this catastrophe?' the people ask. 'Ur – inside it there is death, outside it there is death.'[13] It is a funeral dirge for the city that long pre-dates Ur's actual demise, calling it a haunted and ruined mound.[14] It would eventually become just that.

Throughout the world today, lengthy periods of drought and extreme heat ignite wildfires that leave some cities and regions shrouded in smoke, while others find themselves submerged in floodwaters. Climate breakdown, precipitated by an exponential, human-driven increase in carbon emissions, have already forced many to relocate. Ur had survived the changing of hands of numerous kings, outlasted dynasties and even languages. But without water, it was no longer habitable, so its people slowly trickled out of their homes, workshops, and temples to relocate. The city lay untouched by all but the hot winds and shifting sands, which concealed most of its brickwork for almost 2,000 years.

The palace of Princess Ennigaldi-Nanna itself has an even deeper history than it might seem at first glance. Within its footprint, many strata of habitation overlap and intersect. The ziggurat complex where it sits was originally built well over 1,000 years before Ennigaldi-Nanna's time, but the whole area and its buildings fell into disrepair over many centuries. Her father King Nabonidus took it upon himself to restore the dilapidated area, including the stepped pyramid itself, to its former glory, and even installed his daughter as high priestess to the moon god, resurrecting a long-forgotten religious and political office. What would Nabonidus have encountered at the already historic site in the sixth century BCE?

Modern historians can look to Nabonidus's own description of the building works he undertook for clues. One account known as the 'Ennigaldi-Nanna Cylinder' describes the site of the old palace or *giparu* as a ruin, overgrown with date palms and orchards. Nabonidus apparently cleared away the trees to find the building's ancient foundations and several 'inscriptions of ancient kings of the past'.[15] It is likely that these inscriptions were stamped onto bricks, or impressed onto clay objects buried in the foundations by earlier kings and even the princesses who once lived in the complex. The legacy of the king's distant ancestors was all around him. I imagine that a site so littered with artefacts, ancient even to him, must have had the same kind of haunting impact on him that anyone might feel at a ruin today.

According to the account, Nabonidus found an inscription that bore the name of Princess Enanedu, a high priestess at Ur and the daughter of a much more ancient Babylonian ruler named Kudur-Mabuk. Although no further details about that inscription are given, several clay objects bearing Enanedu's name have been excavated from Ur that might give a sense of what Nabonidus found. One, donated to the British Museum by Woolley, is shaped like a large architectural nail or cone and has two columns of cuneiform on its base. The text dates to the early second millennium BCE and describes the princess's own consecration as high priestess and the renovation of her abode. Could this be the inscription that Nabonidus found among the ruins?[16]

> I, Enanedu, a high priestess tellingly named by an exalted name, daughter of Kudur-Mabuk, against the old base of the giparu lay sound brick, and on its walls, (to which) an inch of plaster (was) applied, I slapped an ell of mud-plaster. Lastly, I entered that house.[17]

In other words, she put fresh brick against the decrepit base of the dwelling and applied extra plaster to its inch-thin walls, a royal DIY home renovation from 4,000 years ago.

During Enanedu's tenure, the dwelling had been 'returned to its place' – a way of describing a building restoration – and a wall had been built around the adjacent burial ground of ancient priestesses. To Nabonidus, these details confirmed that he had stumbled upon the site of the ancient giparu, which he proceeded to renovate for his daughter. Like

Woolley in the 1920s, the king carried out his own excavation to find the remains of the *giparu*. Instead of recording them for posterity in a series of graph-paper note cards and excavation reports, Nabonidus simply rebuilt the temple as it had looked 'in ancient times'.

This nascent type of archaeology – of restoring old things to their former glory – was typical of Nabonidus and his royal predecessors. It was part of a broader strategy to lend credence to an otherwise brand new dynasty. King Nabopolassar, the founder of the Neo-Babylonian dynasty to which Nabonidus and Ennigaldi-Nanna belonged, managed to fine-tune this way of forging a connection between new and old by building things atop ancient foundations and by incorporating elements of the ancient writings into his own self-presentation.[18] Unlike the incomplete records that survive today, Nabopolassar and Nabonidus – and their respective coteries of palace scribes – would have had access to the inscriptions of far more ancient kings, kept in libraries or unearthed during building works. (They accessed material so old that their scribes include references to 'breaks' in these older tablets and missing tranches of text.) They knew what era a historical account belonged to, what king's name was stamped on bricks excavated from a ruin, and they tapped into that history to add to their dynastic prestige. In the process of connecting the new with the old through building excavations and renovations, they also unintentionally established an early precursor to what we now call archaeology.

Neo-Babylonian kings deliberately searched for older inscriptions in the course of such renovations. Nabopolassar's son and successor, Nebuchadnezzar II (of Biblical fame remembered for attacking the kingdom of Judah), could not have been more clear on this point. In his restoration of a temple in Marad, a city on the Euphrates, he 'sought and found its ancient foundation document', a clay or stone document drafted and buried by the king overseeing the project. 'I saw the foundation document of King Naram-Sîn, an ancient ancestor,' reads his account.[19] Ancient might perhaps be an understatement, as Naram-Sîn lived and died almost 2,000 years before Nebuchadnezzar II came to power. Indeed, all Neo-Babylonian kings seem to hark back to that particular millennia-old era. Nabonidus similarly claimed to have rebuilt various temples atop foundations laid by Naram-Sîn and his grandfather, Sargon.[20]

It was into this dynasty with a sustained interest in the past that Princess Ennigaldi-Nanna was born and within its context that we must understand the artefacts found in her museum. Ennigaldi-Nanna's own name is a relic of the past, given to her not at birth but upon her accession to the role of high priestess of the moon god at Ur. We know from one of Nabonidus's own royal accounts that part of his decision to appoint her involved renaming her with an official name. Names in ancient Mesopotamia often take the form of a brief phrase or sentence. For example, Nabonidus's own name means 'Attentive to (the god) Nabû' in Akkadian. Ennigaldi-Nanna is actually a sentence in Sumerian, far older than any language in use during her lifetime. It translates to 'the high priestess requested by the god Nanna', a reference to the Sumerian name for the moon god. No record remains of her original birth name, but it may have been one in her own native language, rather than in the, to her (and us), ancient Sumerian. Her office, after all, was as old as that dead language, so her name had to match its antiquity and, through its age, its power.

Nabonidus and Ennigaldi-Nanna were not the last people between the two rivers to lean on ancient history for political gain, nor to do so by restoring Ur's ruins. Today, the remains of the last Babylonian king's restored ziggurat, whose footprint could fill half a football field, are encased in a modern façade that was built by Saddam Hussein in the 1980s. Atop this modern brickwork sits what little is left of Nabonidus's restored temple. Saddam Hussein had much of the ancient structure rebuilt too as it might have looked 'in ancient times', including the foundation levels and the three ceremonial staircases that lead up to the moon god's temple at the ziggurat's zenith. Following in the footsteps of modern Iraqi rulers before him, Hussein made a concerted effort to link himself to Iraq's ancient past in order to bolster nationalism in the country. He routinely referenced Iraq's history in his speeches and even compared himself to Dumuzi, a Sumerian shepherd god.

Ennigaldi-Nanna's museum reminds us of the importance of an even more ancient history to the people who resided along the banks of the Tigris and Euphrates thousands of years ago. When Nabonidus rebuilt the *giparu* as it once was, he relied solely on the old building foundations for a blueprint. In ancient Mesopotamia as now, old stuff had a special status. Indeed, in some sense, it was in Mesopotamia that history was born with the development of writing and using it to record history. Buried under millennia of debris, the artefacts found in Ennigaldi-Nanna's palace at Ur show that despite the gulf of time and, for some, space, the people who left them behind share much in common with those of you reading this book. Just as the objects in her palace connected her to the distant past, so too do they connect the modern reader to her world and its long history.

2

The Clay Drum

'The First Written Words Started Here'

If the birth of history happens when people begin to write things down, then our own journey must start with the first written words in ancient Mesopotamia. It was with these first words that my own path into the field began. I have always been a bit of a nervous wreck, and as an academic it took years before I grew comfortable enough to deliver a talk in anything but a soporific monotone that could lull even the most over-caffeinated student to sleep. When I managed to land a teaching job at Oxford University, I had to face my new reality of lecturing to an audience multiple times a day, every single day. My first few days were a sweaty, red-cheeked, nervous-stomached nightmare, until one class reconnected me with the clay tablets that had inspired me in the first place – tablets that happened to showcase some of the first words ever written down.

My anxiety followed me up the stone steps to the main entrance of the Ashmolean Museum one cool October morning, where four columns rise up several storeys from the stone slabs of its courtyard. I found my students at the building's side entrance and led them to the study room where two blue trays of cuneiform tablets awaited us on a large table topped with black foam. It took less than a second for the rush of adrenaline at seeing the tablets to sweep away all of my nerves. Before us lay some of the earliest examples of writing in all of humanity's history.

We took our seats around the table in awed silence. I picked up a pale, iPhone-sized tablet whose surface was divided into uneven boxes, some filled with thick dots and others etched signs – a sheaf of barley, a foot, a bull, a divine star. 'Let's start with this one,' I said, recognising what was essentially a very ancient receipt tallying up as many as 400 objects.[1] This was, after all, one of the first tablets I had ever picked up years ago as a student in this very class. It was now my turn to teach others about these moments from the dawn of writing, frozen into lumps of clay and nestled neatly in a bright blue plastic tray.

Amazingly, tablets from this early era of the first attempts to codify a writing system share features with those made by scribes thousands of years later, like the scribe who made the drum-shaped clay museum label from the palace of Ennigaldi-Nanna. In the seventh century BCE, a generation or so before the princess was born, that scribe, called Nabû-shuma-iddin, was pressing a reed stylus into a lump of wet clay. He pinched, rolled, and shaped the slightly slippery, moist clay to form a small cylindrical tablet about 4 inches long and 2 inches in diameter. This drum-shaped piece of clay would fit comfortably into the palm of my hand, solid and smooth apart from the gentle texture of impressed signs.

Nabû-shuma-iddin covered the drum in signs describing the now missing brick of King Amar-Suen. His text leaves behind such a wealth of detail that we need not feel too wistful about the lost brick, which once bore a short inscription in Sumerian, the first known written language used by the people who lived in what is now southern Iraq. The brick, Nabû-shuma-iddin tells us, had been discovered by Sîn-balassu-iqbi, a governor of Ur in the seventh century BCE. In other words, he was recording an archaeological find by one of his contemporaries, much as any archaeologist today makes notes on an ancient artefact and the circumstances of its excavation.

This little drum can unlock for us far more than the possible nature of Ennigaldi-Nanna's collection. It also reveals an interplay in ancient Mesopotamia between history and languages, the shared script of cuneiform, and the main medium on which these have survived: clay. Clay may not look like much. Damp and a bit sticky when wet, it can be grey, beige, brown, or a slightly more exciting reddish brown. This ubiquitous material left the soil in ancient Mesopotamia so rich with nutrients that some people call this land between two rivers the 'fertile crescent'. This silty soil may seem insignificant at first, but it becomes the opener for a major chapter in humanity's ongoing global story. The landscape's wealth of clay helps to enable the birth of the written word.

Nabû-shuma-iddin, a professional scribe, would have spent only a few minutes shaping the wet clay of the cylinder, but would have taken considerably longer to cover it in writing that would have been ancient even to him. On the clay cylinder are four columns of text, written in two different styles of cuneiform script. The first three columns preserve a style deliberately made to look old, just as the 'font' would have appeared on the original brick he was copying from: an attempted rendition of the original Sumerian writing on the brick of Amar-Suen. Although kept alive in scholarly settings, much like Latin was in medieval Europe, Sumerian was no longer spoken in ancient Mesopotamia after about 2000 BCE. Nabû-shuma-iddin would have had to learn it in school, and when he copied the ancient text, he also copied the font style, like we might use a Gothic font to evoke an older text. The signs are so large and elaborate that only a few – sometimes only one – fit on each line. The fourth and final column uses the contemporary and far more streamlined Babylonian style of cuneiform to describe how Ur's governor found the brick.

To give you an idea of how different these two styles look, the cuneiform sign *lugal*, which means 'king', uses seventeen wedges in ancient Sumerian, whereas the later Babylonian version of the sign uses only seven. To see two such script styles from totally different eras in a single work is odd. It would be like using American Typewriter font for contemporary newspaper quotes in a history of the 1960s space race – or even like using cuneiform-like letters in this book's quoted passages from ancient tablets. Nabû-shuma-iddin reprised an archaic style of writing to remain as faithful as possible to the original inscription on the brick he was copying from.[2]

This object captures perfectly the many layers of meaning, language, and history embodied in cuneiform and clay. The cuneiform on the clay drum is itself a museum of Mesopotamia's past – each character contains layer upon layer of history. The individual characters of a writing system in use for thousands of years are bound to reflect stages of history. Each period of cuneiform's use had a unique font style, as well as a language or dialect typical of the era, and even preferences in the signs and words used. Where Shakespeare wrote 'doth', today we say 'does', and what we call 'chaos', he called 'coil'; it may be the same language, but his word choice fitted his era (and genre). Cuneiform, like any writing system, also evolved from one era to the next, as did the languages it was used to write. Each individual character offers us a window onto the past.

One of the first clay tablets I ever held in my hands was the iPhone-sized one at the Ashmolean Museum that I picked up again, many years later on that nervous October morning. On one side of the small clay slab, uneven boxes contain a series of what look like tiny pictures. One character resembles a boot, another looks like a star, and another might be the head of a bull. The other side of the tablet is a different story; it shows a scattering of dots and two other carefully drawn signs – it is a calculation, showing the sum total of all the things pictured on the reverse of the tablet. This ancient accounting record comes from the early period of cuneiform, which ranges from the Late Uruk period from about 3500 to 3000 BCE to the Jemdet Nasr period from 3000 to 2900 BCE, named for the city of Jemdet Nasr where similar developments occurred around the same time. (In fact, this tablet was from the city of Jemdet Nasr.) In its early form, cuneiform signs often looked like the things they represented – a boot might represent something like walking, a star might represent something divine, and the head of a bull might represent that animal.

It felt intimate to cradle that tablet in my palm, like I was touching the unknown, early scribe who also once held the wet clay while tracing pictures of boots and bulls into it. Over time, these realistic signs were streamlined and simplified until they could be impressed rather than traced into clay, creating the distinctive wedge-shaped writing we call cuneiform at the beginning of the third millennium BCE. As the English word 'cuneiform' refers to the script's visual appearance (from the Latin *cuneus*, 'wedge'), so too does the Arabic word *mismari*, which derives from the word for nail. The signs, in other words, look like the marks left behind by nails. The Akkadian word for the script, *sattakku* (or *santakku*), also describes its appearance; it means triangle.

Because cuneiform has evolved in various stages, it is relatively easy to date a tablet based on the writing style alone, even with no knowledge of the language being recorded. Very ornate signs that resemble the objects they represent make it easy to date an object to the early days of cuneiform, while characters that look more like nail prints, wedges, or triangles are a clear giveaway that they are a later version of the script used by people like Nabû-shuma-iddin and even Ennigaldi-Nanna.

To understand the beginnings of writing in clay, we must travel three millennia back in time from even Ennigaldi-Nanna's era and 13 miles from her palace in Ur, upstream on the ancient course of the Euphrates to a city called Uruk.

There, another ziggurat rises out of the sand like a camel's hump, and today at its foot is an unassuming blue sign bearing two lines of white Arabic writing that state: 'The first written words started here'.

What may surprise (or even disappoint) you is that the motivation to create these first written words came not from a deep-seated need for self-expression, but from a far more practical need to record – in essence – who owed beer to whom, and how much. Around 3350 BCE during the Late Uruk period, in the city of Uruk, a man named Kushim (or at least, this is our best guess at how to say this name) was in charge of a storage facility for the basic ingredients of beer production.[3] Almost all texts signed by him concern the two products used to brew all known beer types of this time: malt and barley.[4] Far from a DIY homebrew kit tucked into a basement in Portland, this was an enormous undertaking and a critical cog in the administrative machinery of agriculture in Uruk. At one point, Kushim had to administer 135,000 litres of barley over the course of thirty-seven months, and at another, he was responsible for the production of nine different cereals used to make eight different kinds of beer.[5] This beer provided rations to agricultural workers who harvested products that were stored and redistributed by the temple, which served as the city's religious and economic centre.

Fertile soil and new farming methods increased the number of products for Urukeans like Kushim to keep track of, a phenomenon sometimes known as surplus agriculture. Uruk had a distributive economy, where these agricultural products were funnelled through the temple to its workers and a wider population.[6] Already, one byproduct of successful agriculture becomes readily apparent: the need for middle managers. The sheer volume of stuff being produced triggered a hierarchy of personnel and became a highly bureaucratic affair. People like Kushim managed the products harvested by the people he oversaw and the payments for those people's labour in rations, and he likely answered to someone else higher up the administrative chain.

And this is how not poets or artists or philosophers, but rather middle managers brought about the birth of writing. Imagine being Kushim and having to keep tabs on all of these goods in your head. Most of us would lose track pretty quickly, even instantly in my case as I cannot even remember someone's name within seconds of meeting them, let alone something more complicated like their phone number. Administrators needed some kind of memory aid, which initially took the form of little clay tokens to count and keep track of commodities like barley, oil, sheep, and textiles. These tokens have been found at numerous sites throughout the ancient Middle East, from Turkey in the north all the way to Iran in the east. As methods for counting and accounting, they may have been used as early as 7500 BCE – almost 10,000 years ago. But around 3500 BCE, a rise in the number of commodities being represented signals an uptick in the goods being produced and distributed, and the reliance on tokens to keep track of them.[7]

Some tokens were miniatures of the objects they represented. Complete with a handle just big enough to be pinched between one's forefinger and thumb, a tiny jug found in Uruk represented oil, and a slightly different tiny jug represented beer. They are so adorable that you'd be forgiven for thinking they could be toys instead of an elaborate clay calculator.

Other tokens were more geometric than naturalistic. In Jemdet Nasr, tokens had a variety of geometric shapes. Instead of a tiny jar, an ovoid token represented a jar of oil, a disc represented sheep, and a cone-shaped token represented a small measure of barley. Sometimes, these shapes bore markings, like lines and dots, that provided further information about the object being counted. Regardless of their shape or place of origin, a few of these could comfortably fit into the palm of your hand, like Monopoly board tokens, and were sometimes stored in spherical clay envelopes impressed with markings on the outside to reflect their contents. These envelopes were sometimes imprinted with a seal that added a layer of security and authenticity to the information they contained, sort of like a wax seal on an envelope.[8]

Eventually, things shifted from three-dimensional tokens and envelopes to two-dimensional signs incised into pillow-shaped clay tablets. Traced with the sharpened end of a reed stylus, these signs looked a lot like the things they represented, such as a bowl for food or rations, genitalia for the sexes of workers, and a jug for milk or beer. The early administrators pressed the opposite, unsharpened end of a stylus into clay to represent numbers. Instead of representing thirty jars of oil with thirty ovoid or jug-shaped tokens, for example, a picture of a jar was traced into clay to represent 'jar of oil' and preceded with three impressed dots that could represent the number 30.[9] As with the tokens, there is a limited repertoire of things being recorded, all of which include people, products, animals, and commodities related to agriculture. These early tablets may not seem like much, but they represent a major leap in the development of a technology without which this (or any) book would not be possible: writing.

Writing and agriculture were so closely intertwined that the Sumerian goddess of grain, Nisaba, eventually also became the goddess of writing and patron of scribes. A hymn to her, written down much later than these early tablets and tokens, opens with a dazzling description of the goddess and a tool of her trade: 'Lady coloured like the stars of heaven, holding a lapis-lazuli tablet'. 'May you be the butter in the cattle-pen, may you be the cream in the sheep-fold, may you be keeper of the seal in the treasury,' it reads.[10] A seal may seem out of place in a poem about the goddess of writing. It refers (tragically) not to an adorable marine mammal housed in the treasury, but to an administrative tool that served an integral role in temple accounting. About the size and shape of an AA battery, these cylinder seals were carved with imagery and, later, minute inscriptions that said something about their owner, like an ancient social media avatar. Instead of a photo of me with a dog and a bio that described me as a historian and dog lover, for example, I might have had a cylinder seal engraved with the image of the Mesopotamian healing goddess Gula, depicted with her pet dog. The seal may have included an inscription with my name, patronymic, and occupation.

Carved from a variety of stones, seals said something about their bearers and even about the tablets that they were gently rolled onto to impress the delicately carved scenes and some-times cuneiform signs. A 'sealed' tablet conferred an added layer of authenticity to the document. Like an official letter-head that graces the top of old-school paper correspondence, or a signature at the end of a legal contract, a sealing carried the authority of the sealer, affirmed their identity, or verified a transaction.[11]

These small battery-sized objects radiate a totally unexpected beauty for what is more or less an ancient e-signature. In the *Epic of Gilgamesh*, which tells the story of a legendary king's quest for eternal life, there is a scene where he emerges from a pitch-black tunnel, past even where the sun rises and sets, onto a 'garden of the gods' where jewels stud trees that are made out of precious stones. 'A lapis lazuli tree bore foliage,' reads one line, 'in full fruit and gorgeous to gaze on.'[12] Others glowed with rich red carnelian, coral, and even the metallic sheen of haematite. To me, cylinder seals from ancient Mesopotamia are so 'gorgeous to gaze on' that they look like they could have been plucked from the trees in this divine garden at the edge of the known world. A dark green cylinder seal, as old as the earliest writing in ancient Mesopotamia, shows two people holding back a bull that appears to have broken loose from something. Its horn curves above its head like a long crescent moon, and below it a minute eye – no bigger than perhaps a millimetre or two – stares dead ahead. It drags two lines of rope behind it, depicted down to perfectly spaced knots.[13] A tiny lapis lazuli cylinder from several centuries later glows with such a bright blue it looks like it contains a whole ocean. Three bearded figures wrestle two lions in a stylised scene that looks more like a dance than a hunt. Their muscles ripple with the effort, and innumerable little lines make up the lions' manes.[14] The artistry takes my breath away, even if their function might have been as mundane as a signature or Instagram bio.

Together, seals and early writing provided the much-needed bureaucratic tech to meet the growing demands of agricultural production and distribution in the last half of the fourth millennium BCE in the fertile plains of southern

Mesopotamia. The same circumstances that made the soil fertile enough for agriculture to thrive also left behind the clay that became the medium for recording the fruit of that soil. I find this really moving – that the landscape itself made this leap in human innovation possible, that ingenuity worked in tandem with geology to change the course of history.

These early tablets were perhaps once kept in baskets or on shelves, and were likely discarded after the clay receipt or record was no longer needed, much like I don't think twice before throwing away a Tesco receipt. But like many ancient artefacts, their final resting place was not the place they were originally used and kept. If every object has a story, these earliest examples of writing began as wet clay in the hands of agricultural administrators like Kushim and ended, for the most part, in the trash.

About 5,000 of these early clay tablets were found during modern excavations in the 1950s in a district of Uruk known as Eanna, meaning 'House of Heaven', which was the beating heart of the city's agricultural administration. An architectural layer cake of Uruk's economy, religion, and scholarship, the Eanna district housed temples built alongside and on top of one another, beginning with the earliest monumental architecture of the fourth millennium BCE. Constructed from mud bricks, the temples and terraces of the Eanna would have been an enormous logistical undertaking. One building, charmingly named Building C by modern archaeologists and constructed in the same period that saw the development of writing just over 5,000 years ago, had walls 16 feet high and required over one million bricks to construct.[15] It was one of the largest buildings from this period in Uruk's history. When Building C and nearby structures were originally built, surface pits were dug to lay their foundations. Today, one would expect a truck to pull up to such a cavity and slowly fill it with concrete from a revolving mixer. In ancient Uruk, the pits were filled, instead, with garbage. Cheap and accessible, it made for excellent foundation material. Animal bones, pottery fragments, ash, broken mud bricks, and some of these early proto-cuneiform clay tablets found their way into these pits below the monumental architecture of ancient Uruk.

Ancient trash preserves not just everyday life from 5,000 years ago, the ancient analogues of my Amazon packaging and yogurt pots, but also milestones in human history – in this case, the earliest attempts at a brand new technology called writing. Because the tablets were used as fill for buildings that were constructed around 3200 BCE, archaeologists assume that they must have come from the preceding period in Uruk's architectural layer cake, anchoring the earliest attempts at writing to around 3350 BCE.[16] As far as we know, this is about 200 years before hieroglyphs develop into a writing system in neighbouring Egypt and 2,000 years before the earliest evidence of writing in China.

These tablets from the end of the fourth millennium BCE show that writing did not emerge fully formed overnight, and that it was developed not to write sonnets, but receipts. Tokens, their clay envelopes, and stone seals set the stage for the technology that would ultimately make it possible to write anything down, from these early receipts to later letters between kings and lullabies to comfort a crying baby.

Just as the medium for writing, clay, came from the fertile plains around Uruk, so too did the writing implement. Even today, alongside the slow-flowing waters of the Euphrates in southern Iraq, lush reed beds grow, made up of different varieties of this grass-like plant. Reeds were such a valued resource that a pictogram of a reed bundle represented the name of the fertility and war goddess Inana, to whom the Eanna precinct in Uruk was dedicated. The reed plant even finds its way into an early Babylonian story of the Flood as a communication tool between a god and a king. An entire system of area measurement is based on the reed, which were also woven together to make doors, roofs, and sometimes even whole houses.[17]

Reeds lined canals, rivers, and moats, and covered marshes in southern Iraq where, to this day, the lives of the minority (and marginalised) Marsh Arabs (or *Ma'dan* in Arabic) open up a window onto the lives of their distant ancestors. For millennia, Marsh Arabs have made their home at the juncture of the Tigris and Euphrates rivers, where a flooded grassland has created a micro-ecosystem rich in plant and animal life. Over the last few decades, their synergy with the landscape has come under threat. In the 1990s, Saddam Hussein had thousands of square miles of marshland drained as political retaliation for an alleged rebel presence in this area. By the end of his rule, their once thriving population of half a million had shrunk to around 20,000.[18]

Like their ancestors, these people rely on the marsh's resources, like mud, clay, and reed. In Arabic, a *raba* is a house made almost exclusively of reeds, and a *mudhif* is a similarly constructed house built for receiving guests and celebrating special events, like weddings. Reeds are bundled and interlocked into thick columns, each as wide as two people standing side by side. Several of these columns are then bent into arches to form the backbone of the structure, and smaller reeds are tightly woven across these to form the roof and walls, with small perforations to let light through.

Seeing these structures in the landscape of Iraq's marshes is like looking at scenes from the country's ancient art. Carved from a white stone, one cylinder seal made around the time of the development of early cuneiform is only 3 inches high, but somehow fits two bands of scenes across its small body. It is thick, more like a short stack of adhesive-tape rolls than an AA battery, and at its top sits a dark stone figurine of a ram. Ten tiny overlapping cows are carved in a line that forms the top register, creating the illusion of a moving herd. Along the bottom are the façades of four reed huts flanked by thick reed columns, miniatures of the *raba* and *mudhif* still standing in southern Iraq today.[19]

In ancient times, and indeed now still, different types of reed flourished alongside the rivers in southern Iraq, some better suited to building homes and others suited to pressing into clay, like the *Arundo donax*, or giant reed. Split and sharpened in just the right way, the solid stalk and glossy, waterproof skin of the giant reed made it perfect for being pressed into wet clay.[20] For these early Uruk tablets, one end of the stylus was kept whole to preserve the naturally round end of the stalk, while the other end was sharpened like the tip of a fountain pen. The scribe would press the round end into the clay at various angles to represent numbers, and would use the sharpened end to trace a pictogram to represent the counted commodity.

In the early days of writing, there were as many as 2,000 different signs in use.[21] But as this collection of signs grew, scribes began to compose lists of signs, words, and expressions. These were in essence the first written dictionaries. The earliest surviving fragments of these lists come from about 3200 BCE. Thematically arranged, the lists recorded vocabulary for the kinds of things a scribe might encounter in day-to-day accounting, like types of vessels or professions. One list writes out 125 professions, including the signs for sage, chief, and various types of overseers or managers. These early clay dictionaries might not have been page-turners, but they provided crucial teaching tools, disseminating the new technique of recording information on clay and allowing people to learn the many characters. If the knowledge of the script had been lost with the first generation of scribes who developed it, cuneiform may never have evolved into the multi-millennia writing system it turned out to be, leaving silence in the wake of the Uruk tablets, instead of so many thousands of snapshots of life in ancient Mesopotamia.

Even in this early stage of writing, the lists were standardised, or copied over and over again in the same form that amazingly survives into much later periods. I think this is extraordinary. The first people to write things down knew that they had to do it in the exact same way for others to acquire the skill. Almost as quickly as they learned how to write, they knew to create the tools to teach others the ABCs of cuneiform. Reading these lists, though, it becomes apparent pretty quickly that more is at play than a clay literacy primer.

Cuneiform's scribes – from the ones who wrote the account of 400 things I held in the Ashmolean Museum to the astronomer of 79–80 CE who impressed the last surviving wedge-shaped signs – revelled in complexity. We can see it in the lists that they created, which sometimes include unlikely combinations of signs like a vessel symbol and a pig symbol. The vessel symbol was normally paired with the signs for things like beer and barley – so did this combination mean a vessel that was storing pig fat, or pigs themselves? Today, many scholars offer a different, more exciting explanation for the presence of such unexpected combinations. They argue that compilers of the lists included not just *actual* commodities, but any *imaginable* one to generate as exhaustive a list as possible. The early scribes compiling these lists seem to have had a compulsion for completeness and for creating something new. 'They dealt,' in the view of Marc Van De Mieroop who literally wrote the textbook on ancient Mesopotamia, 'with written reality, not with physical reality.'[22]

Even if writing was developed out of necessity to keep track of people and products, its earliest users managed to apply this new technology to something seemingly unnecessary. They embarked on a kind of philosophy of what was real and what could be real. Perhaps they did this for the same reason that we write violin concertos and build particle accelerators – because we can, because we're human. With this in mind, is it possible to understand these lists as an early attempt to organise knowledge, or even early philosophical endeavour? Were they imposing order onto the world around them or creating a new order through writing? Although we may never be able to answer these questions with certainty, they make me think that we share with the early scribes of ancient Uruk a curiosity about our world and a need to make some sense out of it.

Cuneiform eventually expanded to reflect more than the languages and ideas of these early scribes in Uruk. Unlike

the alphabet used to write this book, cuneiform mixes logograms (characters that stand for entire words) with syllabograms (characters that stand for a finite syllable). To borrow
an example from the same Irving Finkel we met earlier and
his fellow curator Jonathan Taylor, a logogram is like using
an ampersand, '&', instead of spelling out each letter of the
word 'a n d', while syllabograms might spell out the word
'cat' with 'ca' and 'at' instead of as three separate letters, 'c a
t'.[23] Sometimes the logograms can also precede or follow a
word to hint at its meaning.[24] For example, the cuneiform
sign that means 'deity', which looks a bit like a star, precedes
all divine names to signal to the reader that the signs that
follow spell out the name of a goddess or god, rather than
the name of a mortal person. The sign for 'place' follows the
names of cities like Uruk and Ur. In cuneiform, all logograms come from Sumerian, even though they continued to
be used in later texts written in Akkadian, to represent
whole words alongside syllabic signs. For this reason, cuneiform is called a 'mixed system'. This may be familiar to
people who read Japanese, which can incorporate Chinese
characters, known as *kanji*, alongside phonetic and syllabic
scripts.

Cuneiform was initially developed to write Sumerian, but
in the middle of the third millennium BCE, it was adapted to
write the unrelated language of Akkadian, used by various
peoples in the region including eventually the Babylonians
and Assyrians. The way the script was adapted helps make
sense of the 'mixed system'. In the earliest stages of writing,
it was enough for early cuneiform to represent a limited
repertoire of words for professions, commodities, animals,
and numbers in relatively straightforward and obvious ways; a

jar for beer, a face for person, and so on. But what about abstract concepts, like 'happy', or activities like 'to smile'? What about prepositions like 'to' and 'from', and what about grammatical features, like making something plural? After a few centuries of receipts and lists, the writing system began to expand by way of the rebus principle, which uses existing signs and symbols in novel ways to represent new things. This principle exploits how a sign is pronounced and what it means in order to represent more things in the world that are related to those sounds or meanings.

To explain this process, let's begin by looking at a system of symbols familiar to most people who use a mobile phone: emojis. The 💙 emoji represents the word 'heart' in English, but is also used to represent the verb 'to love' as in the perhaps now dated usage of 'I 💙 you', and to mark a message as being well intended like 'hope you're feeling better 🖤'. Combinations of emojis can also be used to create new words, whose meaning is not necessarily related to the original images. For example, the phrase 💣 🐚 🐱 uses the symbols for 'bomb' and 'shell', creating a word whose meaning is unrelated to each element, 'bombshell', to describe a bikini as being outrageously attractive. If we are feeling particularly imaginative (or have too much free time), it's possible to construct entire sentences out of emojis. Using the eye, can, and sea symbols, it's possible to write 👁 🥫 🌊 to mean 'I can see'. If inclined, you could even write 'I love you' with the eye, heart, and ewe emojis. The way each sign sounds is used to represent words unrelated to the sign's original meaning so that a writing system can reflect more sounds and meanings. Scribes in ancient Mesopotamia did something similar with cuneiform.[25]

As a result of this expansion, signs took on many meanings and sounds over time. Like the layers of architecture that tell a story about Uruk's history – from the trash heap foundations to the top of a temple – each cuneiform sign carries layers of meaning that reveal its history. Sometimes, these layers are easy to explain. The cuneiform sign that represents 'house' can represent the word in Sumerian, *e*, and in Akkadian, *bītu*, but it can also represent syllables that sound like those words: *e*, *bit*, *bet*, *bid*, and *bed*. Each of these syllables derives from the original words in Sumerian and Akkadian represented by this sign. In other cases, the meanings and sounds a sign has taken on are more difficult to explain, like one sign used to write the words 'fox', 'liar', 'singer', and 'accountant' that neither sound similar nor share any thematic meaning apparent to a modern reader. Perhaps this compares to how the words 'gnarly' and 'cool' have all come to refer to something excellent, alongside their original meanings.

Cuneiform could have easily been adapted to write Akkadian purely as a syllabic script. In other words, scribes could have dispensed entirely with the signs that stood for entire words – the logograms that had their roots in the way cuneiform was used to write Sumerian – in favour of a writing system whose signs stood only for syllables. This was, after all, the case with another Semitic language that cuneiform was used to write, Eblaite, in what is now Syria. Scribes there stopped using the logograms and opted to limit every sign to a syllable and to spell words out that way. (It was even adapted into an alphabet in the nearby city of Ugarit.) Sumerian's antiquity and prestige, however, had such a firm grasp on the reed styluses of Akkadian-speaking scribes that they preserved these ancient characters in what ended up as a mixed writing system. As a result, scribes like Nabû-shuma-iddin who inscribed the clay drum found in Ennigaldi-Nanna's museum were trained to read and write Sumerian well enough to recognise and write it, and to know the more ancient readings of cuneiform signs. This enabled him to copy an inscription that was, to him, 1,500 years old in a dead language and archaic font. This also means that almost every single cuneiform sign represents more than one thing or sound, making it challenging (but such fun) to read.

To revisit our emoji analogy, this might be like remembering and respecting that ♥ originally represents the internal organ responsible for circulation, as well as eventually taking on the added meanings of a figurative or emotive heart, the verb 'to love', and a stamp of affection at the end of a text message. With time, and as cuneiform signs expanded to take on more meanings, the early receipts and dictionary-like lists did finally give way not just to ancient sonnets, but to epic works of literature, including the legend of how writing was born, of how people first came to press reed to clay.

This mythical account of the birth of writing originally ran to 640 lines, but today we only have various-sized scraps of this story, known as *Enmerkar and the Lord of Aratta*. Almost 100 lines survive on one clay copy that is almost 4,000 years old. It is covered in impeccable handwriting, but unfortunately broken at a diagonal from the top right to bottom left, creating an almost perfect clay triangle. A much smaller fragment of the story preserves only four broken lines on one small nub of clay.[26] The work would have been known in its complete form to scribes like Nabû-shuma-iddin and may even have formed part of a wider literary or mythological tradition appreciated outside of scholarly circles. Modern scholars, however, had to piece it together from these myriad small and large fragments to reveal what some have deemed the 'finest piece of storytelling ever produced' by Babylonian scribes.[27]

King Enmerkar of Uruk, so the story goes, decides to decorate his city and the surrounding region with precious metals and stones from Aratta, a mythical city of splendour located beyond the mountains and adorned richly with gold, silver, lapis lazuli, and 'mountain stones'. This fictional prem- ise actually matches up to the resources of ancient Mesopotamia, a region devoid of natural sources of stone, like lapis lazuli, and metal, like silver, which all had to be traded from beyond the Zagros mountain range bordering modern-day Iran, Iraq, and Turkey. Unfortunately for Enmerkar, trade did not yet exist, so he asked the goddess Inana for advice. She directs him to send a messenger to demand the ruler of Aratta to supply him with the precious metals and stones, claiming Inana's support. The ruler refuses, unless King Enmerkar can solve a series of challenges, which read more like riddles.

In the first challenge, Enmerkar must cart grain from Uruk to Aratta in open nets, a seemingly impossible task that he makes possible by using sprouting barley to close the net's holes and protect the grain from being lost en route. In the second, the ruler of Aratta asks him to bring a sceptre made not of any known wood, reed, metal, or stone – in other words, to make one out of an entirely new material. Enmerkar creates one out of a gluey substance poured into a hollow reed, hardened, and broken away from its natural mould. The final challenge is a fight between the two rulers' dogs, but Enmerkar must find one who is not black, white, brown, red, yellow, or multi-coloured. The Urukean king weaves a garment of a novel colour to wrap around his dog and instructs the messenger to deliver a long speech to his adversary. Exhausted from the increasingly complex exchange between the two rulers, the messenger feels his mouth grow too 'heavy' and 'tired' to repeat Enmerkar's words. To make the messenger's job easier, Enmerkar 'patted some clay and wrote the message as if on a tablet'. In other words, he invented writing.[28]

Both in reality and in myth, the first writing developed out of necessity, made possible by serendipity. The same geological circumstances that made southern Mesopotamia fertile enough for surplus agriculture also left behind rich deposits of clay, which allow for the birth not just of writing, but of humanity itself. According to Mesopotamian mythology, clay becomes the medium that the gods use to make the first human beings (and then human beings go on to record those very creation myths in the same material).

In one Sumerian creation myth that survives on clay tablets made by Babylonian scribal students in the early second millennium BCE, the mother goddess Ninmah used clay to create a series of human beings. One of her first creations had perpetually opened eyes, and was assigned the fate of musician. Another could not give birth, and was assigned the role of serving the queen. Ninmah even fashioned one 'with neither penis nor vagina', an early reference to nonbinary gender in an important creation myth. Ninmah's son Enki was then given a turn. He shaped a baby and instructed Ninmah to pour ejaculated semen into a woman's womb to create a newborn in its image. 'It could hardly breathe,' the story describes, its ribs were shaky, its lungs were afflicted, its heart was afflicted, its bowels were afflicted. With its hand and its lolling head it could not put bread into its mouth. Its spine and head were dislocated. The weak hips and the shaky feet could not carry it on the field.

Anyone who has held a newborn may relate to this description of a baby with a barely functioning digestive system, a neck too weak to hold their own head up, and no control over their tiny limbs and perpetually clenched fists. Horrified at this ostensibly useless creature, Ninmah demanded what fate she was expected to decree for it. Although much of the passage that follows is fragmentary, Enki's reply was presumably something along the lines of 'figure it out'.[29]

Humanity came from clay, which formed the beginnings of a writing system in Uruk that would ultimately preserve some of its inhabitants' greatest surviving achievements – their first counting and accounting, dictionaries, early philosophical ideas, and eventually the literature and myths that reveal how they understood their own beginnings. The writing system reflected the landscape, and the mythology reflected the writing system.

In the very first tablets found among the rubbish in Uruk, it is impossible to say with certainty what language is being recorded. Even modern scholarly interpretations of these rely on the well-established meanings of similar signs from later periods to read these early records. The combination of numbers and signs, and the lists, otherwise offer no linguistic information. Grammatical endings like the plural -s at the end of an English word or a past-tense marker like -ed at the end of a verb, which would provide clues about the underlying language, are missing. The earliest examples of texts that include linguistic clues like these come from the start of the third millennium BCE, when cuneiform is no longer a fledgling technology used solely to keep track of beer and sheep, and when signs are no longer traced, but are impressed to create the iconic wedges of cuneiform. At this point in cuneiform's development, it is without any doubt being used to record the Sumerian language, and within 500 years, it gets adapted to write the unrelated Akkadian language. Eventually, it was used to write about a dozen others, including Hittite, Ugaritic, and Old Persian.

In Leonard Woolley's day, the decipherment of cuneiform was still incomplete,[30] but he knew enough to read (with some mistakes) the clay tablets unearthed at Ur, including the 'key' left behind by Nabû-shuma-iddin. Despite his own limited understanding of Sumerian (indeed, he read Princess Ennigaldi-Nanna's name initially as Bel-shalti-nannar), Woolley disparaged the scribe's copy of the ancient brick for its errors. 'The scribe, alas!' he writes, 'was not so learned as he wished to appear, for his copies are so full of blunders as to be almost unintelligible, but he had doubtless done his best, and he certainly had given us the explanation we wanted.'[31] This is a gross exaggeration. Nabû-shuma-iddin was writing in a language that had been 'dead' for 1,500 years, and the mistakes are akin to a few typos. Hardly rendering a text of forty lines unintelligible, the few minor errors he makes are a reminder that speakers of Sumerian were as far away in time from Nabû-shuma-iddin as the scribe himself was from Woolley, and highlight the great lengths to which the scribe and his contemporaries went to preserve their long history. Sumerian was as important to them as it was ancient; the antiquity that made it so difficult for Nabû-shuma-iddin to read and write the language made it all the more important to remember. To some degree, Nabû-shuma-iddin would have known that the brick discovered by the governor that he had attempted a copy of was centuries old, but would he have known it was over 1,500 years old? Babylonians knew about their ancestors, preserved their languages, and respected their age, but could they have known exactly what that age was?

During the course of his reign, Ennigaldi-Nanna's father Nabonidus renovated several temples, like the one to the moon god at Ur where she served as high priestess. He also renovated the Ebabbar temple to the sun god Shamash about one hundred and fifty miles away in a city called Sippar. This temple, Nabonidus had decided, was too small to house its divine resident, and in the course of expanding it, he discovered its original ground plan. A royal inscription from the tenth year of his reign gives an elaborate backstory for this to inflate the king's legitimacy in the eyes of the gods. According to the inscription, the temple – which had, in fact, been renovated in the preceding few decades by one of his predecessors, Nebuchadnezzar II – 'had fallen to pieces and turned to ruins in distant days, over which sand dunes and dust heaps, massive piles of earth, were heaped so that its ground plan could not be determined, its design could not be seen'. The god Marduk sent forth four winds and a great storm that swept away the sand dunes, dust heaps, and massive piles of heaped-up earth to reveal an *even more* ancient foundation. There, the king made a discovery that confirmed the foundation's age.

> I discovered an inscription bearing the name of Hammurabi, an ancient king who had built Ebabbar and its ziggurat for the god Shamash on top of the original foundations 700 years before Burna-buriash.[32]

Nabonidus isn't quite right here – Hammurabi, in fact, reigned in the eighteenth century BCE, only about 400 years before Burna-buriash, not 700 years. If Nabonidus stretched the temporal gulf between Hammurabi and Burna-buriash, he may well have done the same for the time that separated Burna-buriash from himself. To him, the foundations must have seemed very old indeed.

It may be unfair to compare Nabonidus's attempt at dating Hammurabi's reign to that of today's scholars who have the benefit of hundreds of thousands of texts, including ones with objectively datable events like eclipses, and radiocarbon dating to calibrate those dates. Early scholars of Mesopotamia made similar errors to those made by Nabonidus. A French-German Assyriologist named Jules Oppert, in 1863, dated the beginning of Hammurabi's reign to 2394 BCE. About seventy years later, the scholar François Thureau-Dangin shuffled this date forward to 2003 BCE. These early scholars were muddling through a fraction of the texts known today, written in what was then a newly (and only partly) deciphered writing system. In 1950, scholarly consensus moved the date even further forward to 1792 BCE, which remains the most widely accepted, although alternative accounts and arguments for the different dates persist.[33] History is messy, whether it's done from the basement of a library in Oxford, or from a Babylonian palace on the banks of the Euphrates.

Regardless of Nabonidus's imprecision, he had some sense that a very long time had passed between the first building works at the Ebabbar temple and his own restorations. Nabû-shuma-iddin, the scribe who composed the clay drum, would have shared this awareness and maybe even reverence for history. In his account of the discovery of the now lost brick, he describes how it was uncovered during an attempt by a governor named Sîn-balassu-iqbi to find the foundation of a temple complex in Ur. In the course of searching for those foundations, the governor found the brick whose ancient inscription Nabû-shuma-iddin then took the time not only to copy verbatim, but even to copy in the same writing style, on a drum-shaped 'museum label'. Just as architecture layered one civilisation upon another – forcing archaeologists today to dig and ancient kings to await divine winds to sweep the dust away – so too did cuneiform. Each sign preserves its Sumerian past, despite being redeployed to write the unrelated language of Akkadian, and every scribe trained in this multi-layered writing system would have had to learn something about their history.

Ennigaldi-Nanna's own ancient Sumerian name preserved a part of her distant past embodied in that dead language, just as her role in Ur revived a nearly dead religious and political institution. She would have known she was following in the footsteps of priestesses who pre-dated her by over 1,000 years. Living in a resurrected palace, populated with ancient objects excavated from its foundations and environs, it is easy to imagine that she would have had some sense that the brick described in the clay drum and even the drum itself represented something whose age was difficult to quantify. These layers of language, culture, and history are baked into the multivalent meanings of each cuneiform sign.

Nabû–shuma–iddin's clay drum introduces the beginnings of Mesopotamian writing in clay, and the crossroads of language, culture, and meaning baked into each cuneiform sign. In this sense, it does provide a key. It unlocks for us the many layers of the cuneiform writing system and the sounds and meanings of each individual sign that shift from one epoch to the next. Whether or not the clay drum was specifically 'the earliest museum label known', it connects the objects in Ennigaldi-Nanna's collection to one another, to their own distant past, and to our own understandings of how to record and preserve history.

3

The Brick of Amar-Suen

Mesopotamia's Building Blocks

The first clay tablet I ever held – essentially a mundane accounting record – would have meant little more than a work email to the scribe who drafted it. But, for me, it was a handshake with a stranger that transported me from a lonely room in the Ashmolean Museum to the busy, bustling neighbourhood of ancient Uruk. Holding old things is the closest I will ever come to time travel, to connecting with those who came before me, so even that receipt felt like magic.

There's no reason to think ancient people didn't also experience this sense of time travel when stumbling across relics from times long gone. Even something seemingly dull can become extraordinary when viewed in that light. The clay drum, or 'key', that tells us so much about the history of cuneiform is also a record of an ancient discovery of a brick.

The inscription narrates how Sîn-balassu-iqbi, who was Ur's governor at the time, found the brick among the debris while in search of the foundations of a temple. The brick may have stopped the governor in his tracks simply for its antiquity, evident from the writing style and language, and possibly its original use. He would have realised it was not from the previous dynasty, or the one before that, or even the one before that. Could its sheer antiquity have moved the governor to keep it and have a record made?

Anyone who loves history will relate to the impulse to record this find and keep – maybe even display – an artefact. But when it comes to something as humdrum as a mud brick, even the most devoted history lover might want to ask why. Bricks were not exactly rare and beautiful artefacts in ancient Mesopotamia; in fact, they are one of the most common archaeological artefacts from the region. Any kind of construction work would unearth thousands of them, and they would normally be reused as part of any building or rebuilding project.

Despite their lacklustre appearance, bricks fill the display cases of the British Museum. Walking into the museum's cavernous room known simply as 'Enlightenment' feels a bit like walking into a life-sized diorama of the library of an eighteenth-century antiquities collector. The shelves that line its two-storey-tall walls display ancient Greek pottery and statuettes, fossils and fine china, and myriad other artefacts tucked among leather-bound books. Filled with ancient objects, rocks, and old books open to a particular page, glass-topped display cases and collector's cabinets interrupt the gallery's long nave. Among the many objects on display are about thirty mud bricks from ancient Mesopotamia. They feature the inscriptions of kings as early as Ur-Nammu (c. 2100 BCE) and as late as Nebuchadnezzar II (c. 600 BCE), but despite the differences in age all the bricks have more or less the same form and are made from the same materials.

These thirty or so bricks deemed worthy of special display in the British Museum are but an infinitesimal part of the number made and used over thousands of years in ancient Mesopotamia. It took millions of bricks, for example, to build a city wall. The ancient *Epic of Gilgamesh* tells the story of King Gilgamesh who allegedly ruled Uruk for over a century during the Early Dynastic period, from about 2900 to 2340 BCE. Later kings credit him with building the city's walls, as do the myths about him that would have been impressed into clay and recited aloud in royal courts. Whether Gilgamesh was a real person or purely fictional (or somewhere in between), the city wall he supposedly built is very real. Parts of the wall are still visible today, though its size and state of disrepair make it nigh on impossible to excavate fully. And this is no wonder. First constructed in the third millennium BCE – that's to say 5,000 years ago – it is up to 16 feet thick in parts and 5.5 miles long, fortified by hundreds of towers. Archaeologists estimate that over 300 million baked mud bricks and over two million working days of labour were required to build the literally epic wall.[1]

Just as the basic materials for writing came from the fertile landscape surrounding the Tigris and Euphrates rivers, so too did building materials. The brick and mortar of their many buildings were essentially mud and more mud.[2] Brickmakers shovelled and trod over mud mixed with chopped straw and sometimes animal dung, and water. They filled standard-sized moulds with the resulting mixture. Once formed, the bricks were sometimes baked, but most were laid out to dry in the sun for two weeks or more, after which they were ready to be used. As a result, brick production was sometimes seasonal with a preference for the spring and summer to avoid rainfall that would sabotage any attempts to dry or lay bricks.[3] Although pretty solid when new, the bricks would fracture over time as the straw decayed, leaving behind a landscape littered with millions of ancient building blocks.[4] (The very thing that made them decay, interestingly, leaves behind enough ancient DNA to reveal the exact plants that grew in Mesopotamia at the time.[5])

Ancient builders stuck those bricks together with pretty much the same mixture that bricks were made from – mud, chopped straw, and water – left wet to serve as mortar, but in important construction works like a ziggurat, bitumen was used. This sticky substance had manifold uses in ancient Mesopotamia. In major building works, the water-resistant material was used along with reeds to bind mud bricks together, as described in an almost foot-long clay cylinder covered in cuneiform from the time of Nabonidus. He describes his building work at Ur where builders used bitumen to seal together baked bricks, some of which were stamped with a short inscription dedicating the temple and detailing the king's renovation of its central stepped pyramid. The most conspicuous bitumen pits were those near the city of Hit, which was such an important site and source of this multi-purpose material that it forms the architecture of the Akkadian word for bitumen, *iṭṭû*.[6]

I find it impossible to picture the sheer number of bricks that would have been laid out at any one time to dry on the sandy, stepped plains of ancient Mesopotamia. There is some modern help, however. Over the past few years, a team of Iraqi and German archaeologists have been making modern mud bricks as part of a restoration project for the ruins of the ziggurat at Uruk.[7] This restoration work is to try to save the exposed areas of ancient brickwork in parts of Uruk. Making modern mud bricks with wooden moulds with the same ingredients as the surviving bricks from thousands of years ago, the small team was producing an astonishing 450 bricks each day. Laid out in lines to dry in the sun, the hundreds of bricks look like rectangular soldiers in uneven infantry squares, an ancient army resurrected to protect the world's first city. Seeing them like that, it's easy to forget the many thousands of years that separate these bricks and us from those that built the cities of ancient Mesopotamia.

But this production line was only in the hundreds. Why, when there were so many millions of bricks used in ancient Mesopotamia, would this one brick have stood out to Sîn-balassu-iqbi? A clue might lie in the copy of the brick's inscription found on the clay drum. 'Amar-Suen, the one called by name by the god Enlil in Nippur,' reads the opening line. Amar-Suen is the name of the king when the brick was made sometime during his rule between 2046 and 2038 BCE. He's referred to in the inscription as a 'mighty king, king of Ur, king of the four quarters'. This is a typical opener for the kind of brief royal inscriptions that were stamped onto bricks in ancient Mesopotamia, naming the king directly and calling him the king of the known world. The text also refers to the city of Nippur, situated about 90 miles up the Euphrates from Ur. Nippur was the home city of Enlil, the supreme god of the Sumerian pantheon who bestowed divine legitimacy on royal rule in Mesopotamia from his home city. So if you were a king in ancient Mesopotamia, you were a king because Enlil said so, and he said so from Nippur.

Despite its standard opening sentence that essentially lays out his claim to the throne, this was not quite a run-of-the-mill brick. From the scribe's transcription, we learn that the brick was not from a city wall or a temple or a palace, but rather had been part of the plinth that held up a pair of golden statues of the moon god Nanna (or Sîn in Akkadian) and his wife, the goddess Ningal. Perhaps it was this detail that gave the governor pause 2,500 years ago. While bricks were ten a penny, he might have hesitated to discard something that once held up the golden, earthly embodiment of a goddess. Even more persuasive was the next line: 'As for the one who removes these statues of my gold from a storehouse, may the god Nanna, lord of Ur, and the goddess Ningal, lady of Ur, curse him.'[8]

As we know, this particular brick was never found. Maybe it crumbled over time, or an ancient passer-by found it among the ruins and took it home for display or reuse. Excavators in Ur did, however, find five other bricks like it with nearly identical inscriptions. The cuneiform signs pressed into those bricks are almost as pristine today as they were millennia ago when King Amar-Suen supposedly built the golden statues and placed them on their brick pedestals. A different, equally ominous, curse threatens anyone who encounters these bricks: if someone damages the pedestal, it reads, the moon god and his divine wife will 'bring his offspring to an end'.[9] Could the governor have known about these other bricks and their more extensive curses that extended to destroying the pedestal? Did they make him feel sufficiently anxious about the end of his genetic line that he decided to keep the brick he found for posterity?

The most ordinary bricks – curse not included – can reveal the most interesting, and sometimes unexpected, details about life between the two rivers. Even the thing about them that seems to make them less special – their sheer number – is informative. Their use seems to expand especially during the era that followed the development of writing, in the Early Dynastic period that spans much of the 2000s BCE. This window of time was an age of innovation and of firsts, and of the legends inspired by the many changes that occurred in this centuries-long era. The way people begin to use bricks in this period tracks major social and political changes, telling us a lot about the people who made and laid out these building blocks under the baking sun.

Bricks had many different ways of outliving their purpose as building materials, just as the brick of Amar-Suen became something much more than an earthly bit of construction. Many medical rituals from the region called for the use of a brick. In an ancient therapy for someone who feels troubled, the patient is instructed to remove a brick from the threshold of his house, and place it in an oven with the implication of burning it.[10] Even to this day in certain Middle Eastern traditions, the threshold is a liminal place between the safety of one's home and the danger of the outside world where evil can collect, so to remove one of its bricks for a symbolic burning might have helped cleanse the man or his house of whatever forces caused his troubles.

Bitumen was also used in a ritual to protect a baby against the demoness Lamashtu, a hybrid of human and animal whose face was so terrifying there seems to be no consensus on what exactly she looked like – perhaps a rabid dog or lion, or even a bird of prey. Despite her mostly human body, she had talons and claws for hands and feet, and her *modus operandi* was to terrorise pregnant women and babies. She offered a demonic explanation for the same inexplicable losses we still face today in pregnancy and the first few vulnerable months of a baby's life. In ancient recipes, bitumen gets used alongside other things that stink, like animal dung and sulphur, to protect babies from her clutches.[11]

In Mesopotamia, witches and warlocks spent a lot of time turning their dark arts against others, infecting them with all kinds of misfortune, from financial ruin to severe illness. One such witchcraft-induced illness left the victim with paralysis, sexual dysfunction, and the sudden onset of muteness. In the ritual to heal him (and it is a him in these texts), the ancient doctor must fashion figurines of the warlock and witch thought to have caused the symptoms. Each figurine's right hand should clutch its mouth, and its left hand its anus, before the patient crushes each one with his foot and sets them on fire. The instructions are detailed – graphic, even – and specifically state that each figurine must be made of clay, dough, tallow, wax, and bitumen.[12] A man suffering from depression and premature ejaculation must also touch bitumen 'when his semen is dripping' to leave him purified.[13]

Magic and ritual may seem to have no place in a medical context, but in ancient Mesopotamia supernatural beings were as much a part of the fabric of reality as today's microbes – invisible without the aid of technology like the microscope. In the absence of knowledge about these microscopic organisms, the physicians of Mesopotamia came up with their own explanations, like demons and witches, and remedies that could tackle such terrifying forces. The ingredients for these remedies and rituals often incorporated ever-present elements like clay, brick, and bitumen. These building blocks must have had enough literal and symbolic power to battle the forces behind some of life's scariest medical experiences.

Brick and bitumen are therefore far more than the building blocks of ancient Mesopotamia's multi-million-brick walls, its temples, and statue bases. They give us a way into so many aspects of life in ancient Mesopotamia, partly because of their symbolic importance. Mud, plants, and the bubbling bitumen pits from places like Hit come together to create earthly homes for gods and people, so why shouldn't the ingredients for something so important also work their way into other elements of everyday life? They provided the material not just for buildings, but for magic and myth-making and medicine (and maybe even an ancient museum). These building blocks tell us so much about normal people, and the mythological, religious, social, and political institutions that underpinned their lives.

The Early Dynastic period showcases just how well bricks track major historical developments. This was the era of Sumerian cultural and linguistic domination, and a period of astounding innovation and development of human society that comes to an end with the rise of King Sargon of Akkad, generally dated to 2334 BCE. If the legend of Gilgamesh is to be believed, he would have ruled Uruk sometime during this period, in the early part of the third millennium BCE – centuries before Amar-Suen's dynasty rose to power in nearby Ur and he laid the brick at the base of the golden statue of Ningal. Gilgamesh allegedly oversaw the construction of Uruk's multi-million-brick wall two centuries before the Great Pyramid of Giza was built and more than two millennia before the Greek historian Herodotus would set foot in the region.

However, dates for this period should be taken with not just a pinch, but a heaped tablespoon of salt.[14] It is only the later periods whose dates we can know with some certainty thanks largely to ancient Mesopotamian scholars who made rigorous records of astronomical phenomena in the first millennium BCE. Their observations can be dated precisely – even down to the hour, including a total solar eclipse that happened on 15 June 763 BCE, which happens to be the event that anchors all dates that follow and the handful of centuries just before.[15] For the periods that precede this moment, the best historians can do is orient events in relation to each other.[16]

So, in this centuries-long, imprecisely datable span of time known as the Early Dynastic period, various Sumerian city-states rose and fell, unified by the use of the Sumerian language, but not unified under any one ruler. What characterises this period is the intense innovation that blossomed, from the further development of the cuneiform writing system to the rise of cities and new kinds of architecture. It is an era of many alleged firsts in human history, including perhaps one of the most crucial innovations: the wheel.[17] The wheel would have transformed ancient societies, connecting people and cities, facilitating trade, easing agricultural labour, and even speeding up the production of high-quality pottery (the Tupperware, Amazon packaging, and art of the ancient world) with pottery wheels. Where and when the wheel is invented is a topic of eternal debate, but the earliest known evidence for the use of the wheel on a vehicle appears in an early cuneiform sign. At least five clay tablets from Uruk from the end of the fourth millennium BCE, when pictographic early signs still resembled the objects they represented, include one sign that looks like a sledge sitting atop two perfectly round impressions.[18]

Whether the wheel was 'invented' by Sumerians or not, one thing the Early Dynastic period did was bring people together in larger numbers than ever before, creating ever-bigger towns and cities. It is easy to see how an increase in innovation followed as a byproduct of urbanisation (two heads, after all, are better than one). Over time these settlements coalesce into city-states whose rulers would survive into later legends as figures from an era of great kings.

People in these growing cities needed places to live, as did their gods and leaders. Architecture naturally expanded in this period; with innovation and urbanisation came the need for structures like homes, palaces, and places of worship. They even needed protection from neighbouring cities, and from around 2700 BCE, we begin to see city walls – like the 5.5-mile-long one that encircled Uruk.

One particularly astonishing feat of construction from this era is a sprawling building complex known today as the Plano-Convex Building uncovered in the city of Kish, just over 100 miles northwest of Uruk. This modern name comes from the shape of its bricks, formed by patting the excess mud at the top until the brick resembled a loaf of bread, leaving the bottom part flat (plano) and the top slightly rounded (convex).

Their shape meant that they had to be laid in a V-shaped, herringbone pattern, where one course was laid on its side at a tilt with the other laid with an opposite tilt. The loaf-shaped bricks that went into these very early buildings can reveal much about the people who made them, laid them, and inhabited them, as well as the institutions that informed their daily lives.

The modern name for Kish's ruins is Tell Uhaimir, which in Arabic means 'Red Mound' to reflect the colour of bricks used in many of the site's monumental buildings during its millennia of occupation along an ancient branch of the Euphrates.[19] One of the first city-states in history, it was a site of political importance during the Early Dynastic period, and Sumerian legend even has it that kingship – the very concept of rule by a king – descended from heaven to take its seat at Kish. Incredibly, archaeological digs of the site have actually uncovered evidence that seems to support this mythological picture. After a major expedition in the early twentieth century, archaeologists revealed the Plano-Convex Building to be a huge structure with tens of rooms surrounding a great court. Buttresses still survive to a height of about 5 feet along the thick, external wall of the trapezoid-shaped building, hinting at a once much-taller structure. Paved with bricks set in bitumen, the entrance leads to a series of well-connected chambers en route to a large courtyard, whose central feature is now a grave. Fragments of decorative shell inlay, which would have once flecked wooden furniture, walls, or other art, peppered the intact brick flooring in these rooms. Other features stood out to the excavators, like drains that led to bitumen-lined brick pits where water could collect, several workshops including one with a wine or oil press, kilns and ovens, and a headless statue. Several more graves found throughout the building, however, suggest that it was probably abandoned by the end of the Early Dynastic period, and signs of fire and looting suggest this abandonment was not voluntary.[20]

Another extensive building had much in common with this building made of plano-convex bricks. Fragments of luxury material were found crushed throughout many of the rooms, like shell and mother-of-pearl that were once fixed to other pieces of art. Statues, for example, might have had mother-of-pearl eyes, or game boards might have had squares made with the shiny shell plaques. A frieze in one room shows limestone inlaid figures about 8 inches high in a military procession complete with prisoners and animals; in another, a mother-of-pearl inlay depicts a banquet scene, featuring musicians who appear from the iconography to be women.[21] But the lavish life lived between its mud brick walls came to an abrupt end and, like the Plano-Convex Building, it was abandoned after a short period of use and its remains served as a cemetery.

There's something unusual about these sprawling structures, with their beautiful art, and their eventual use as makeshift cemeteries. Made with such care, they seem to have had no apparent religious function in their décor or design. Perhaps even more telling is the fact that, in ancient Mesopotamia, no one abandons a temple. If anything, kings rebuilt and renovated temples over and over again, like Ur's ziggurat complex. These monumental buildings, archaeologists think, were palaces, possibly hinting at a major political innovation: the advent of kingship as an institution separate from the temple.[22]

In Uruk, during the period of the earliest writing just a few centuries before, it was the Eanna temple district that was the city's heart. The temple was not only the earthly home of the goddess Inana, but it was also a social and economic centre. It was the temple that organised agricultural labour and distributed goods to a wider population. While the city had a leader, that role was inextricably tied to and carried out in the temple. The architectural remains in Kish show that later on things shifted; people made a new kind of building to house not a god or goddess, but a king. Citizens went to great lengths to construct and decorate palaces for their kings, moulding and laying every individual brick of a new institution that was important enough to warrant this level of attention and artistry.

This is not to say that the temple or religion declined in importance in the Early Dynastic period. Kish also boasts impressive temples from this period, which mark religious developments and, in particular, the rise of city gods and the symbolic importance of such sites in the landscape. Each city took on a patron deity for whom the primary temple was consecrated. The patron god of Kish was Zababa, a warrior god whose epithet was 'Crusher of Stones'. At Ur, we know by now that the moon god reigned supreme, and the importance of his cult was such that only a daughter of the king could be worthy to serve as his high priestess and earthly wife. A temple was understood to be the 'house' of a god, so much so that 'temple' was, in fact, written with the cuneiform sign *e* (pronounced like the vowel in 'get'), the word for 'house' in Sumerian.

That such a great many bricks were laid to shore up these political and religious institutions and movements shows the symbolic importance of these places – and the people who lived in and among them. This helps to explain why these cities were so densely inhabited and why these buildings survived for so long, often still standing thousands of years after construction.[23]

Such grand temples, palaces, and other monumental structures stand out to us today, but it's important to remember that they were surrounded by much smaller buildings that tell a different, complementary story about life in ancient Mesopotamia. Bricks, after all, were also used to build people's houses. For the first part of the Early Dynastic period, the archaeological evidence for private homes is sparse, not for want of ruins, but for their location deep under the arid earth. Some sites are best left underground and undisturbed to preserve their fragile remains, which can be partially resurrected by other means, and some sites simply have yet to be excavated. The use of remote sensing technologies, like imagery from satellites and drones, has allowed archaeologists to map the remains of whole cities without lifting a trowel, and the handful of sites where houses have been excavated layer additional details onto that digital picture. Archaeologists have used remote sensing on various cities, including Ur and Lagash further north, to learn about the layout of cities and the density of residential areas down to the width of streets. This level of detail may sound extraneous, but it allows historians and archaeologists to paint a picture of everyday life. How far did someone have to walk to get from their house to the nearest temple? Did street width permit two carts to pass each other, or were they just wide enough to fit a solo donkey? Where did canals interrupt or connect architecture, or create boundaries within a city?

The images also show that in the shadows of (usually well-excavated) palaces and temples lie densely packed neighbourhoods of private homes.[24] We don't need to look far beyond the traditional courtyard houses of Al-Kadhimiya district in Baghdad today to picture these ancient abodes. These homes would have been centred around at least one open-air courtyard, paved typically with a tiled floor, bordered by brick walls, and decorated with sometimes colourful painted wooden doors and windows. Each door would lead into a room on the ground floor. One house may border another or be separated from it by a narrow, sometimes winding gap.[25]

For the same reason that houses in Greece are painted white to prevent overheating, or older buildings in Britain have small windows to avoid draughts in winter, architecture must accommodate the climate. Archaeologist Mary Shepperson captures beautifully what architecture really means for life, then and now. She writes:

> There are two periods of about five days each, one in the Spring and one in the Autumn, when the weather in southern Iraq is quite nice. Outside of those brief pleasant interludes, it's either cold, windy and rainy, or roasting, windy and dusty. In the past, before electric heaters and air conditioning, the only thing standing between human beings and great physical discomfort was architecture.[26]

In residential areas in Mesopotamian cities, houses might have been jammed together to allow buildings to shade each other and to minimise the amount of surface area exposed to sunlight.[27]

The layout of private homes had to accommodate not just climate and geography, but everyday needs, including the less than glamorous ones. Innovations from the Early Dynastic period therefore also include the all-important toilet. Toilets begin to appear in the early third millennium BCE at various sites in ancient Mesopotamia, including Ur. Cylindrical shafts were dug into the ground and padded with perforated pottery rings. Atop these shafts sat a small drain opening or sometimes a square-shaped seat built of none other than the trusted mud brick.

But where did the waste actually go? Depending on the city's infrastructure, it might simply seep into the ground, or get carried through a drainage system once flushed manually with rinse water. Woolley gives a particularly detailed description of Ur's early second millennium BCE lavatories, which did not benefit from central drainage. Unlike those lucky enough to relieve themselves in temples or palaces, 'the ordinary citizen', Woolley writes, 'had to make his own arrangements for the disposal of his sewage'.[28]

These houses and cities leave behind traces of the architecture of everyday life. Mud bricks built up the walls that kept people cool and close together, and buttressed their toilets. They tell us about more than just ancient attempts at air conditioning and waste management; the slightly broken, often still buried bricks that people used to build their homes provide clues about how they coexisted. Crammed together in the shadow of those towering buildings, private homes confirm the success of these institutions in maintaining some level of social cohesion. This is perhaps the ancient Mesopotamian rendition of 'if you build it, they will come' – and they will bring with them not just their innovations and political ideas, but also their toilets.

As well as living in these houses, many thousands of people would have been involved in the hard work of building the homes, gigantic walls, and splendid palaces. Some people's job was to dig up the mud from canals or gather the straw and reed to mix with the mud. Other people mixed the materials together and cast them in the mould, while others baked the resulting bricks or laid them out to dry. There were many steps in the production process, and many different people involved in every step.

The colossal task of making millions of bricks meant an equally colossal taskforce was needed, so just about anyone could be roped into construction work, even a highly trained astronomer like Tabiya who in a clay letter begged the Assyrian king in the seventh century BCE not to abandon him to the task of making bricks.[29] Letters from ancient Assyrian officials to the king in the first millennium BCE even give a sense of people pulling their hair out to secure the workforce and raw materials to keep up with brickmaking quotas. This desperation is captured in the saga of a shepherd named Ilu-piya-usur and the stress he caused his superiors in the eighth century BCE. Ilu-piya-usur was tasked with providing 300 bales of straw and reeds for brickmaking, and not only did he fail to produce the required bales, but he also 'stole the sheep in his charge and went away, seeking refuge in a temple' (and all this after also stealing money from another man). Even after these multiple crimes in one fell swoop, the official was willing to excuse everything as long as the shepherd just provided the much-needed materials for brickmaking. It seems the need for the straw and reed was far more urgent than the need for punishment.[30]

It was normal practice to stamp bricks with a cuneiform inscription that described the building, the god to whom it was dedicated or the king who oversaw the building work. The technology used to write these inscriptions is, in a way, a variation on the earliest printing press, dating as far back as the Sargonic period, which picks up where the Early Dynastic period leaves off with the rise of King Sargon around 2340 BCE. An orphaned king left to float in a basket down a river before being recovered by a gardener, Sargon eventually rose to power after defeating key Sumerian city-states. He founded what many agree is the world's first empire, which was equal parts conquest and construction – and within that, an exciting technological innovation tantamount to the world's first portable printing press.

Instead of having a scribe write an inscription over and over again on select bricks, a highly skilled and time-consuming task, a sizeable and specially made stamp bearing a cuneiform inscription meant that anyone could impress messages into a brick in mere seconds. One of these stamps still survives today, from the time of one of Sargon's successors (and grandsons), King Naram-Sîn around 2250 BCE. On this square clay stamp with a curved handle, the contours of the cuneiform characters pop out in relief and also in reverse so that, when pressed into the wet mud of a freshly made brick, they impress a readable inscription that looks a lot like something a scribe might produce with a reed stylus. 'Naram-Sîn, builder of the temple of the god Sîn', it reads simply.[31] It was precisely this technology that was used to stamp the brick of Amar-Suen with the inscription about the golden statues and the great curse, faithfully copied onto the clay drum, or museum label, found in Ennigaldi-Nanna's palace many centuries later.

But it was not just people who stamped the moist mud surfaces of bricks laid out to dry. In more happy accidents from history, we also see the paw prints of dogs imprinted onto the mud bricks as they scampered over freshly made moist mud bricks. Dogs were an important part of life in ancient Mesopotamia, where they guarded homes and cities, they helped people hunt, and they may have helped them heal alongside Gula, the goddess of medicine. As they so often do today, they accompanied soldiers into battle, which gets depicted in art alongside chariots and horses, and recorded in administrative texts that describe their provisions.[32] Sumerian proverbs give sweet glimpses into the way people interacted with and relied on their canine companions, such as 'The dog understands, "Take it!" It does not understand, "Put it down!"'; and 'A dog which is played with turns into a puppy.' Or a personal favourite, 'Fate is a dog, walking always behind a man.'[33] My own ten-year-old black Labrador follows me around like a shadow, lying quietly at my feet when I sit at the dining table or panting cheerfully at my side when we go for short runs. He is, unequivocally, the best dog in the world (as is every other dog in the world). I cannot think of a more beautiful – and less stressful – way to understand the inescapability of fate than as a doting dog at my heels.

Perhaps this was the case with brickmakers in Ur who laid wet, stamped bricks out to dry. One of these bricks bears the stamped inscription of King Ur-Nammu, and just to the left of the cuneiform signs are two paw prints of a dog that weighed about 20 kilograms (44 pounds), the size of a full-grown Border Collie or mastiff puppy.[34] Four paw prints cover another one of Ur-Nammu's bricks.[35] Were the dogs following the brickmakers, or were they strays who were so thoroughly surrounded by the moulded mud cubes that they couldn't help but step on them in search of food or shelter?

Did the brickmakers shoo them away, or chuckle at the paw prints left for posterity before feeding them bits of bread and meat?

Even before Woolley's excavation of Ur in the twentieth century, the building blocks of life in ancient Mesopotamia were visible on the surface. The mound that once buried the ruins of the great city was so covered in flecks of dried bitumen that locals called it Tell al-Muqayyar, 'Mound of Pitch'. Brickwork poked out of the tell, hinting at the monumental ruins below the rocky sand of southern Iraq's desert. People's houses, the palaces of their kings, the pedestals for their statues, and the ingredients in their medical therapies drew from these basic materials, hewn from the landscape around them.

The opening lines of the *Epic of Gilgamesh* invite readers (or listeners) to inspect the brick walls surrounding Uruk. Anyone would see that the bricks were baked, not sun-dried – in other words, that they were strong and solid and built to last, like King Gilgamesh himself. Among them is a cedarwood box that encloses a secret tablet made of lapis lazuli that records the whole tale of Gilgamesh. I like to think that the walls are doing more here than simply providing the most impossible-to-find hiding place for the bright blue stone tablet. The walls bore witness to it all. Its bricks were laid by his people under his watch, and those bricks towered over him upon his return to Uruk after a life-changing journey. In some sense, the walls saw the most important moments in Gilgamesh's story; they were there for it all.

As something that surrounded people in ancient Mesopotamia, it makes sense for bricks to carry stories and secrets,
to embody history and even people, and to symbolise something important enough that these humdrum mud building
blocks find their way into myth and medicine. It perhaps also
made sense for an ancient governor of Ur to delight in finding a far more ancient brick that once held up a statue, and to
deem it important enough to get a scribe to copy it faithfully
enough that today, even without the brick itself, it is easy to
picture. The object carried a story that warranted remem-
brance. If Gilgamesh did indeed exist in the era of great kings
of the Early Dynastic period, then he perished in antiquity
alongside his subjects. The millions of bricks he supposedly
had laid to erect Uruk's walls, however, remain. Even if he
doesn't join them in weathering the extremes of time and
erosion, Gilgamesh would be happy to learn that he has
achieved the only kind of immortality allowed mere mortals:
he is remembered.

4

The Statue of King Shulgi

How to Be a Good King

My toddler often asks me to tell her the story of Gilgamesh's quest for eternal life. It is usually in the middle of the night after yelling for me in the baby monitor, interrupting a sleep so deep that I barely know my name upon waking – only that I am mommy and must get up. Half stumbling from my room in a panic, I feel my way to her door and wade through a shallow sea of board books and battered building blocks until I reach the edge of her bed. 'What's wrong, my love?' I ask in Arabic. Her three-year-old reply in English sounds so loud that I'm worried it will wake my infant son. 'Um, Mom, can a Portuguese man-o-war come to our house?' (She actually calls them Portuguese man-o-warts, a detail that I hope I never forget.) After reassuring her that their tentacles are really too long for them to live anywhere other than the ocean, I can feel her mulling it over quietly in the dark. 'Okay,' she finally concedes, but by now she feels awake enough to ask for the story of Gilgamesh. 'The one,' she clarifies, 'where he looks for Uta-napishti.'

Thinking of the Babylonian lullabies to quiet crying babies, I picture parents in ancient Mesopotamia hushing their toddlers in the darkness, lest their wails wake the *kusarikkum*, a deity with a bison's body and a human head who guards the home. I kneel at her bedside next to a dimly lit penguin-shaped night light and grasp her tiny hand before recounting Gilgamesh's quest to the edge of the known world, past the cosmic gates at the base of twin mountains where the sun rises and sets, in search of the key to immortality. Instead, he finds answers to questions he never even knew to ask.

I have to modify the many myths about Gilgamesh to suit a mind forming one million neural networks every second, but my daughter knows his world and the cast of characters who populate it. The mud brick walls of Uruk rise up in her imagination. She can picture the steppe outside the city, where Gilgamesh's beloved companion Enkidu found life among the animals he fought to protect, and the forest of gemstones beyond the cosmic gates. My toddler's familiarity with and love for stories of Gilgamesh is not unusual (although the level of detail may signal a specialist *in situ*); Gilgamesh was a household name throughout ancient Mesopotamia's long history, and so it remains to some degree today in the Middle East. Remembered as one of the earliest great kings in the region, he begins his royal career as a tyrant but ends it as a king who has grown to understand the value of protecting and preserving his community. His position in Middle Eastern culture – and particularly in Iraq – is in part thanks to his reputation as one of the great Sumerian kings who, according to legend, ruled the first city of Uruk for over 100 years with a wisdom that only someone as old as the Flood itself could impart. Stories about his superhuman strength and depth of knowledge filled royal courts for well over a millennium.

The earliest surviving poems about Gilgamesh would have been recited at the royal palaces of the short-lived Third Dynasty of Ur, the period that follows the fall of Sargon's empire, as entertaining tales of a legendary king who had lived around 500 years before. The Third Dynasty of Ur, also known as the Ur III period, was founded by Ur-Nammu, the king who began construction of the ziggurat at Ur. During this period, the Sumerian culture and language is resurrected (after Akkadian had displaced it under Sargon and his successors) for its final living hurrah before it becomes relegated to the ivory – or mud brick – tower of cuneiform academia. Although the Third Dynasty of Ur only lasted about a fleeting century – from c. 2100 to 2000 BCE – it is the best-documented period in the region's history. This is partly because the highly organised state of this period relied on a lot of red tape to maintain its administrative machinery. Clay tablets preserve transactions, loans, letters, court cases – an almost bottomless resource for economic and political history. Alongside these ostensibly dry administrative texts survive works of literature, hymns, and even medicine. Some 120,000 clay tablets held in collections around the world, along with an indeterminate number in the Iraq Museum, survive from this short window of time to document everything from the accomplishments of kings to the death of a sheep.[1]

In excavating Ennigaldi-Nanna's palace at Ur, Woolley and the team stumbled upon a statue fragment from this very period, carved out of diorite, a dark polished stone, and covered in cuneiform characters. It was clear to the excavators that the statue had broken to pieces in antiquity, but its remaining piece beautifully preserved a cuneiform inscription that names Shulgi, the longest reigning monarch of the Third Dynasty of Ur – indeed, one of the longest reigning kings in ancient Mesopotamia's history. The fragment that preserves Shulgi's cuneiform 'tattoo' looks like little more than an uneven sphere, perhaps once part of a stone statue's shoulder. Many other more complete statues of this famous king have been found, and they show a man with large eyes, thick eyebrows joined together over a sloping nose, and narrow lips.

Shulgi's rule lasted almost half a century, from 2094 to 2046 BCE, which we know thanks to texts that capture his yearly accomplishments, like 'year the city of Der was restored'.[2] There's even a reference to his own daughter becoming high priestess of the moon god, like the much earlier Enheduanna and much later Ennigaldi-Nanna, as the 'year En-nirza-ana, the en-priestess of Nanna, was installed'. These pithy 'year-names' give a sort of highlights reel of any king's rule, and tell us that Shulgi, in many ways, was the ideal king – a real-life Gilgamesh. He inherited the empire from his father, Ur-Nammu, who rather unusually died a violent death in battle – a very bad sign in ancient Mesopotamia that should have put a pretty much instant end to Shulgi's rule. Instead, Shulgi went from strength to strength. He grew the empire and even created a standing army. The year-names from the last half of his rule take on a decidedly military character, referencing campaigns in almost every cardinal direction that would expand the empire's footprint.[3]

A good king, as we will see, does all of these things and more. Hymns that praise his deeds layer some of the ideal traits of a king onto his real accomplishments. In one, which is written in the first person, he lists those of his accomplishments that tally with those ideals, such as the somewhat unsubtle 'I have perfected my wisdom just as my heroism and strength'. The poetry of 'I am a fierce-looking lion, begotten by a dragon' finds balance with more literal descriptions of laying down highways and planting gardens. He even supposedly ran something like an ultra-marathon from Nippur to Ur, a distance of almost 125 miles, in an impossibly short number of hours. Over the course of 400 lines, the hymn highlights his exceptionalism for posterity, and it records praise worthy of a king who wants to be – and indeed still is – remembered.[4] Although perhaps not as much of a household name as Gilgamesh, he must have come pretty close back in the day.

By the time Shulgi ascended the throne, the traditions of kingship and its ideals had long since been established in ancient Mesopotamia, like those immortalised in the poems about Gilgamesh, recited and remembered in Ur's royal court. Gilgamesh resonated not only for the very human issues his stories tackle, like love and grief and a fear of one's mortality, but for the ultimate lesson he learns about what it means to be a good king. The poems that celebrate Gilgamesh's exploits would have been part of the repertoire of courtly entertainment. Its earliest iterations take the form of Sumerian stories, sung aloud or otherwise performed in the courts of the Ur III kings, where poetry and music played an important part of royal and religious life. The ziggurat at Ur during this century-long era would have boasted a staff of priests, butchers, sex workers, seers, singers, and musicians. Lists of such staff from Girsu, a major administrative hub of the Third Dynasty of Ur, include various types of musicians and several kinds of singers. Instruments would have been a common sight, and we can picture musicians like Dada who, during the reign of the penultimate king of the dynasty, took receipt of no fewer than nine pairs of string instruments known as *sim* that had broken and been repaired.[5]

These entertainment professionals undoubtedly included in their performances the, at the time, standalone Sumerian stories about Gilgamesh and his companion Enkidu that would eventually get incorporated into the work of literature we now call the *Epic of Gilgamesh*. In one of these early versions, Gilgamesh and Enkidu travel to the great Cedar Forest of what is now Lebanon to defeat its guardian, Humbaba. In another, Enkidu descends to the Underworld to retrieve an instrument that Gilgamesh had lost. When Enkidu gets trapped there, Gilgamesh asks him about the fate of people who lived and died in various ways, like a palace eunuch or a man who died in battle. One of the most poignant couplets in all of Sumerian literature appears near the end of this story: 'Did you see my little stillborn children who never knew existence?' Gilgamesh asks. His dead companion replies, 'They play at a table of gold and silver, laden with honey and ghee.' All of the other ghosts that Enkidu had described in the Underworld suffered ongoing trials in their afterlives. Other works of cuneiform literature describe the Underworld as a 'gloomy house' whose dwellers wear feathers for garments, eat dust and clay, and 'see no light'.[6] But not so it seems for those who died too young to know anything other than their mothers' heartbeats. Traditions about

Gilgamesh don't shy away from the most anguished of life's questions, especially ones centred on mortality and loss.

The majority of these early Sumerian poems about Gilgamesh survive on clay tablets drafted by eighteenth-century BCE Babylonian scribal students – about 200 years after the fall of the Ur kings in whose royal courts such tales were probably sung aloud. It was around this time that traditions about him begin to appear in the Akkadian language, where his adventures with, and eventually without, Enkidu are fleshed out in a Babylonian version of the *Epic of Gilgamesh*. While the story resonates today as an early example of the hero's journey that tackles many of life's most challenging questions, what belies this is the transformation of Gilgamesh into a good king.

At the start of the legend, Gilgamesh terrorises the citizens of Uruk with his rule. Two-thirds divine and one-third human, he stood at almost 6 cubits – around 9 feet – tall with strength as mighty as a meteorite, described as 'a lump of rock from the sky'. Instead of using his strength to protect and serve his people, he wielded it to brutalise them. He forced the men to build the 5.5-mile wall around Uruk and, for his entertainment, to fight each other in sporting matches that left them exhausted. He forced himself on the women, letting 'no girl go free to her groom'. It was the women, in the end, who begged their goddesses and gods to spare them from this semi-divine tyrant. (Needless to say, I leave these details out of my daughter's version of Gilgamesh's story, in which Enkidu also doesn't die, and the two make friends with Humbaba because he loves trees . . . I take some liberties.)

From clay thrown into the wild steppe outside of Uruk, the goddess Aruru fashions Enkidu to be Gilgamesh's match.

'An offspring of silence', born without the cries of a woman in childbirth, Enkidu comes into being as a full-grown man, as wild as any other animal in the steppe outside of Uruk. He eventually approaches the city to take on the tyrannical Gilgamesh, who in the meantime dreams of a man whom he would love deeply and who would also be his saviour. The language of the epic suggests that Gilgamesh and Enkidu were far more than friends.[7]

My favourite summary of this first part of the epic comes from, of all places, an episode of *Star Trek: The Next Generation* that finds Captain Jean-Luc Picard stranded on a planet with a Tamarian, a species that communicates exclusively through metaphor derived from their history and mythology. After spending hours trying unsuccessfully to communicate, the two sit by a fire in the middle of a wood as night begins to fall when they are suddenly attacked by a quick-moving creature in the dark. The creature strikes the Tamarian and, as the alien lies dying, Picard finally realises that his travel companion communicates through stories. At the alien's request, Picard falls upon one of the earliest and most enduring works of literature, the *Epic of Gilgamesh*. His face animated by flickering flames of their makeshift hearth, he recounts what he can remember of the story, and of the pair Gilgamesh and Enkidu:

> They became great friends. Gilgamesh and Enkidu at Uruk . . . But Enkidu fell to the ground, struck down by the gods. And Gilgamesh wept bitter tears, saying, 'He who was my companion through adventure and hardship, is gone forever.'[8]

And just as Gilgamesh watched Enkidu die, Picard watched helplessly as the Tamarian captain passed away.

It is only after Enkidu's death, in fact, that Gilgamesh's journey begins, as the loss drives him to seek out the secret knowledge of immortality from the Babylonian Noah figure, Uta-napishti. It is this quest that is the making of Gilgamesh, and the start of his transformation from godawful to good king. Hounded by grief, he crosses an ancient mythical landscape that eventually takes him to twin mountains where the sun god rises and sets – the limit of the known world in Mesopotamian cosmic geography. He manages to convince its half-human, half-scorpion sentinels to let him pass into a pitch-black region beyond those mountains that eventually opens up onto a divine garden filled with breathtaking trees made of carnelian, lapis lazuli and coral, and, eventually, a seashore. On finding Uta-napishti there, Gilgamesh hopes to receive the secret to everlasting life from him, but instead is told that wandering in search of this unattainable goal is actually shortening his life.

According to Uta-napishti's account of the Flood, the supreme god Enlil decided to send a deluge to destroy humankind, but the mischievous god Ea, who had a soft spot for humanity, finds an indirect way to instruct an 'exceedingly wise' man (Uta-napishti) to build a boat and save as many living creatures as possible from the coming flood. To build a boat, however, Uta-napishti would need help from his fellow citizens, meaning he would have to lie – or stretch the truth at least. Following Ea's instructions, he makes a promise to his people laced with a warning. The supreme god, he tells them, 'will rain down on you bread-cakes, in the evening, a torrent of wheat'.[9] The ambiguity here stems from some good old-fashioned puns that foreshadow the storm to come. The word for 'bread-cakes' in Akkadian is *kukku*, which plays on the word *kakku*, 'weapon', and the word *kibtu*, 'wheat', has a homophone that means 'misfortune'. The plural form for wheat used in this couplet, *kibātu*, also sounds a lot like the word for 'heavy', *kabittu*. Had Uta-napishti lied to his fellow citizens about cake and wheat, or had he warned them that the morning would bring rain so heavy it would serve as a weapon against them?

It may nevertheless seem callous to ask your neighbours to help you build a boat in a single day and then leave them all to die. But in the older, longer version of the Flood story, he had to excuse himself from a feast he hosted due to the emotional toll of his task as 'his heart was broken, and he was vomiting gall'.[10] In some ways, Uta-napishti provides a model for ideal kingship: an exceedingly wise man who obeyed the gods at great emotional cost and who did what was needed to ensure the survival of humanity.

While he never uncovered the secret to eternal life, Gilgamesh found something just as valuable: a model for a good king and a depth of wisdom that would shape his rule. Uta-napishti teaches Gilgamesh an important lesson on the fragility of life: 'No one sees the face of death,' he reminded the younger king, 'no one hears the voice of death, and yet furious death is the one who cuts man down.' Death is inevitable. Eternal life lies not in the survival of any individual, but in the survival of the community – of humanity.

Gilgamesh's story evolves considerably from the earliest Sumerian versions that would have been sung aloud in the courts of kings like Ur-Nammu and Shulgi, to the latest surviving fragment written by a trainee astronomer named

Bel-ahhe-usur in the 130s BCE. Somewhere in between these two temporal poles, around 1000 BCE, a scholar named Sîn-leqi-unninni edited the tale into a standard version that would be copied in the same form for centuries, what we now call the *Epic of Gilgamesh*. Tellingly, Sîn-leqi-unninni also added a prologue that spotlights wisdom in Gilgamesh's transformation from cruel to kind king. His version emphasises the depths of wisdom that Gilgamesh would ultimately gain from his failed quest for eternal life that would enable him to rule in a way that protected and preserved his community. Wisdom enables a good king to rule with justice, to be pious, to protect his people by constructing city walls and winning wars, and to build a strong state. In some ways, the epic warns against tyranny, while also giving a blueprint for how to rule well, and the Gilgamesh of its ending remained a symbol of a wise, ideal king for all rulers who followed him.

When she was three, I took my daughter to the Ashmolean Museum in Oxford to see Gilgamesh's name written in cuneiform on one of the most important documents from ancient Mesopotamia. Shaped like a three-dimensional prism about a foot tall, this slab of clay is known as the Sumerian King List, and the copy I sought out with my toddler came from around 1800 BCE. Just as its modern title suggests, it lists hundreds of kings of the region, both mythical and historical, along with the dates of their rule. Once mounted on a spindle, like a rotating display case in a shop, it now sits atop a pale light in a glass museum cabinet. As I lifted my daughter up to bring her face to face with what the label described as 'one of the most famous objects in the museum', she stared in silence before announcing matter-of-factly, 'Mom, that's not Gilgamesh. It's just a brick.'

Gilgamesh, so the Sumerian King List tells us, ruled for 126 years, an impossible length of time that blends mythology, ideology, and history in a way that's typical of Mesopotamian historical records. Also listed is the mythical superhero Lugal-banda, an ancient Flash endowed with superhuman speeds who supposedly ruled Uruk for 1,200 years. A king called Etana is thought to have ruled the city of Kish for 1,500 years. Legend tells of his trip to heaven on the back of an eagle to retrieve the 'plant of giving birth' that would help him and his wife have a baby (infertility is not a new problem). Like Gilgamesh, such characters also appear in literary works in Sumerian and, later, Akkadian. Figures like Etana, Lugal-banda, and Gilgamesh are mythologised to highlight their superhuman greatness as kings and, by extension, the greatness of kingship in Mesopotamia.

History, memory, and antiquity were important in ancient Mesopotamia and it was not unusual – or even problematic – to blend history and myth. The older a thing or person or event was, the more important it was. Kings regularly sought to root their royal activities and even identities in bygone ages. The Sumerian King List, as a record stretching into a past so distant no sources even survive to corroborate it, allowed later kings to associate themselves with such a long history of greatness.[11] The people who wrote the list were attempting the very same thing I am in this book – a history of their ancient past. To me, this is what makes the text so special. It is a prism-shaped window onto ancient understandings of history, a home-grown presentation of the past.[12]

For Assyriologists, it might compare to a historian 5,000 years from now constructing a timeline of the twentieth century partly through Marvel comics as a genre whose alternate history is, indirectly, a source of history. The Marvel stories navigate the framework of modern history with real cities like New York and real events like the Second World War. The characters, however, are larger than life like Jane Foster in *Thor* who, just like the legendary Gilgamesh, travelled beyond the known world, or like Barry Allen in *The Flash*, who moved with superhuman speed similar to Lugal-banda. Saturated with myth and fiction, the Marvel universe still draws from reality and allows artists to rewrite history in a way that occasionally allows good to prevail over evil. If a historian of the future could find a way to unpick fact from fiction, to separate the real from the ideal, they might be able to reconstruct a basic timeline of major events from 1939 onward – and how some wish they had turned out instead.

The Sumerian King List also helps us answer a question that historians and archaeologists continue to puzzle over: where did the very idea specifically of a king come from? In the Early Dynastic period, there was not one king who ruled over the region, but individual rulers of city-states who all coexisted (and occasionally came into conflict). As time wore on, the idea of one supreme ruler seems to have taken root and eventually flourished into the concept and institution of a king. According to the Sumerian King List, the concept of 'kingship' quite simply 'descended from heaven' to take its seat in the city of Eridu, according to the later tradition, or

Kish, according to the earlier one. The reality is quite a bit messier than this.

One of the earliest written documents from Mesopotamia, from just before 3000 BCE, is a tablet covered in signs that look like circles, circles within circles, and half circles. These are, in fact, ancient numerical symbols, recording calculations of the areas of several fields by a scribe using an early form of geometry. A small cluster of signs that stand for whole words follow each calculation, which represent the titles of high-ranking officials, and among these are the signs 'lord' and 'wife of the lord'. Could this be an early allusion to some kind of rulership, or at least to the concentration of power in the hands of one person?[13] If so, this could be one of the earliest known records of such a phenomenon anywhere in the world.

'Lords' and kings were not quite the same gig, though. Early city rulers like the 'lord' did not have the same responsibilities, expectations, and divine backing of kingship proper that were part of the deal in later periods of ancient Mesopotamia's history. How, then, did things move from 'lord'-ship to kingship? Was kingship simply the inevitable culmination of social stratification? It may be that the emergence of a single ruler was a logical consequence of early urbanism in the region; improvements to farming and the resulting food surpluses freed people up for non-agricultural activities, which may have encouraged social stratification. Even ancient social ladders had a top rung. Some modern scholars have suggested that kings emerged as a natural consequence of conflict and set the stage for a more lasting political institution that followed bloodlines in lieu of ability. Other more speculative theories are based on the idea that these early rulers were seen as earthly husbands of the goddesses who dominated the early pantheon of ancient Mesopotamia. While there are more gaps than answers, by the end of the third millennium BCE, it is kings, rather than 'lords' or other equivalent titles for sovereigns, that are in charge of the region.[14]

As well as the land of the living, these great kings also populate the Underworld: the cemeteries of ancient Mesopotamia. Buried near the foundations of Ur's ziggurat, archaeologists have discovered about 2,000 graves of some of the city's ancient residents. The vast majority of these, dated to the Early Dynastic and Sargonic periods, consisted of simple burials – typically a single pit with a body laid in a coffin or wrapped in reed with a handful of personal items, like pottery and jewellery.[15] Sixteen tombs, however, were clearly a cut above. They contained multiple chambers that entombed the bodies of Ur's elite together with grave goods of such extraordinary splendour that Woolley dubbed them 'royal tombs'.[16] These tombs preserved an array of gold and gilded objects, ox-drawn chariots, musical instruments with gold fittings and mother-of-pearl inlay, battle-axes, ornate headdresses, and more.

Overshadowing the dazzling finds, however, were sinister signs of human sacrifice. Over 100 attendants followed some of the tombs' main occupants into the afterlife, buried in what Woolley called 'death pits'. Elaborately dressed and surrounded by musical instruments, their deaths or their corpses may have formed part of a mourning or funerary ritual.[17] In the largest of these, known as the Great Death Pit, seventy-four people, including adolescents, met a violent end. The remains of one of the only skulls complete enough to undergo a CT scan show that the person – a woman in her late teens or early twenties – met her end by blunt force trauma. The blow that ended her life was delivered with a hafted weapon like an axe, similar to weaponry found in a nearby tomb and ones depicted on cylinder seals found at contemporary sites. The skull also showed signs of being cooked and embalmed with mercury, both practices associated with the preservation of human remains.[18]

In one particular tomb, excavators found the remains of a forty-year-old woman that told an unusual story. So spectacular was the untouched tomb that Woolley sent a telegram, written in Latin to prevent anyone who might intercept it from understanding its message and looting the site, to the directors of the British Museum. 'I found the intact tomb, stone built and vaulted over with bricks,' he wrote in 1927, before giving an abbreviated description of a woman 'adorned with a dress in which gems, flower crowns, and animal figures are woven. The tomb is magnificent with jewels and golden cups.'[19]

His description leaves out details that might have made the directors bristle. Her skull had been compressed under the weight of all the dirt that had filled the tomb for so many millennia. Rows of teeth were frozen into a morbid, two-dimensional smile framed by flattened gold ribbons, leaves, and hoops, and the lapis lazuli triangles of her beaded necklace. In order to display the impressive jewels in the 1928 British Museum exhibition of the artefacts, Katharine Woolley had to make a model head and rather bouffant wig big enough to fit everything. (The face she gave the model generated some controversy for not looking enough like ancient Sumerian statues, which presumably looked somewhat like Sumerian people, and led another excavator at Ur to make a competing model in that style with higher cheek-bones, wide-open eyes, and a dramatic unibrow.[20])

In the middle of the third millennium BCE, when the woman was buried, her final resting place was a mud brick chamber with a vaulted ceiling. She was laid upon a bier, perhaps made of wood, and her corpse surrounded with gold and silver bowls, alabaster jars, and a wooden lyre decorated with a silver bull and shell inlaid designs, among other fine objects. Her body was decorated even more glamorously. Woolley described her as 'covered with beads of gold, silver, lapis-lazuli, carnelian, and agate . . . they were astonishingly numerous and of exceptionally fine quality.'[21] The bodies of three others were found in the chamber, adorned with little more than beads and, in one case, some weaponry. At some point before excavators unearthed the chamber in the 1920s, its roof had collapsed, leaving the woman and her grandeur crushed under the weight of brick, dirt, and debris.

Who was this woman, buried not only with such finery in a vaulted underground room, but also with other people, perhaps to accompany her into death? Three gold pins held her garment together at the shoulder, and attached to each was a cylinder seal made of lapis lazuli, one of which answered this question. 'Puabi', it reads, followed by the title 'queen', or *eresh* in Sumerian. Extraordinarily, the seal mentions no man or king in relation to her. Is it possible that she may have ruled with some autonomy, rather than in relation to or with reliance on any man? No other available contemporary sources name her, so her named role as a queen remains shrouded in mystery.

But how plausible is it for a woman to have ruled in ancient Mesopotamia? From the historical evidence, queens seem less commonplace as kings, but there are glimpses of women in power. According to the Sumerian King List, the city of Kish was ruled by at least one bartender-turned-queen named Ku-Bau sometime around 2400 BCE.[22] The passage reads:

> Ku-Bau
> the woman tavern-keeper,
> who made firm the foundations of Kish,
> was king, 100 years she ruled.

This handful of ostensibly dry lines about Ku-Bau's rule describe a unique historical moment. If the list is accurate and Ku-Bau did rule Kish around 2400 BCE, that makes her the earliest confirmed woman in power in the ancient Middle East. Ku-Bau also enjoys the title of *lugal* or 'king', instead of any terminology for queen, which suggests she ruled in her own right much like Puabi might have around the same time.

As more sites are uncovered throughout ancient Mesopotamia, evidence of women in power may become less of an exception. A royal cemetery at Umm el-Marra to the east of Aleppo in what is now Syria from around the same period yielded the kind of finds that make us question just how much of an exception it was to find women in positions of power. Strikingly, one woman was buried in a tomb that contained various items of silver and gold, and a foot-long bronze spearhead, inviting modern scholars to re-evaluate more than one assumption about gendered activities and rule in ancient Mesopotamia.[23]

Almost 2,000 years after Puabi and Ku-Bau, the Assyrian queen Sammu-ramat would wield such power in the court that she would inspire the later Greek legend of Queen Semiramis. In his *Histories*, the Greek historian Herodotus credits her with building the fortifications of the banks of the Euphrates. 'Before that,' he writes, 'the whole plain used to be flooded by the river.'[24] The Greek physician Ctesias of Cnidus mentioned her in his now lost works that survive only in their retelling by the first-century BCE Greek historian Diodorus. According to him, Queen Semiramis was fed by pigeons before being found and raised by shepherds. While married to her first husband, she accompanied the Assyrian King 'Ninus' on a military campaign to Bactria, which she helped him conquer. She eventually married him after her first husband took his own life. King Ninus then died, leaving her to rule his empire, and in her role as queen, she founded Babylon and enhanced a palace in Media, a region in north-western Iran that once fell under the control of the Medes.[25] After a failed military campaign in India, she ascended to heaven, and on earth she became worshipped as a pigeon or dove.

Her story also finds its way, with some variations, into Roman, Jewish, and Armenian legend. For an Assyrian queen to have survived into the much later traditions of diverse cultures, and even found herself deified to a degree, is remarkable, but no more so than what we do know of her actual life. The real Sammu-ramat may not have been married quite so many times or have turned into a dove upon her death, but her list of accomplishments as queen is unique.

Contemporary historical records confirm that Sammu-ramat ruled the vast Assyrian empire much like a regent in the years between the death of her husband, Shamshi-Adad V, and the ascension of her young son, Adad-nirari III, to the throne in the ninth century BCE. She also held the royal title 'the woman of the palace' or *sēgallu* in Akkadian, typical of Assyrian queens during this era who managed an array of responsibilities parallel to those of the king. Queens supported temple institutions and participated in rituals designed to guide political decision-making, like omens and oracles. All over the empire, they managed households and palaces with extensive holdings of land and hundreds of employees. They were closely associated with scorpions, given how fiercely female scorpions defend their young, and the seal found on the body of a young queen named Hamâ shows both a scorpion and a lion at her throne. 'In many respects,' writes historian Dr Saana Svärd, 'the queen's actions were comparable to those of the king.'[26] The notable exception to this is a queen's military role (with Sammu-ramat as the exception even to this exception in battling the Hittites alongside her son in 805 BCE).[27]

Assyrian queens wielded exceptional power, even when it was the kings who ruled. Queen Naqia in particular deserves to be as much of a household name as Cleopatra. Mother to King Esarhaddon, she had such power that statues of her were put on display – at the time unprecedented for a queen – and was the only Assyrian queen to leave behind a royal building inscription. In it, she describes her construction of a palace in Nineveh with foreign labour, 'enemies' defeated in battle who made the building's bricks.[28] Scholars at the time even compared her to the antediluvian mythical sage Adapa, a comparison reserved for kings.[29] She oversaw political and military matters, and one letter from a governor at the fringes of the Assyrian empire named Na'id-Marduk recounts to her a raid by the Elamites. He promises to keep her apprised and even addresses her as 'my lord', a title enjoyed only by kings in royal correspondence.

Women like Ku-Bau and Sammu-ramat were unusual in a region whose people were typically ruled by kings. These kings left behind copious chronicles of their deeds for their people, their gods, and, happily, for future Assyriologists to pore over. Statues like those of Shulgi, tattooed with cuneiform signs that name him as a 'king of Ur' and 'king of the lands of Sumer and Akkad', preserve their dedications to deities and their deeds. Bricks stamped with their names memorialise the city walls, temples, and palaces they built. Poetry describes their trials and triumphs, and some like Gilgamesh enter the realm of legend as an exemplar of the Mesopotamian king. From the legacy these kings left behind, can we tell what made a king popular, or successful, or, importantly, 'good'?

Even as one civilisation fell and another rose in its stead, it seems the answer to what made a good king remained more or less the same, weathering the passage of time and many political and cultural shifts. From the inscriptions of Sumerian kings of the third millennium BCE to the clay barrels of Nabonidus set into niches of Ur's ziggurat in the sixth century BCE, kings went to great lengths to portray themselves to their people and their gods as worthy of rule in related and sometimes even identical ways. Perhaps this is comparable to modern-day political candidates; they must prove to their constituents that they are worthy of the vote, as individuals and as party leaders. A slight deviation from social expectations, a big enough misstep to call into question a leader's character, or failure to comply with party principles can derail a campaign (with some notable exceptions in recent memory).

Although chosen by the gods and not by popular vote, a Mesopotamian king had to continually justify that choice by fulfilling certain pre-established criteria. A good king was a just king who protected the weak and vulnerable. King Ur-Nammu who built Ur's ziggurat boasts in his collection of laws, 'I did not deliver the orphan to the rich, I did not deliver the widow to the mighty, I did not deliver the man with but one shekel to the man with one mina (i.e. 60 shekels).'[30] Just as a good king served the people, he also had to serve the gods by maintaining, building, or rebuilding temples, and ensuring provisions for the gods in these earthly, mud brick homes. Kings also had to go to war, and in some eras, battles served ideals of expansion, not just defence. The gods expected kings to be protectors, lawmakers, religious leaders, builders, warriors, and more – kings had to earn their position and continually show the gods that they were worthy of it.

Kings may have reigned supreme over mortals, but the gods reigned over *them*. Far from the absolute sovereignty of early modern European monarchies, a Mesopotamian king had to justify himself and his right to rule from ascension to death. Actions may speak louder than words, but in Mesopotamia, those actions mean nothing if not written down and displayed for the gods to read. Many of these get recorded in a genre known today as royal inscriptions, which were commissioned by kings to record their deeds.

The surviving body of Sumerian royal inscriptions alone

covers a total of 25,000 lines.[31] Scribes impressed, stamped, and carved the cuneiform characters that record these deeds into a variety of objects – the bricks laid for a temple, the clay cones buried in that building's foundations, the body parts of statues, vases, bowls, ceremonial weapons, and even the school exercise tablets of students from centuries later. Typically, a Sumerian royal inscription includes the name of the relevant king with his titles, a dedication to a particular deity, and a great act of some kind.

It is precisely this kind of royal inscription that appears on the diorite shoulder of King Shulgi kept in Ennigaldi-Nanna's museum. Short and sweet, it begins with a slightly broken reference to putting 'sustenance fields' in order and goes on to describe the king's dedication of a statue to the goddess Ninsun: 'Shulgi, mighty man, king of Ur, king of the four quarters, presented this statue to the goddess Ninsun of Ur'. However brief this inscription may be, it does tell us something interesting about how Shulgi wanted to present himself. The goddess Ninsun is none other than the mother of Gilgamesh; it is her hereditary imprint that leaves him two-thirds divine. Throughout his reign, Shulgi tries to position himself as Ninsun's son, a brother of Gilgamesh, to tap into this divine heritage and promote himself as an ideal model for kingship.[32]

While royal inscriptions may embellish a king's deeds or heritage, or even ascribe divine will or intervention to them, they still record historical events – some, like reorganising a field, perhaps less exciting than others. Many of Shulgi's inscriptions also record his military triumphs, including a brief but graphic one found in the city of Susa in what is now Iran, which describes how the king 'destroyed the land of

Kimash and Hurtum, set out a moat and heaped up a pile of corpses'.[33]

This practice of self-promotion continues well into the first millennium BCE. The great kings of Assyria set down lengthy narratives of their feats, especially ones that showcase the empire's military might. A barrel-shaped clay cylinder written sometime between 704 and 681 BCE records the many military campaigns of Sennacherib, the fourth king of the Neo-Assyrian dynasty. Its opening captures in one fell swoop almost every desirable feature of a good king; Sennacherib calls himself a great, strong, and unrivalled king who is also a 'pious' and 'reverent' shepherd. He is a 'guardian of truth who loves justice, renders assistance, [and] strives after good deeds', but he is also a 'virile warrior' who, like a 'bridle', controls those who refuse to obey and 'strikes enemies with lightning'.[34] This is actually among the least graphic of Sennacherib's accounts of how he treated enemies who refused to submit – we will get to the disembodied heads on spikes a bit later – but like anyone today struggling to draft a standout 'About Me' section on LinkedIn, he is showing his range. He can be equal parts charitable and brutal, dole out good deeds by day and violent punishment by night because it's all in a day's work when you are a king in ancient Mesopotamia. And like any good king, Sennacherib knows that his engraved stone CVs are being reviewed not by a potential new boss (or a college ex who doesn't yet realise that LinkedIn lists your profile visitors by name), but by the gods.

Despite the many centuries separating Shulgi from Sennacherib, both rulers present themselves in similar ways, with parallel values of kingship. Although formulaic and, at times, repetitive (perhaps not unlike some of today's political rhetoric), these puff pieces – which cover limestone palace reliefs, prism-shaped clay columns, diorite statues, nails, bricks, and countless other objects – tell us a great deal about how these kings wanted to present themselves and how they wanted to be remembered once they were gone.

This propaganda isn't just found in writing, but was communicated through art too. Elaborate gypsum reliefs once built into the walls of a palace at Nimrud show Ashurbanipal (the last great Assyrian king and Sennacherib's grandson) overpowering a lion in a typical hunting scene. The king's muscular forearms are interlocked with the equally chiselled front legs of the lion, who stands upright mid-attack. The wild lion symbolises the chaos of the world outside the city gates, on which only a true king can impose order and against which only a true king can protect his people. (In reality, the lions were caged and maybe even left to grow hungry and weak – or drugged – before the hunt to ensure the king would prevail over the otherwise powerful animal.) If you look closely at the carved image of the king, you can see two styluses tucked into his textile belt. According to Ashurbanipal's inscriptions, he not only hunted lions and battled enemies, but he also learned the wisdom of the god of writing, Nabû. His claims to wisdom encompass complex mathematics, obscure texts written in Sumerian and Akkadian, and antediluvian inscriptions on stone whose meanings are hidden or sealed.[35] It is worth bearing in mind that the first king to add scribal prowess to his list of achievements was none other than our Shulgi.[36]

Ashurbanipal went even further than most to demonstrate his interest in intellectual pursuits; he is famous for his 'library', which consists of about 32,000 clay tablets that were excavated from Nineveh, the Assyrian capital at the time of his rule. Unfortunately, the tablets were found during the nineteenth and early twentieth centuries before more systematic archaeological methods became standard, which means their findspots are not listed with as much precision as would be the case today. The tablets were actually found at different sites throughout the capital, including two different palaces and two temples at the northwest corner of the city wall, rather than in one neat building that we might imagine as a 'library' today.[37] Much like Woolley's museum label for Ennigaldi-Nanna's collection of antiquities, the 'library' label is a bit of a modern construction that has become part of the collection's history. Inaccurate as it may be, it has stuck (so we will keep using it).

It was the content and quality of the tablets that led early archaeologists to interpret the thousands of tablets as having hailed from a royal library. They cover all manner of scholarship – collections of omens, medical treatises, star maps, astronomical reports, dictionaries, works of literature, and more – and could all be seen as vital information for a king looking to sustain his rule. Hundreds of the tablets also end with a signature section, or colophon, that names Ashurbanipal himself as the owner, compiler, and even copyist of the tablets. A handful of letters also show the king's interest in compiling a learned collection. The king wrote letters to far-flung scholars to request copies of tablets in their collections so he could add them to his own. 'Write out all the scribal learning in the property of Nabû and send it to me. Complete the instruction!' read one letter to some scholars based in the city of Borsippa, over 300 miles to the south of his capital. Ashurbanipal's royal CV was not just about power and might, but also showed the wisdom of a learned scribe and scholar.[38]

Among the tablets thought to hail from the Library of Ashurbanipal are some of the best-preserved copies of the *Epic of Gilgamesh*, including the chapter that recaps the Flood story. The first person to read that particular tablet after it spent millennia underground in Nineveh was the English Assyriologist George Smith in the late nineteenth century, and he allegedly got so excited about stumbling upon a pre-Biblical story of Noah's Ark that he stripped down and ran naked through the halls of the British Museum. At the end of the epic, when Gilgamesh returns to Uruk after gaining so much wisdom on his quest, he asks the ferryman who accompanied him on his journey home to survey four key sites: the city, its date-grove, its clay-pit, and the temple of Ishtar. These four sites represent four activities – the home, agriculture, crafts, and religion – that express the totality of human life and society. They reflect family, food production, industry, and the *vita contemplativa*, all tucked safely within the city's walls.[39] It is over this that Gilgamesh, like all good kings, must rule, and it is this life that he must preserve – not the life of an individual, but of humanity. A good king does that by doing all the things kings show off about in their royal inscriptions. To protect life within their walls, they must be equal parts judge, builder, scribe, shepherd, and sometimes also warmonger.

Gilgamesh would perhaps be happy to learn that despite his anxiety about death, almost 5,000 years after he supposedly ruled, he lives on in many ways. His story has inspired poetry, films, music, and even video games from the Middle East (as well as my favourite *Star Trek* episode). Not unlike the towering statues of ancient Mesopotamia, a statue of Gilgamesh astride a bull by Iraqi artist Hadi Hamza Al-Taie was recently erected in Baghdad and the sculpture sits atop a thick ziggu-rat-like pyramid made of brick engraved with large cunei-form characters. Thousands of years after the kings of Ur heard verses about his exploits sung aloud in their courts, Gilgamesh remains a symbol of what it means to be a good leader. His journey instilled him with the basic principles of public service that any leader today understands; individual power comes from an empowered whole, and history will remember well those who rule with the survival of their community in mind, rather than just the next election cycle.

5

The School Tablets

Ancient Babylonian ABCs

I really struggled to learn Sumerian. I used to stress and often even sweat my way through every Sumerian class, taking chaotic notes in messy handwriting that I would then find myself unable to read when it came time to revise for exams. My brain craves structure – routine, rules, regularity – which Akkadian grammar elegantly accommodates. Sumerian, on the other hand, is the earliest language that cuneiform was used to record and remains only partially deciphered. It is not much of an exaggeration to say that there might just be as many interpretations of Sumerian as there are people who study it. My research at the time was focused on tablets that had been written in the later (and completely unrelated) language of Akkadian. So why on earth did I need to learn Sumerian? Only years later would I encounter a proverb that a Babylonian student copied down around 1800 BCE that would answer my question with a question. 'What kind of a scribe,' it reads, 'is a scribe who does not know Sumerian?'[1] Not a very good one, is the suggestion.

What offers me some comfort is that, like me, the Akkadian-speaking Babylonian students along the Tigris and Euphrates rivers thousands of years ago also had to learn Sumerian, which even then would have been a dead language. The Old Babylonian period (2000–1600 BCE), which followed the fall of the Third Dynasty of Ur, left behind some of the richest evidence for formal education in ancient Mesopotamia. It's a period in Mesopotamia's history known for its school tablets, which survive in such abundance that they have allowed modern scholars to reconstruct step-by-step how fledgling scribes learned how to read and write. Their often circular-shaped clay tablets might show a teacher's neat writing on one side and a student's messy attempt at a copy on the other. This isn't a million miles from the modern phonics workbooks that children are taught with today, where typeset ABCs appear at the top of each page, and a young child must attempt to copy the letters over and over again below that ideal version. My daughter occasionally comes home from nursery with her name spelled out in shaky letters under the steady all-caps exemplar of her teacher. Her copied letters look huge and messy, like parts of them are trembling with lines that fail to connect where they should. More than once, the letters have looked unrecognisable, like side-by-side drawings of wiggly worms on red sugar paper that nevertheless make my heart sing. I pin these onto the wall of art in our kitchen that to me rivals the modern calligraphy art of eL Seed, but to anyone else might look like worthless scribbles.

Although impressed into clay, ancient school tablets show the same phenomenon in cuneiform. The first wedges of young students look understandably clumsy. The wedges tilt at unexpected angles, often drawn far too large for the tablet size, or they wobble across an incised ruling, presumably made by a teacher to show the student how to write in a straight line. (Another proverb stresses the importance of good handwriting: 'If a scribe knows only a single line, but his handwriting is good, he is indeed a scribe!'[2]) Ancient students, and indeed even seasoned scribes, sometimes ran out of space and had to cram characters together to make them fit on the tablet. The rare drawing of a star, a fish, and, in one case, the teacher reassure us that our bored schoolday doodles stand in a long tradition.

Excavators at Ur came across a few of these school tablets in Ennigaldi-Nanna's palace – tablets with some of these heart-warming features that appeared to date to the same period as the princess's residence in the sixth century BCE.[3] In his memoir, Woolley describes 'a very much ruined room' where the tablets were found, half-buried in a dusty, crumbling space. He noticed that many showed the messy, mistake-riddled work of what could only have been young students. He even spotted a reference to a 'boys' class' on one such tablet, convincing him that there was a school on site.[4] 'That the museum should be connected with a school,' in his view, 'is no matter for surprise.'[5] Despite his conviction about this link, he gives no further details about the 'boys' school', so I spent an ungodly amount of time trawling through the online archive of artefacts found at Ur in an attempt to find this particular tablet.

What I eventually found was a really quite unremarkable fragment shaped like a jagged triangle. Based on its shape and the orientation of writing on it, it likely once formed the bottom-left corner of a rectangular clay tablet, like the torn corner of a paper homework assignment today. It lists types of wood, such as cedar or juniper, one of many word lists used to teach vocabulary and signs in ancient Mesopotamian schools. Woolley's graph-papered excavation card for this broken bottom corner includes the Sumerian phrase *e banda*, 'house of the boys', which was written at the end of the clay fragment. Next to it, Woolley has scrawled the brief note, 'Probably material of the school'.[6]

To most, a broken bit of homework from 4,000 years ago looks like little more than part of a sandwich you might discard. To me, it carried a special kind of magic that most other ancient artefacts lack. We know so much about adults from the ancient world, like Queen Sammu-ramat, the beer-brewer Kushim, and even the fugitive shepherd Ilu-piya-usur who preferred to hide in a temple than source straw for bricks. Comparatively speaking, we know very little about young people from the ancient world, and a lot of what we do know comes from contexts I can barely bring myself to read about, like burials. When did babies start to talk? What nursery rhymes did they sing? What wondrous questions did they ask (and did they too wonder about Portuguese 'man-o-warts')? Given how much more interesting, energetic, and curious (and also adorable) my own kids are than I am, I find the overall silence of our sources on the lives of children quite sad, but school tablets from ancient Babylonia afford an antidote. They tell not just a story about education, but one about children who were really not so different from kids today.

In some cases, these kids left behind unexpected marks beyond the usual practice lines and doodles. In the eighteenth century BCE, over 1,000 years before Ennigaldi-Nanna moved to Ur, a child of about twelve lifted the corner of a clay exercise tablet to his mouth and bit down, immortalising his little teeth marks in clay. Was he feeling particularly hungry or curious about the taste of clay during that day's lesson? Had he just wanted to break the tablet to prevent anyone from plagiarising his work?[7] We may never know the reasons, but we do know enough about his setting to catch other glimpses into his life. From where the tablet was found, we know the pre-teen lived in Nippur, a city along the Euphrates that lies halfway between Babylon and Ur, during the Old Babylonian period. This was an era known for political struggle and consolidation, large-scale construction, and legal reform.

By the time this boy sunk his teeth into his homework, Nippur was already integrated into a growing empire under the leadership of King Hammurabi, who rose to power in 1792 BCE and set to work on expanding and consolidating the Babylonian empire for the duration of his forty-year reign. For two centuries before his arrival, the political landscape of what is now southern Iraq had been fractured by the fall of the Third Dynasty of Ur around 2000 BCE. The collapse of the large and highly centralised empire founded by Ur-Nammu and expanded by his progeny, including Shulgi, left behind a power vacuum that several cities tried to fill. The first half of the Old Babylonian period is characterised by a political tug of war between two major dynasties based in the cities of Isin and Larsa, followed by an era of expansion and consolidation under Hammurabi. Rather than calling himself 'Babylonian', though, Hammurabi would have identified as an Amorite.[8]

(His real name reflected that heritage; it was actually Hammurapi, a name that means 'the great dead ancestor is my kinsman', but early scholars misread his name with a *b* instead of a *p*, and like so many historical blunders in Assyriology – from the 'library' of Ashurbanipal to maybe even the 'museum' of Ennigaldi-Nanna – the mistake has stuck, and we will stick with it for now.[9])

Hammurabi was a king whose power and fame long outlived him in the region. One of his great achievements as a ruler was uniting northern and southern Mesopotamia after this long period of political instability. As skilled in statesmanship as in battle strategy, he undertook building projects and partook in religious rituals that would strengthen his legitimacy as a king. He was so important in the history of Mesopotamia that much later kings like Nabonidus used him as a reference point in their claims to legitimacy, and much later scholars even claimed to descend from his court sages.

But what Hammurabi is perhaps most famous for is his collection of laws, immortalised not just on a black stone column that today towers over visitors to the Louvre, but also on the many thousands of clay tablets written by students throughout ancient Mesopotamia who had to copy out these laws as part of their training to become scribes. The collection preserves almost 300 laws, each phrased as an if-then statement that presents a legal scenario and its outcome. 'If a man accuses another man and charges him with homicide but cannot bring proof against him,' reads the first half of the first law, then 'his accuser shall be killed'. (In other words, a false accusation of murder will land the death penalty for the accuser.) The range of legal scenarios covered by the provisions chiselled into Hammurabi's diorite stela and copied on clay school tablets is sweeping. In one, a woman innkeeper faces the death penalty for failing to report a meeting of criminals in her pub. Another covers medical malpractice for surgery gone awry on a person's head. The laws deal with every element of life in society – construction, property, inheritance, grievous bodily harm, abortion, assault, incest, marriage, divorce, adoption, adultery, loans, debts, wet-nursing, witchcraft, perjury, and what should happen if your ox accidentally gores someone. Just as Babylonian students had to copy down these laws, students of cuneiform today often begin with them. The first full sentence I ever read in cuneiform was from Hammurabi's first law.

School tablets like these multiple copies of Hammurabi's laws survive in such huge numbers and exquisite detail from the Old Babylonian period that it sometimes feels as if they were left behind on purpose for future students to piece together the experiences of their ancient counterparts. And the most abundant and best-studied examples come from the religious centre of Hammurabi's vast empire, Nippur, where we found the tooth-marked clay workbook of a twelve-year-old. It's from these throwaway scraps of homework that we can learn so much about education and the daily lives of schoolchildren.

'Schoolboy, where have you been going so long?' reads the first line of a Sumerian story that students had to learn in the final stages of their education. Although they likely spoke the Babylonian dialect of Akkadian at home, students learned Sumerian at school – just as some children today might learn Latin at school while speaking English at home (or how students in the Middle East learn literary Arabic in school despite only speaking a colloquial or local dialect). The story's opening word of 'schoolboy' comes from the Sumerian words *dumu eduba*. *Dumu* means 'son' or '(male) child', and *eduba* translates literally to 'house that distributes the tablets', or more simply to 'tablet house'. The schoolboy, then, is the 'son of the tablet house', and the word for teacher translates to 'father of the tablet house', perhaps suggesting something about the close, almost familial relationship that might have existed between teacher and student.

Today, we call the story *Schooldays*, or in dry Assyriological parlance *Eduba A*, as it is one of many such tales about daily life at school. There are at least fifty-seven fragmentary copies of this story about a fictional boy who goes to the *eduba*. In response to the story's opening question, the unnamed kid tells us where he has been:

> I recited my tablet. I ate my lunch.
> I prepared, wrote, and finished my tablets.
> They set out for me my lines,
> They prepared my hand-tablet for me during the afternoon
>   meal.[10]

His mother has packed a lunch of 'two breads' (an ancient sandwich?) for that meal and in the schoolboy's first lesson, the teacher recites words for him to copy onto a tablet. So far, a fairly unremarkable day at school. But this mundane list of activities takes a dark turn on a day the student arrives late to school. Fear tears at his heart, and we learn that he faces beatings for minor missteps, like messy handwriting, sloppy clothes, or clumsy Sumerian speech. By the end of *Schooldays*, the student believes that learning to write deserves such sacrifices, and he goes from wretched schoolboy who faces beatings to an exalted 'man of wisdom' who garners respect even from his own father. *Schooldays* as a work of literature celebrates the gifts of literacy and wisdom that education imparts, calling the graduate a 'hero' and ending with praise for Nisaba, the goddess of writing and a patron deity of scribes.

As part of their education, scribal students had to copy down many similar stories about life at school. In another story, when challenged to recite the school rules, a student quips, 'If you were to ask me about the rules of the school, I would be speaking from sunrise until sunset, and I wouldn't be able to finish my assignment!' He even calls these rules 'limitless'. I can't help but compare this to the single golden rule we had in my fifth-grade classroom in Saudi Arabia, which was scrawled in cursive on a banner above an algae-green chalkboard so large it took up most of a single wall: 'Do unto others as you would have them do unto you'.

This story gives us an incredibly clear picture of the day in a life of a Mesopotamian student – you would rise before dawn, eat breakfast, and pack up your stylus to take to school, where you would repeat out loud the teacher's lessons on arithmetic and vocabulary. As well as recitation, 'the student will lay out words on his exercise tablet and his lexical list', for the teacher to correct, and if they fail to do so, the senior student and teacher, we learn, can slap him.[11]

Like any work of literature, these fictional stories probably reflect some of the lived reality; but equally, like any work of literature, the stories may exaggerate elements of life in the *eduba* for the sake of pedagogy or humour. They stereotype and generalise. Even if we take the stories' details at face value, they reduce education over the course of millennia in ancient

Mesopotamia to the experiences of a handful of boys around 1800 BCE.

Thankfully, though, we don't need to rely entirely on fiction to reconstruct fact. In the ruins of a house in Nippur, known in excavation reports by the underwhelming name of 'House F', excavators found the Mesopotamian equivalent of hundreds of pages of homework. Nippur would at the time have been about the size of Hyde Park in London, and its highest point swelled nearly 65 feet above the plains of Iraq with a canal meandering through its centre. To its east rose the monumental brickwork of a ziggurat with a temple to ancient Mesopotamia's supreme god Enlil, as well as a residential neighbourhood where House F was found.[12] One of Nippur's early lead archaeologists, Donald McCown, described the area with an awe that borders on reverence: 'When I first saw Nippur on a bright fall day . . . I was overwhelmed by its size, the dunes of sand covering the ruins, and the air of desolateness.' He worried, though, about the magnitude of the task and the possibility that he and his team might find nothing of note beneath the barren landscape.

Instead, they found a city that would become central to our understanding of the social, political, and intellectual history of ancient Mesopotamia. 'Here,' he wrote, 'the oldest recorded literature in the world was written down in cuneiform on clay tablets.' While the artefacts may seem old to us, he stressed that the material 'was already old when copied 3800 years ago by the scribes to preserve it for their posterity'.[13]

The treasure trove of school tablets found in House F and the vicinity in Nippur is essentially the detritus of learning. Practice tablets were tossed aside at the end of a long day, much like students and teachers today discard scrap paper with arithmetical calculations or rough drafts of essays. Yet again, our understanding of history gets pieced together from piles of trash. Like the earliest examples of writing used as fill for the foundations of a building, these clay tablets were discarded with all the pomp and circumstance of tossing a dated to-do list, but today, they make up a major chapter in ancient Mesopotamia's already rich intellectual history.

Why, though, would this particular house be so rich in trash turned archaeological treasures? It was otherwise much like other homes in the surrounding area, with a courtyard surrounded by three rooms, and an additional back room (which could alternatively have been a second courtyard). The crumbled remains of benches appear in one of the rooms. Very little about this mud brick house stands out until you count the number of clay tablets found within its walls. In the surrounding neighbourhood, archaeologists excavated a total of about 200 tablets and fragments, but House F yielded 1,425 in the first season alone. This house was clearly an *eduba*, an ancient school.[14]

Together with similar buildings found in Nippur, Ur, Kish, and other cities in ancient Babylonia, this school has made it possible to reconstruct every stage of the Babylonian scribal curriculum in the early twentieth century BCE, and by extension other periods of Mesopotamian history. It is difficult to stress how remarkable a find this is in such an otherwise unremarkable house. Here, kids threw away their scribbled notes without a second thought, and certainly without thinking about what their clay scraps would one day convey to people thousands of years in the future. They tell us about the daily lives of schoolchildren, about the Sumerian sandwiches prepared by their mothers, and about what little wiggle room they had to daydream and doodle, which they found a way to do anyway. They tell us about how people learned, what sorts of stories might have mattered to them, and, ultimately, what steps they had to take to prepare for the life of a scribe and scholar.

The fragments of scholastic life exhumed from the ruins of House F give a sense of each phase of education on the journey to becoming a scribe who had command of cuneiform and its languages, who had practical skills like multiplication, and who was well versed in both everyday documents like contracts and the elevated prose of Sumerian literature.

The first school lessons a child might receive were focused on the simple act of how to impress a single wedge or sign into a flattened mass of wet clay, which they did over and over again, reed stylus in hand. Amazingly, one of the signs copied by students in this first stage of education – the equivalent of a cuneiform ABC exercise – looks like the sign that represents the sound 'a'. (I cannot overstate how much I love this coincidence.) These tablets show endearing early attempts by children to write the basic building blocks of cuneiform script. The lines look unsteady, and the signs oversized. Fingerprints and sometimes even fingernail impressions interrupt the impressed tetrahedrons to suggest that these youngsters had not yet learned to comfortably hold a tablet without leaving unwanted marks.

Practice makes progress, though, and students moved on to

basic lists of signs and words that, remarkably, reproduce or revisit the earliest texts from the dawn of writing. The teeth-marked tablet from Nippur preserves more than the kid's dental records; it also preserves part of a list of cuneiform characters and words known as *Proto-Ea*, which lists Sumerian signs and their pronunciation. Such lists preserved and taught the correct usage of cuneiform signs and vocabulary that students had to master well before moving on to anything like the *Schooldays* story. Sometimes, a teacher would copy out signs on the left side of a tablet for a student to replicate on the right side – sort of like the shaky letters of my toddler's name next to her teacher's neat lines. Other times, as in some of the finds from Ennigaldi-Nanna's palace, a teacher would copy part of a list on one side of a tablet, and the student would reproduce the same on the other side. In this way, students learned the building blocks of the writing system and the languages it was used to record.

The next phase of education introduced more advanced lists and mathematics, which students had to learn to help them carry out practical calculations in their future roles as scribes. Students first had to copy down and likely memorise lists of measurements and their equivalences, the ancient versions of the number of feet in a mile or millilitres in a litre. Lists of measures of capacities, weights, surfaces, and lengths served as the introduction to numeracy. They then had to learn lists of reciprocal pairs (a sort of divisions table) and multiplication tables, the latter not too distant from what is expected of, say, a modern nine-year-old. (Had you asked me to tell you the result of 8×7 thirty years ago, I'd have blurted the answer out instantly, whereas now, I need to use my phone's calculator function to double-check.)

They were then taught to apply this knowledge to more complex calculations, which occasionally took the form of word problems like the ones that left me mystified and stressed as an elementary school student. As a kid, I remember staring at paragraphs that mixed words and numbers until the combination swirled like alphabet soup in a sink. Carrying that out in cuneiform feels impossible to me; the wedges seem to dislodge from the clay into a similar whirlpool of confusion. One such cuneiform maths assignment lists twenty-three word problems (be still, my anxious heart) relating to a 'little canal', where students must calculate measurements of time to dig a canal, its dimensions, and even wages of its diggers. For example, one problem asks students to determine how many days it would take to dig a canal given its dimensions, while another, conversely, asks them to calculate its dimensions given the number of days a canal's excavation took. They learned to calculate the areas of triangles, trapezoids, and circles, likely the foundation for work relating to the area measurement of fields.

These everyday exercises preserve some astonishing snapshots in the history of mathematics. One 4,000-year-old tablet features a faint circle in its centre with numbers in various positions around it. Among these, just above the circle, is the number 3, which is thought to be the earliest known approximation of pi. Another tablet shows an accurate calculation of the square root of 2 and a diagram that suggests knowledge of the Pythagorean theorem, well over a millennium before the Greek philosopher was even born. Similarly, another tablet known today as Plimpton 322, named after one of its modern owners, has made headlines several times in the past few decades for showcasing Babylonian knowledge of the Pythagorean theorem. Each of the tablet's four columns lists a number, including integers that satisfy the formula, familiar to many, of $a^2 + b^2 = c^2$.[15]

What could this have been used for? Professor Eleanor Robson, who came to Assyriology as a mathematician, was able to deduce that this tablet was most likely a 'list of regular reciprocal pairs'. Plimpton 322 was a kind of Mesopotamian spreadsheet with pre-loaded calculations of the Pythagorean formula that teachers and students could reference without having to do those calculations from scratch. The list was constructed with basic techniques taught in schools, likely for use in the classroom. Although the Pythagorean equation as we know it is nowhere written down in clay, by 1800 BCE Babylonians must already have understood its principles and applications.[16] I find these immortalised leaps in maths' ancient past by children and their teachers absolutely stunning to behold.

Despite this, at the time they served a purely practical function to help students learn how to do the kind of maths they would need in their lives as scribes. All school texts had this didactic, scratch paper purpose. But the earliest pi, the shaky cuneiform ABCs, and lengthy works of literature like *Schooldays* may – and I think, should – leave us moved. These are intellectual milestones impressed into clay, alongside the literal fingerprints of ancient children, a beautiful reminder of the sheer breadth of what cuneiform preserves from lives long gone.

Although stories like *Schooldays* mostly record the education of boys, the earliest named author in history was, in fact, a woman. This extraordinary first is credited to a woman named Enheduanna, who was a prolific poet and also the first high priestess to the moon god in Ur, the same role filled two millennia later by Ennigaldi-Nanna. Enheduanna's claim to authorship is not straightforward. Not a single clay manuscript signed by her survives from her lifetime, almost 4,500 years ago in the 2300s BCE. Instead, later copies of her work name her as the original author. In fact, the earliest copies of her poems were made by none other than the students of Old Babylonian schools just like House F.

In the Old Babylonian period, the idea of studying or copying work written by a historical figure from five centuries earlier would have had quite a bit of appeal, perhaps just as I had to read Shakespeare and Chaucer in high school. The same deep reverence for the past that placed Sumerian at the heart of scribal education also ensured a place for the past's famous figures in the same curriculum – whether it was fictional characters like Gilgamesh and Uta-napishti, or an indisputably flesh and blood person like Enheduanna. Where an original work might be missing, however, it was enough to attribute authorship to an earlier figure to lend a piece of literature more credibility.

The content of Enheduanna's poetry might have given students as much pause as her antiquity. One of her poems, which was copied out by scribes in training, even shows flashes of feminism in its praise of the Sumerian goddess of love and war, Inana. Even a brief excerpt shows that Enheduanna was endowing the goddess with immense might.

To destroy and
To create, to plant
And to pluck out
Are yours, Inana.

. . .

To turn brutes
Into weaklings
And to make the
Powerful puny
Are yours, Inana.[17]

The Sumerian pantheon that the goddess Inana fits into is one dominated by gods. The head of the gods was Enlil (analogous to Zeus in ancient Greece), Enki was the god of wisdom, and war was covered by various gods, such as Ningirsu. In some works of Sumerian myth, Inana is portrayed as coy, and in others, she is rather ambitious. But in Enheduanna's poetry, she is unapologetically powerful, 'a stubborn and defiant female force', to quote Dr Sophus Helle, the most recent modern translator of her work.[18] Enheduanna portrays Inana in a position of great power in a pantheon that otherwise made little room for such a powerful goddess.

Enheduanna's work – and her very existence as a named author – perhaps hint at a strong 'female force' in early writing in Mesopotamia. The patron deity of scribes, Nisaba, was actually a goddess. Unfortunately, the surviving evidence shows that it was less usual for girls and women to write than men. We occasionally see the impersonal sign-off 'hand of a female scribe' at the end of a piece of writing with a cuneiform gender marker that tells us the student is a girl, and some girls even leave behind their names in school assignments, like one Belti-reminni who signed a basic list of words. Her handwriting also matches that on a clay copy of a playful and pun-filled ode to an agricultural tool.

Women also worked as professional scribes, though the evidence is again sparser than that for scribes identified as men. In the Old Babylonian period in a city called Sippar, a community of women, known as *naditum*, lived together in a cloister. The women in this temple community were assisted by scribes who recorded official documents and business transactions, from lease contracts to lawsuits, and these scribes were also women. One scribe named Amat-Mamu worked for at least four decades, longer than most careers today.[19] Almost twenty records were made by a scribe named Inana-Ama-Mu who signed her name with the Sumerian word *dub-sar*, meaning 'scribe' from the Sumerian words for 'tablet' and 'write'. Importantly, she did not add any gender-identifying elements to her profession, only to her name; she signed as a 'scribe' not a 'female scribe', which is written *mi-dub-sar* in Sumerian.[20]

The professional work of these cloistered female scribes suggests that they would have received the final phase of scribal education, which introduced more complex works, like proverbs, mock legal contracts, and eventually works of Sumerian literature like the *eduba* stories and Enheduanna's hymns. To truly become a scribe, in other words, you had to show mastery not just of your multiplication tables and clay vocab lists, but also of poetry, literature, and, ultimately, Sumerian. According to one poem from the Babylonian era, a good scribe who works hard to attain these skills will enjoy 'wealth and abundance' (but not before enduring 'grief').[21]

During the Covid-19 pandemic, I was asked to make an audio recording of me reading a section of an early Sumerian version of a Gilgamesh story in the original language for the new Ancient Middle East gallery at the Ashmolean Museum. I said yes, and then I did what any normal person might do after being asked to recite Sumerian 4,000 years after the language's demise: I panicked.[22] Much of Sumerian is mono-syllabic, so the words don't roll off the tongue the way they might with the lengthier words of Akkadian. There is a beau-tiful staccato to them that, to me, lends them better to a chant than a melody. I have no idea how someone in ancient Ur's royal court might have sung these lines of the Gilgamesh story, but I ended up chanting them in the style of an *adhan*, or call to prayer in my home country, and then reading them the way I would an excerpt from a modern novel.[23] In a way, studying this learned language helped bring me as close to the ideal Mesopotamian scribe as one can be in the twenty-first century CE, as well as to the imperfect ancient, perhaps also somewhat panicked and at times grief-stricken, students who strived towards that ideal.

Sumerian literature is in many ways a product of scribal education, which required these texts to be reproduced in various ways. In fact, most of what survives of that literature comes exclusively from schools, where students also learned Sumerian proverbs, which are quite honestly some of my favourite lines from the millions left behind in clay. Although they were primarily constructed and copied to help students learn elements of the language, they also preserve snapshots of everyday wisdom, morality, and even humour. 'Who can compete with righteousness?' one asks before adding, 'It creates life.' Another seems to prefigure a modern saying about the grass being greener: 'You don't speak of that which you have found. You talk only about what you have lost.' In a world that suffers increasing polarisation thanks largely to social media, one perhaps still resonates several thousand years later: 'A heart never created hatred; speech created hatred.' Finally, one that rings true particularly for me, who was taught as a girl in the 1990s only to be seen and not heard, deals with gender-based double-standards in behaviour: 'A chattering girl is silenced by her mother. A chattering boy is not silenced by his mother.'[24]

Some are more graphic. I sometimes listen to podcasts while I run, and one morning, I put on Keegan-Michael Key's ten-part podcast on the history of sketch comedy. In the first episode – to my unadulterated delight – he brings up what is essentially the first known fart joke from a Sumerian proverb. In fact, several proverbs reference flatulence in some way. 'Something which has never occurred since time immemorial: a young woman did not fart in her husband's embrace' is one that many may take issue with. 'Like a flatulent anus, the mouth produces too many words' might meet with less opposition.[25] Feel free to remind anyone who maligns your potty humour that we have been making fart jokes for a very, very long time.

Proverbs served as memorable tools to teach students not morality, but even more Sumerian. Embedded into these collections of maxims might be word associations, visual and phonological puns, and other tools to help students master the language and the many layers of meaning in cuneiform writing. The Sumerian proverbs remind us of the bilingual nature of education in ancient Babylonia. Students and scholars were first and foremost translators. Scribes stayed loyal to

Sumerian, despite the growing temporal gap between them and the language's ancient speakers.

In ancient times, as now, students got bored. My favourite testimony to this is a millennia-old doodle – one clay tablet crammed with proverbs and a literary excerpt of a story about an enslaved girl also captures a child's drawing of an angular, seated figure who either has a very long stick-figure arm, or perhaps wields a stick.[26] Could a bored student have resorted to doodling the teacher?

Drawings on clay tablets are unfortunately rare, so the ones we do find feel like gold dust. Another notable example is what Irving Finkel calls 'the oldest drawing of a ghost in the history of the world', which is quite simply breathtaking.[27] Finkel, who brought cuneiform back into my life that London summer day, stumbled upon a tablet dated to the 300s BCE that gives instructions for banishing a ghost from your life. Alongside these written instructions is one of the very few drawings in clay that survive from ancient Mesopotamia. Written by a scribe named Marduk-apla-iddina, one side of the tablet details a ritual for getting rid of the ghost (it involves making two clay figurines, one of the ghost and one of a woman who can entice him to the land of the dead where he can no longer trouble the living). The other side of the tablet appears blank, 'like nothing at all at first sight', in Finkel's words.[28] But when hit with light at just the right angle the clay reveals the shallow lines of two human figures. On the left, a barefoot man with a long beard holds shackled hands before him, attached to a rope. On the right, a woman draped in long garments appears to pull the rope. She leads the ghostly figure of the man to eternal life in the land of the dead below, the Mesopotamian Underworld.

A handful of doodles and drawings capture other idle or imaginative moments, like the practice wedges of a new student alongside a drawing of a fish, complete with fins.[29] Another student used nothing but fingernails to draw two arched eyebrows above eyes that give way to a wide nose. Is it too much of a stretch to imagine this to be a caricature of the teacher or school attendant?

To fill some of the idle moments of free time between arduous lessons, it appears that Mesopotamian students also played board games. Among the detritus in the ruined room of Ennigaldi-Nanna's palace where Woolley found the school tablets, excavators also came upon what looked like abaci, or checkered counting boards to help with mathematical calculations, but were more likely game boards etched into mud bricks. Some of these are arranged in a grid, while others follow the pattern of an ancient board game with a single row of squares that juts out of such a grid to form what to me looks like a heavily pixelated Minecraft hammer. This game is sometimes called the Royal Game of Ur, which takes its name from several famous examples of a game board, complete with gaming pieces, that were found in graves at Ur's Royal Cemetery. A similar gaming board was also found in House F, the school for the young scribes in Nippur. Perhaps students who ate their lunches of 'two breads', as described in *Schooldays*, moved pieces across these squares during breaks between lessons.

The fact that similar types of game boards and school tablets were both found in Ennigaldi-Nanna's palace was enough to convince Woolley that the princess also ran a school in her palace, perhaps not unlike House F. But it's also feasible that the school tablets may have just been discarded there, and reused as building materials. They may have originally come from a small school run near the site before Ennigaldi-Nanna's arrival in Ur, or may have come from a different part of the city, where several private homes functioned as scribal schools in the first millennium BCE. Their potential for reuse should come as no surprise. The exercise texts, scratch pads, practice wedges, and bite marks of early students were never meant for posterity.

Of the tablets found among the remains of Ennigaldi-Nanna's rooms, only a handful are obviously the work of students. Unlike school tablets from the Old Babylonian period of 2000–1600 BCE, the tablets used by students 1,000 years later were often made from recycled clay, and the resulting poor quality has left behind a mostly fragile, fragmentary collection. Despite this, the tablets found by Woolley remind us what was deemed important enough to be used as learning material in ancient Mesopotamia. The poems, stories, laws, signs, maths exercises, and proverbs were shaping young minds (or at least, the minds of those who attended schools), not just in the Old Babylonian period but for hundreds of years. Evidence shows that even 1,000 years after House F was a lively school, the basic steps in the school curriculum had changed very little. Was this because education in Mesopotamia was in many ways founded upon a sense of antiquity, a curriculum built around a language seen as important due to its age and heritage? Education was bilingual in a way that bridged the Babylonians' yesterday and their today. Rather than studying contemporary Babylonian poems, students copied Sumerian hymns attributed to Enheduanna who had lived and died centuries earlier. And it was Hammurabi's laws from around 1750 BCE that still kept the scribal students of 550 BCE awake at night. The countless school tablets that preserve this reverence for history also open up some beautiful moments. Even now our ambitions remain the same – just like the child in *Schooldays* who entered school a wretch and left an exalted 'man of wisdom'.

6

The Cone of Kudur-Mabuk

The Birth of Science

When I was pregnant with my daughter, Comet NEOWISE graced the night skies. A glowing rock with its arced tail hung suspended in the darkness, as if the world had hit pause. Night after night, I would stand in our garden and stare up at it. Maybe pregnancies are supposed to feel as magical as a comet that only comes into view every 7,000 years. A single cell turns into a trillion during the time it takes the planet Venus to move across the night sky. Two hearts were beating in my body at the same time. My belly swelled with the promise of life, but after two years of miscarriages, I struggled to feel anything but fear and grief. Only in the moments that I stood barefoot in the grass each night to watch this blazing comet did I feel some sense of peace. Even if my whole world hinged on the cell division in my uterus, NEOWISE reminded me that the world was far bigger than my belly and that I was but a blip in a beautiful universe so filled with wonder that I can hardly stand it.

Thousands of years ago, people on the banks of the Tigris and Euphrates shared in that wonder. They, too, looked up. They bore witness to the same quiet comets we will see in our lifetimes, like Halley's Comet in 164 BCE and maybe even NEOWISE millennia before that. They marvelled at shooting stars and the same planets we still watch take baby steps across the sky over many months. They observed eclipses with such regularity that they generated methods, still in use today, for calculating the dates of their appearances.

These phenomena meant something even more tangible to Mesopotamian astronomers and their kings than NEOWISE did to me on those spring nights. A single eclipse completely changed the destiny of Ennigaldi-Nanna, as the alignment of sun, earth and moon triggered a religious reshuffle that would land the princess in Ur. On 26 September 554 BCE, over the course of almost two hours, a shadow stretched across the face of the moon over Babylon. A barrel-shaped clay tablet covered in cuneiform describes Ennigaldi-Nanna's rise to power and the eclipse that inspired it. 'The Fruit', as the moon gets described, 'became darkened'.[1] This partial lunar eclipse was seen by Babylonians as a message from the moon god, but what did it mean exactly? An eclipse could portend many things, most of them bad, but Nabonidus interpreted this one as a request from the moon god Sîn to appoint a high priestess in the god's home city of Ur. His court scholars, however, appear to have disagreed. One even turned up at the king's palace with a basket of tablets to try to match up the king's interpretation to anything recorded in his clay textbooks full of omens, but to no avail. Nabonidus never-theless insisted this was what the moon god was telling him, and he commissioned professionals to carry out fresh omens to confirm it – a royal Babylonian version of fake it until you make it. He employed some highly trained scholars to perform a ritual on a sheep's innards, known as divination – or the attempt to elicit divine signs from earthly phenomena, includ-ing animal remains – to confirm whether or not the eclipse was itself a divine sign from the moon god, calling for a high priestess to be appointed in Ur.

Multiple sheep met a premature end so that the king's court scholars could find signs of the moon god's desire in their entrails. If you read enough signs, you eventually find the message you're looking for. He asked the professionals to perform one final divination to ask about the suitability of his own daughter, Princess Ennigaldi-Nanna, for the role, which (perhaps unsurprisingly) returned an affirmative answer.[2] In another one of his royal inscriptions, Nabonidus gives a step-by-step account of this divinatory hoopla, and in another he reduces it to but a few lines to highlight his attentiveness to revelation:

At the request that he (Sîn) made of me, I became frightened, (but) I was attentive and did not deny his request and consented to his command. I elevated (my) daughter, my own offspring, to the office of en-priestess and I named (her) Ennigaldi-Nanna.[3]

The account makes the consecration of his daughter sound more like a sacrifice – I gave and renamed *my own daughter* for this role – perhaps an apt characterisation of a life of divine service. The job of high priestess, after all, came with a burdensome set of responsibilities, from leading important rituals related to the harvest to acting as estate manager for great tracts of land in and around Ur. Despite the challenges his daughter would face, Nabonidus stressed his attention to the divine command and his many attempts to get the message right.

Different methods of divination could complement, or even contradict, each other, and kings relied on every means at their disposal to interpret the will of the gods and make the right decisions. Nabonidus's dogged determination to interpret Sîn's message relied on a fundamental premise about knowledge in Mesopotamia: its divine origins. Certain scholars, known as 'diviners' or 'seers', underwent years of training to access this knowledge, which their clay textbooks exhort them to keep secret from the uninitiated. From the mundane, like a bird perched on a city wall or a mole on the left side of someone's face, to the exceptional, like a lunar eclipse, every observable phenomenon could be interpreted as a divine message or sign. The gods communicated to those trained in the art of reading natural phenomena as divine writing, but communication was not just one way. Just as deities like Sîn scrawl their signs across the night sky, so humans – and more specifically, kings – could impress into clay messages for their goddesses and gods to read, like prayers.

As part of this ongoing dialogue, kings sometimes hid these messages in places where only divine eyes could see them. When they built or rebuilt important buildings in ancient Mesopotamia, such as temples, they buried such offerings in the foundations. From the end of the third millennium BCE, these offerings were sometimes placed in a brick box, sealed at its top with a reed mat smeared with bitumen and capped off with a few more bricks, some of which bore an inscription setting forward accounts of the building work. The offerings within the box could include small statues or figurines with short inscriptions dedicated to the gods on them or smaller, uninscribed objects, like beads and date seeds.[4] Longer dedications appeared on tablets shaped rather like bricks, whose words carried such important inscriptions that the tablet itself was occasionally made of stone instead of clay. It is one thing to impress cuneiform signs into clay, and quite another to chisel them painstakingly into stone. The skill required to do this coupled with the expense associated with sourcing costly stone tell us that the messages were considered extremely important. Today, it would be like sending a letter instead of an email to announce something as momentous as a baby's birth, or even travelling to deliver a letter or news in person. The added effort is proportional to the importance of the message.

Dedications to the gods were also written out on large clay nails or cones, which measured about the length of your hand, from wrist to fingertips. I've always thought these look a bit like clay Cornetto ice cream cones, covered not in the criss-cross of waffle print, but in the tiny lines and triangles of cuneiform script. One cone was found in Ennigaldi-Nanna's palace, and is part of the collection of items that Woolley saw as a museum. The cone had once been intentionally buried somewhere in the ziggurat complex below the brick pavement floor over 1,000 years before Ennigaldi-Nanna became priestess. It may have been rediscovered and excavated in the princess's time, possibly during building works, and recognised as historic.

For Ennigaldi-Nanna to take up her new role after the lunar eclipse message to Nabonidus, her father had to rebuild the entire temple complex in Ur, which had fallen into disrepair. In previous eras, the high priestess to the moon god lived in a small palace within the ziggurat complex, including Enheduanna in the third millennium BCE and Enanedu in the second millennium BCE. The many priestesses who preceded Ennigaldi-Nanna, in fact, inhabited this dwelling both in life and death. Their traditional burial ground was essentially in the palace's backyard, so that successors could continue to provide them with offerings of food and other items they might need in the afterlife.[5] In a sense, the priestesses became a multi-generational family who shared a home that had, by the time Nabonidus arrived, turned into a ruin. When he decided to resurrect this ancient religious role (or when the moon supposedly told him to), he rebuilt the palace and temple complex upon its ancient foundations.

The renovation work unearthed quite a few relics from times past, much like today's building works might occasionally reveal past treasures like Roman ruins or Viking hoards. (The construction of London's Crossrail network unearthed so many artefacts that the Museum of London crafted an exhibit around the finds in 2017, which included 8,000-year-old stone tools and a Tudor throwing ball.) Nabonidus described the ruins he found at the site as overgrown with palm trees and littered with dusty rubble. He cleared away the trees and debris to uncover the original foundations of the dwelling, where he 'discovered inside it inscriptions of ancient kings of the past'.[6] Could Nabonidus himself have been the one to have found the clay cone that had been buried here 1,000 years earlier and added to Ennigaldi-Nanna's museum?

If he was, would he have felt a sense of awe in connecting with a long-gone king who had once renovated the very same temple complex for his own daughter, or a sense of validation in deciding to do the same?

The clay cone bears the name of Kudur-Mabuk, a foreigner from what is now Iran who began his career as a high official and ended it as a regent in the nineteenth century BCE. His daughter Enanedu would rise to the role of high priestess of Ur, just like Ennigaldi-Nanna many centuries later, and his sons would go on to become kings.[7] Interestingly, Kudur-Mabuk never ascended to the throne himself and in inscriptions such as the clay cone found in Ennigaldi-Nanna's museum, he describes himself as a sort of tribal chief instead. At the start of the short message pressed into the clay, which was created during the reign of his son, Warad-Sîn, he calls himself 'Father of the Amorite land' (the same ethnic and social group as Hammurabi who would rule just a century later). The message then goes on to recount Kudur-Mabuk's construction of the temple for the god Nanna, the Sumerian name for the Akkadian moon god Sîn. He built the temple as high as a mountain, and made its 'head touch heaven', according to the cone.[8] Inscribed with this dedication to the moon god, the cone was then buried deep below the brick pavement floor of a temple. Its messages and those on the many offerings deposited in architectural foundations of temples were meant not for human eyes, but for a divine gaze. They were Kudur-Mabuk's way of showing the deities who ultimately justify his rule that he was doing his job, that he was being a good ruler.

Kudur-Mabuk's cone highlights a crucial element of knowledge and learning in ancient Mesopotamia: revelation. The idea that deities were constantly disclosing truths to the people trained to understand them motivated and shaped all manner of scholarly enquiry, from medicine to astronomy. Against the backdrop of constant communication with the divine, scholars made individual and generational leaps in the history of science and particularly in the history of astronomy. Reading divine messages in the sky, year after year after year, eventually gave the ancient scholars enough information to construct mathematical models for astronomical phenomena. Around 500 BCE, their nightly observations even led them to develop the zodiac, which is still in use today. The unassuming clay cone from Ennigaldi-Nanna's museum shows us this extraordinary world of divinely inspired science in ancient Mesopotamia, where empirical science was inseparable from the supernatural messages scrawled among the stars (and the insides of sheep).

The people trained to read divine signs in the natural world were serious, court-appointed scholars who drew on centuries of knowledge, much of which was cemented in the middle and end of the second millennium BCE during what is known as the Kassite period. If we rewind about 1,000 years from Ennigaldi-Nanna and Nabonidus, we find ancient Mesopotamia at a political turning point. The empire originally built by Hammurabi fell in 1595 BCE when the Hittites, a civilisation based in what is now Turkey, sacked Babylon. Famously, and catastrophically at the time, the Hittites stole the city's statue of the god Marduk. From where we sit now, several millennia away, this may sound like a minor offence

– unfortunate and maybe even annoying, but otherwise superficial. Divine statues in ancient Mesopotamia, however, were believed to actually embody the deities they represented. When the Hittites took the statue of Marduk, they robbed the city of the god himself, the patron god of Babylon and head of the Babylonian pantheon. The city's population would have experienced the theft as a palpable loss, analogous perhaps to the loss felt by the people of Mosul in 2014 when Daesh reduced the shrine of Nabi Yunus (Jonah) to rubble.

After the Hittites sacked and abandoned Babylon, rulers with names in a new language began to assume roles of political power in the city and its environs. Enter stage left, the Kassites. Scholars today are still trying to piece together a more complete picture of who the Kassites were, what their language sounded like, and where they came from. What we do know for certain is that the Kassites considered themselves different enough from the local Babylonians to distinguish themselves as such in the written record.[9] In a record of one of the earliest Kassite kings, Agum-Kakrime, he takes credit for returning the statue of Marduk to Babylon about twenty years after the theft. In the same account, Agum-Kakrime describes himself as king of Kassites *and* Babylonians, 'the king of the wide land of Babylon'.[10] That he distinguishes the Kassites and Babylonians suggests that the Kassites formed a separate group within Babylonian society.

Despite their foreign origins, the Kassite rulers stressed continuity with the previous era of Babylonian rule, and one way they did this was through language. Instead of introducing their native language into ideology and administration, they continued to use Sumerian and Akkadian as the primary written languages of their empire. In fact, of the over 12,000 clay tablets known to have survived from this period, not a single one is recorded in the Kassites' native language.

Among these tablets are a fascinating cache of hundreds of letters found not in Babylonia, but in nearby Egypt, that bring together the earliest known international diplomatic correspondence in history and reveal the extent of Kassite scholarly influence. We call them the Amarna letters, for the city on the east bank of the Nile where they were discovered, and they are an absolute delight to read, reminding us that even 3,000 years ago, the people in charge had to follow pre-established rules of diplomacy but that they were also just people. Luckily for us, the *lingua franca* of diplomacy during this era was Akkadian, recorded in cuneiform on clay, which ensured the survival of well over 100 of these missives. Local scribes throughout the ancient Middle East had to go to the great trouble of learning Akkadian to correspond with other empires, but even if they were fluent in this foreign language it is still pretty easy to pick out some of the Amarna letters in a cuneiform tablet line-up thanks to the poor quality of their grey, grainy clay compared to the uniform, smooth clay from Mesopotamia. Fragments of seashells and grains of sand leave some of the tablets looking almost pixelated, and holding one with anything but the lightest touch causes dried clay to flake off from its edges. In horror, I almost managed to do this once when the fibre on my cotton-gloved finger stuck to the corner of an Amarna tablet, rather like Velcro. With a grace I have never managed to replicate, I disentangled the glove's thread from the tablet's edge, preventing a precious millimetre of millennia-old dried clay from flaking off.

Despite having all the wrong resources to write in cuneiform, Egyptian pharaohs went out of their way to write in it, and Mesopotamian scribes even set up a school in Amarna to teach this writing system.[11] Letters between the great powers spill the proverbial tea of Late Bronze Age politicians. Egyptian pharaohs, including a very young Tutankhamun, Kassite, Assyrian, and Hittite kings wrote to each other regularly, and these letters document the minutiae of diplomacy and gift-giving, and preserve some surprisingly human moments among kings. One letter from the Kassite king Kadashman-Enlil to the pharaoh Amenhotep III complains that the pharaoh detained his messenger unduly, sent a gift of gold that looked like silver, and neglected to invite him to a particular feast (Mesopotamian for 'guess my invitation got lost in the mail').[12] Another from the same Kadashman-Enlil begged the pharaoh to send one of his daughters for a diplomatic marriage or, failing that, to send 'any beautiful woman as if she is your daughter' so he could claim this diplomatic connection. Besides, he reasoned, no one in Babylonia would know the difference.[13] Even imagining the high stakes involved in these exchanges, it really is hard not to smile at the unabashed humanity of these kings.

The Amarna letters have filled many a book of their own, such is their historical import, giving broad brushstrokes of fourteenth-century BCE political history, the main cast of characters, and how they carried out diplomacy. What they tell us here is that the Kassites oversaw an era of extraordinary political and cultural connections in the ancient Middle East. Kings exchanged not just gifts of furniture and sometimes sub-par gold, but their own people. Even if it seems the Egyptian pharaoh never sent family members abroad, Kassite and Assyrian kings sent their daughters in marriage, shared their brightest teachers of cuneiform, and even bid farewell to some of their best-trained physicians. A doctor named Rabâ-sha-Marduk began his career in Babylonia in the thirteenth century BCE and ended it in Anatolia among the Hittites. A letter from the reigning Hittite king Hattushili III to Kadashman-Enlil assures the Kassite king that Rabâ-sha-Marduk is alive and well in his court, and had even married a royal relative and settled down in 'a nice house'.[14] From the heartland of ancient Mesopotamia, including both Assyria and Kassite Babylonia, scribes and scholars travelled to Egypt, the Levant, Anatolia, and even as far west as the Aegean.[15] Academic cuneiform texts have been found throughout these regions, from the sign lists that helped students learn the script to advanced literary compositions and astronomical texts.[16] When scribes in Egypt, Syria, Turkey, and beyond learned cuneiform script to write the diplomatic correspondence, they had to learn the same things that students in the Babylonian heartland learned as part of their education. The spread of cuneiform writing, then, went hand in hand with the spread of cuneiform scholarship and knowledge.

One of the more lasting legacies of the Kassites was their contribution to the wealth of shared knowledge and scholarship in ancient Mesopotamia. Experts today think that most of the standard textbooks, from medical therapies to astronomical textbooks, used by scholars throughout the first millennium BCE were first drafted in the Kassite era.[17]

Vast tranches of cuneiform scholarship are exclusively dedicated to deciphering the continual messages from the gods and goddesses, as knowledge in areas like astronomy depended on understanding a world populated by divine signs. True knowledge and wisdom came from the ability to interpret those messages correctly. It is no exaggeration to say that the task of interpreting all natural phenomena was (and still is) a gargantuan one. Ancient scholars had to find a way to tame the dataset, so to speak. To do so, they divided their observations into two overarching categories: the stuff observed in the sky above and the stuff observed on the earth below. This deeply ingrained twofold division even appears in the Mesopotamian origin story about the creation of the world. A Babylonian epic known as *Enuma elish* opens with a description of the primordial world: 'When on high, the heaven had not been named, firm ground below had not been called by name'.[18] Even in this primal state, before heaven and earth were even named, the world was divided into above and below.

Scholars therefore relied on reading signs and omens in these two realms, and during the Kassite era several 'textbooks' for guiding these were definitively written down. These clay reference works listed countless omens, or sets of observations with their linked predictions, from a possible coup to a peace treaty on the horizon. Scholars would comb through these to help them interpret the world around them.

Observations made 'below' on earth were compiled into a clay textbook made up of over 100 tablets known as *Shumma Alu*. In this extensive work, scholars compiled observations of terrestrial events, like the behaviour of animals, the location of a city, or the appearance of plants, which got paired with a prediction about phenomena or events in the human sphere, like a divorce, good fortune, or war. For example, 'If a black cat is seen in a man's house,' reads just one of the tens of thousands of examples from *Shumma Alu*, 'that land will experience good fortune.'[19] Features of people's faces and bodies could also be interpreted as divine signs of events to come, as could the appearance of newborn babies, the content of dreams, the colour of water in a well, and so much more.[20]

In the night sky in particular deities embedded their messages for a trained audience of astronomers, just as kings embedded their own messages to the gods deep below the earth in clay cones and other engraved objects. Observations of something in the sky, like a partial lunar eclipse or the position of Venus, are seen to indicate a political, social, or even personal outcome, like the death of a king or a difficult childbirth. To help them interpret signs 'scrawled' across the night sky, scholars relied on another clay textbook known by its first few words, *Enuma Anu Enlil*, which translate to 'When Anu and Enlil', the most important gods throughout all periods of ancient Mesopotamia.

This may all sound unastronomical and even unscientific to a modern reader, but two considerations should give us pause before passing such judgement. First, divination relied heavily on empirical observation, a cornerstone of any scientific endeavour. Today, as was the case thousands of years ago, without using a telescope we can see five planets from earth: Mercury, Venus, Mars, Jupiter, and Saturn. Without some training, or a reliable app, it is not always easy to find them, but a handful of clues make it possible. Planets don't twinkle the way stars do but, rather, shine uninterrupted, and some shine in striking ways. Mars, for example, sometimes glows with a visible orange or even reddish hue. Venus is so bright that on a particularly dark night when the moon is but a sliver, it can cast shadows. The Sumerian name for Venus, *dili-bad*, in fact translates to 'shining', and poetry often emphasises the planet's radiance. A Sumerian song praises the goddess Inana, identified with the planet Venus, describing her as 'radiantly ascending at evening' and 'filling the heaven like a holy torch'.[21] The far more distant Jupiter is similarly bright, and its Akkadian name translates literally to 'white star', whereas Mercury is so tiny in the night sky that it is easy to miss.

People in ancient Mesopotamia looked upon the same sky as we do now, and they were supremely knowledgeable about it after meticulous observation. Take the seventh-century BCE astronomer Balasî, for example. He served in the court of Esarhaddon, a Neo-Assyrian king remembered for his military successes, as well as a lifelong, mysterious illness that left him regularly ill. Balasî wrote a letter to his king where he complains about another astronomer whom he calls an 'ignoramus' for being unable to distinguish between Venus and Mercury.[22] To be fair to Balasî, stargazers today will know that it is almost impossible to confuse the two; Venus is the brightest object in the sky after the moon, while Mercury is a minuscule dot that is almost impossible to find without knowing where to look. Balasî slates his colleague, writing that he 'does not know . . . the cycle . . . or the revolutions of Venus', a reference to perhaps the most telling feature of all visible planets.[23] Planets noticeably move from night to night against the backdrop of a fixed pattern of stars, and each of the five visible planets follows the same path over and over again. Balasî's reference to Venus's 'revolutions' shows his knowledge of the planet's synodic period, or the time it takes for it to return to a particular point in the night sky as viewed from earth. To observe and predict these paths requires nightly observations, accumulated over months or years.

As astronomers like Balasî looked to the skies each night, they measured their observations against lists of omens collected and copied by generations of scholars who came before them, including Kassite scholars. Astronomers today might similarly look at the night sky and reference a textbook to better understand something they notice – be it a newly detected pulsar or a returning comet – and those textbooks will also be based on earlier observations of scientists who came before them.

The astronomical omen textbook, *Enuma Anu Enlil*, is encyclopaedic. It covers the fronts and backs of seventy clay tablets for a total of about 7,000 omens, some of which are brief sentences, and others extensive paragraphs. 'If Jupiter becomes steady in the morning,' reads the first line of one omen from the sixty-third tablet of *Enuma Anu Enlil*, 'enemy kings will reconcile.' This textbook was set down in a standard form during the end of the Kassite period around 1100 BCE and used by later astronomers like Balasî as guides to understand the meaning of their nightly observations.[24] If Balasî observed Jupiter at dawn, in other words, he can confidently tell the king not to worry about war with the empire. Another portent pairs an observation about Venus with an economic prediction: 'If Venus wears a red crown, year of remission of debts.'[25] If one night Balasî noticed that Venus somehow had a reddish hue, he could report to the king that debts should be forgiven.[26]

The link between observation and prediction seems random, even nonsensical, without reading between the cuneiform lines, and this brings us to the second feature of omens that should make us think twice before dismissing these texts as unscientific. Special types of reasoning link these observations of Venus and Jupiter with the political and economic life of people millions of miles away. To understand the connection, we need to think about the people writing them down; how they understood reality, how they wrote about it, and the cuneiform writing system that they used to do so. Take Venus's red crown and the remission of debts for a year. The cuneiform sign used to write 'red' in Akkadian, *sa*, is pronounced in the same way as a different cuneiform sign that forms part of the word for debt, *nig-si-sa*. The connection between observation and prediction is therefore a simple pun. This kind of wordplay – or sign play – is one of the many strategies that connects an observation and its predicted outcome, though the two may seem unrelated.

What of the connection between Jupiter's steady appearance at dawn and the reconciliation of enemy kings? In ancient Mesopotamia, the planet Jupiter was associated with the god Marduk, the head of the Babylonian pantheon (just as the god Jupiter was supreme among ancient Roman deities). As such, the planet connotes rulership and, along with that, the stability that ideally goes with successful rule. Observed on its own then, without any additional remarks like its proximity to the moon or its location in a particular constellation, Jupiter being 'steady' embodies the idea of stability for a king's reign, which in the human sphere can translate, among other things, to peace between enemies. As a counterexample, another omen pairs the disappearance of Jupiter behind the moon with enmity in the land; the absence of Marduk and his rulership from the sky means a land vulnerable to conflict and strife. This kind of conceptual analogy frames countless cuneiform omens about celestial phenomena.

Sometimes, the connection is more obvious. An astronomer named Nabû-ahhe-eriba, who served in the court of

King Esarhaddon and eventually Ashurbanipal in the seventh century BCE, wrote a brief report of one evening's observations on quite a small tablet. That night, he had noticed Mercury in Capricorn and two stars, Piscis Austrinus and Corvus, or the 'Fish star' and 'Raven star', as they were called in ancient Mesopotamia. To explain the significance of the stellar sightings, he quotes an omen: 'If the Fish star stands close to the Raven star: fish (and) birds will become abundant.'[27] It's not hard to imagine the connection between the sighting of two stars named for fish and birds, and the appearance on earth of actual fish and birds. (Funnily enough, just like Balasî did, Nabû-ahhe-eriba also addressed an alleged sighting of Venus in Aries when, in fact, the planet was not yet visible, calling the person who made the original report to the king 'a vile man, an ignoramus, a cheat!'[28])

The omens of *Enuma Anu Enlil* and similar collections also order their observations according to really specific patterns. For example, many interpretations rely on the meaning of left and right to give different results. In ancient Mesopotamian omens in general, the right side is typically associated with a positive outcome and the left, with a negative one. This sort of left and right symbolism is of course not unique to ancient Mesopotamia. As a child in Saudi Arabia, I learned from a young age to eat with my right hand and open the bathroom door with my left hand: in other words, to do clean things with the right hand, associated with purity, and dirty things with the left, associated with impurity. This left versus right set-up can be seen, for example, in descriptions of a star observed near Venus; if the star appears on the planet's right, 'there will be plenty in the land', but if on its left, 'there will be misfortune in the land'.[29]

However, if something negative is associated with the right side of Venus, that triggers a negative outcome, like multiplying a positive and negative integer in a maths problem yields a negative answer. If something negative is associated with the left side, that conversely triggers a positive outcome; after all, two negatives make a positive:

> If Venus is dimmed at her right side, women will have
>   difficulty giving birth.
> If Venus is dimmed at her left side, women will have easy
>   childbirth.[30]

Other concepts helped the ancient Mesopotamians organise these huge datasets, like the cardinal directions of north, south, east, and west; various colours; the timing of phenomena; and other opposites, like up and down, or bright and faint. Although omens must have had some basis in observation, scribes with obsessive attention to 'completeness' sought to fill out these schemas as completely as possible, which sometimes led to imagined scenarios, or phenomena we would consider to be impossible, like a lunar eclipse appearing to be green or Jupiter passing through a constellation it never crosses.

Scholars in Mesopotamia were, in short, trying to impose order on a chaotic world. They were trying to make as organised and complete a record of everything around them as possible in an incredibly systematic way. Science, after all, is an attempt to make sense of reality, to impose order on a vast world. In ancient Mesopotamia, science was not just about observing the natural world, but about categorising it in a way to fill out and even complete the observable picture.

If this sounds familiar, that is because we have already encountered this impulse among the earliest written texts from ancient Uruk. The sign lists from the dawn of cuneiform writing did something similar – they generated impossible objects, like a vessel filled with a pig, to try to fill in as complete a reality as possible, and even perhaps generate a new reality through the writing system itself. This attempt at systematisation and completeness, which often includes things that defy the limits of what we deem possible, is typical of ways of organising knowledge in ancient Mesopotamia.

When I began my Master's degree in Assyriology many years ago, I was certain that I would focus on the earliest clay tablets from Uruk – texts like the records of Kushim (the beer brewer) and the lists of vessels, traced with the detailed pictographic images of proto-cuneiform. What could possibly be more interesting than the birth of writing? However, the more I learned, the more I found myself drawn to the much later medical and astronomical compendia of the Kassite scholars, the Assyrian astronomers, and the last guardians of cuneiform science in Babylon and Uruk. My path changed, and I ended up studying the history of science instead. Translating passages about the stillness of Halley's Comet in the night sky 2,000 years ago above Babylon, was, to me, translating something about what it means to be human. This is the history of people trying their best to make sense of the world around them and, as part of that effort, poring through every phenomenon ever recorded – actual or potential, real or imagined – in clay.

Night after night, astronomers like Balasî and Nabû-ahhe-eriba read the 'heavenly writing' in the skies and set the stage for major developments in the history of astronomy. Instead of solely predicting events on earth based on what they observed in the heavens, astronomers began to develop ways to predict other astronomical phenomena. Even just writing that sentence makes my heart palpitate (in a good way) and my palms sweat (less good, but still a sign of my excitement). I wish we could collectively get up and dance about this watershed moment because it marks the point at which centuries of observation get poured into an entirely new science. The leap from interpreting phenomena purely as divine signs to interpreting phenomena *purely as astronomical phenomena*, and noticing patterns that enable predictions of other astronomical events, is an enormous one.

For example, by the eighth century BCE, scholars were regularly predicting eclipses. Given that an eclipse could mean death for the king, it is unsurprising that it was a priority to figure out a way to predict and plan for them. Scholars go from observing lunar and solar eclipses over and over (and over and over) again to being able to predict an entire eighteen-year eclipse cycle and, eventually, to generating mathematical formulae to express that cycle. This period of about eighteen years, eleven days, and eight hours that governs the recurrence of lunar and solar eclipses is called the Saros cycle, possibly from the Akkadian word *sar*, which refers to a very large number, or the Greek word *saro*, which means sweeping. A handful of Saros cycle texts that give the months of eclipse possibilities arranged into these cycles of eighteen years survive from the last half of the first millennium BCE. Some of them look like clay spreadsheets populated with dates.[31]

To help organise their nightly observations, astronomers also developed a celestial coordinate system that continues to be used as a tool in modern astronomy: the zodiac. Its ultimate origins may reach back to an idealised lunisolar calendar used in ancient Mesopotamia from the third millennium BCE, which divided the year into twelve ideal lunar months of thirty days each with an extra month inserted to realign the calendar with the solar year as needed.[32] A lunar month is the time it takes for the moon to go through all of its phases, from the nearly invisible sliver of a new moon to a crescent, half moon, full moon, and back down to the sliver again. The god Marduk is credited with creating this cycle in the Babylonian creation epic *Enuma elish*. 'At the beginning of the month,' Marduk tells the moon, 'you shine with horns'. He commands it to swell into a circle and then 'wane at the same pace and form in reverse'.[33] The passage marries poetry, mythology, and science to describe the moon's cycle. With or without Marduk's input, this process takes an average of about twenty-nine and a half days, but some months are shorter or longer depending on how far away the moon is. Ancient Mesopotamians noticed these variations and called it an even thirty to simplify things. (Similarly, in English common law, a lunar month used to mean twenty-eight days, or exactly four weeks.) This made it easier to calculate something as mundane as interest rates or decide when rents are due, instead of waiting for the precise night the moon returned to being a little sliver, or new, and declaring that the start of the month.

In the fifth century BCE, this temporal division of twelve months, each comprised of an even thirty days, gets mapped onto the sky and, more specifically, onto a band of the sky that the sun, moon, and planets move along known as the ecliptic, so named as also being the band where eclipses take place. The zodiac divides the ecliptic into twelve sections of 30 degrees each, named for a particular constellation, so Capricorn is the 'Goat-fish', Gemini is 'Twins', Leo is the 'Lion', and Scorpius is the 'Scorpion', and so on. Defined mathematically, the divisions of the zodiac made it easier to describe movements of the celestial bodies; for example, the location of a planet could be either at the beginning, within, or at the end of a particular zodiacal sign.[34]

The zodiac ended up playing an immediate role in a group of several hundred cuneiform tablets that record astronomical phenomena beginning in the late seventh (or early sixth) century BCE in Babylonia.[35] Known in antiquity by a phrase that translates to 'regular watching', they are today called the Astronomical Diaries for their sustained, nightly observations of events both in the sky and on earth. The planets in particular are described in relation to the twelve zodiacal signs to make it easier to locate them.

> Venus, until the middle of the month, was in Virgo, until the end of the month, in Libra; Mercury, in the beginning of the month, was in Cancer, Mercury's last appearance in the east in Leo; Saturn was in Capricorn. Mars was in Pisces. That month, the river level receded 8 fingers, total: 30 was the *na* (gauge). That month, on the 6th day, the satrap of Babylonia from Seleucia, which is on the Tigris, entered Babylon. On the 9th day, merrymaking took place everywhere.[36]

I will be the first to admit that some of these fragments make for less riveting reading than the manual for my dishwasher (if that manual had been partly eaten by my dog, leaving large tranches missing or illegible). But the Astronomical Diaries preserve extraordinary moments in history. One records a sighting of Halley's Comet in the autumn of 164 BCE.[37] Some of them record early epidemics, like a diary from 567 BCE that mentions a possible outbreak of 'coughing' and another that mentions 'recovery of sick people in the land' from an unnamed illness.[38] In one from 323 BCE, a deceptively simple line of cuneiform signs records a turning point in history: 'The 29th,' it reads, 'the king died'.[39] That king was Alexander the Great.

The generational knowledge and accumulation of observations in the Astronomical Diaries made possible the development of another new science in the last half of the first millennium BCE: mathematical astronomy. The decades and centuries of recorded data allowed scholars to construct mathematical formulae to reflect, predict, and even measure the same phenomena. Some of that maths will send shivers up your spine, and I say that as someone who truly does not love or even really understand maths. One cuneiform tablet actually made headlines in 2016: 'Signs of Modern Astronomy Seen in Ancient Babylon,' read the *New York Times* headline. Written sometime between 350 and 50 BCE, this little square-shaped tablet was looted in the nineteenth or twentieth centuries, as were so many tablets that date to the final centuries of cuneiform scholarship, most likely from Babylon before finding its way into the British Museum collection.[40] It looks a bit like a piece of baklava, but its slightly tilted characters – a typical script style of this later period – reveal a complex geometrical model that has rewritten the history of astronomy.

Using the zodiac as a coordinate system, the tablet plots the movement of Jupiter along the ecliptic from its initial appearance at two sixty-day intervals. Each of these intervals, when plotted on a graph, generates the image of an uneven trapezoid, whose areas together reflect the distance travelled by Jupiter. The tablet's modern decipherer, Mattieu Ossendrijver, clarifies that the trapezoids describe the configuration of the planet not in *actual* space, but in 'mathematical space'. It is, in other words, a 'highly abstract application' and 'an application of astronomy that was totally new'.[41] This technique was previously thought to have originated in Europe in the fifteenth century CE.

These developments were ultimately made possible by a cosmology that populated the world with divine signs, as well as a drive to interpret those signs, and, ultimately, to predict and prepare for events in the social and natural world. Even with all of these developments, the motivation still seemed to hinge on finding a way to predict things in the human sphere. Instead of witnessing a separation of astronomy from divination and revelation, the last centuries of cuneiform science preserved this esoteric conception of knowledge. The zodiac, the advanced mathematics, the fine-tuned observations all fit within an ancient epistemological architecture of divine revelation that the cone of Kudur-Mabuk slots into; as humans buried messages to deities in the world below, so those deities left messages in the world above for astronomers to decipher.

The latter, of course, were far more important. What the gods had to say could foretell an era of war or peace, could give hints about whether or not a woman would survive childbirth, or determine if a loan would be forgiven. Humanity's messages to deities were far more limited in scope – dedications of objects like the cone, written records of kings fulfilling ideals of rulership – but were part of the same ongoing conversation. For the god Nanna, for example, Kudur-Mabuk left behind a cone to let the god know that he had built a temple so high that its roof touched the heavens, so beautiful that the god would have no choice but to rejoice within its walls.[42] It makes me wonder if the ancient Mesopotamian scientific enterprise was, unknowingly, also a message to the gods. As kings built temples to be lofty but earthly homes for their gods and goddesses, the scholars of ancient Mesopotamia showed those same deities that they understood their heavenly writing. They were reading it, taking notes, passing those on to later generations, and reading it some more. Did those deities look down from their heavenly abodes or peer up from their deep underwater dwellings to witness this multi-generational scientific enterprise? Did they notice the leaps in innovation, from the early omen lists to the forerunners to calculus?

The sky was not the only divine clay tablet that gods could use to inscribe their signs onto. They could also choose the far more gruesome tableau of a dead sheep's entrails, and this type of divination – known as extispicy – belonged to an entirely different but complementary discipline, which was still scientific in its methods. Among the types of scholars whose careers hinged on their ability to read those signs was the diviner, or *bārû*, which literally means 'one who sees', or 'seer'. Unlike the astronomers we have met so far, such professional seers didn't need to wait for Venus to move or an eclipse to appear. They could provoke answers from the gods to questions posed by clients, including queens and kings, through the entrails of a sheep.

To provide an answer about a client's future, the seer would whisper a straightforward yes or no question (Should I journey to Babylon? Will my pregnant wife live?) into the ear of the living sheep before ritually slaughtering it. In the time between asking the question and carrying out the killing, the god Shamash would have written an answer on the sheep's liver and intestines in cryptic 'writing' that only a diviner was trained to read. As celestial phenomena were sometimes called 'the heavenly writing', so the sheep's liver was sometimes called 'tablet of the gods'.

That writing took the form of unique features on parts of the liver that had arcane names like 'the Path' and 'the Presence', which are lobes of the organ where it borders the stomach. 'The Finger' is a band of tissue that separates two other lobes of the liver, and 'the gall bladder' is, mercifully, the gall bladder. Whether such features were present or absent carried special meaning, and some could bear particular marks, like being split or firm or bulging; any one of these things carried divine meaning. When learning how to carry out these readings, or 'take' an omen, trainee diviners relied on clay models of livers with these various parts labelled, similar to how medical students today are trained to know highly technical terminology for the human body. They also consulted lists of omens that pair features of the liver with possible outcomes, just like *Enuma Anu Enlil* did with astronomical phenomena and events on earth. 'If the Presence is covered by a membrane,' reads one such ominous prophecy, 'the king will contract a serious illness.'[43] While omens like this one may sound bizarre to a modern audience, they formed part of a momentous heart-to-heart between a highly trained seer and an attentive deity. The liver provided an organic clay tablet, in a sense, on which the gods could impress their answers to the initial yes or no question posed. The gods took the time to 'write' on the different areas of the liver – the gall bladder, the Presence, the Path – but that writing was far from straightforward to read and required an indirect, but systematic approach to its interpretation.

In carrying out an extispicy, the diviner would note the relevant features on the liver and comb through compendia of such liver omens in order to determine which of these marks had a positive outcome and which had a negative one. If a sheep has more than one gall bladder (three, to be specific), this could give a positive outcome: 'there will be harmony and well-being in the land'.[44] The diviner would then tally up these negative and positive values at the end of his reading, and whichever value outweighed the other would determine whether the answer was yes or no. In some ways, it resembles a divine 'pros and cons' list done in a highly technical way with reference to clay textbooks and a bloodied liver.

In the seventeenth century BCE, a Babylonian diviner used a sheep to perform this type of divination to determine the well-being of a woman named Beltani. Beltani, who must have been suffering some form of illness, posed a question about whether or not she would get well. On examination of the sheep's entrails, according to the brief report, there was a protrusion at the top of the Presence, the right of the Finger was split while the left was cleft, and 'the gall bladder is stable on the right side', among various other features noted. The diviner also observed twelve coils of the intestines. Overall, for Beltani, 'it is favourable but has adverse signs and a check-up is necessary'.[45] A small tablet fragment dated to two years later also addresses the well-being of someone named Beltani and gives a firmly favourable response.[46] Though these tablets might deal with two unrelated people with the same name, I like to think that the same Beltani went back for that check-up and found her health issues resolved.

People who could afford the services of such specialist scholars often consulted them before making a major deci-sion, like whether or not to undertake a journey, or for reas-surance about events to come. Today, when I worry about my health, I consult my GP instead of a diviner. When I need to decide whether or not to take a trip to visit family in America, I weigh various considerations on my own, like the price of flights and the often onerous visa requirements. How much will it cost my bank account and mental health to go through the often humiliating experience of applying for a visa (not to mention the further humiliation of being 'randomly selected' every single time for extra checks at airport security and immigration)? For me it's about deciding whether the trip is worth the time, price, or stress. In ancient Mesopotamia, a further step could tip the scales in favour of a yes or no: consulting a seer to read the sheep's liver, or 'tablet of the gods', and give an even more definitive answer.

Alongside people like Beltani of ancient Babylonia, divin-ers served the royal court to help kings make decisions well into the first millennium BCE. Neo-Assyrian kings relied on the expertise of seers to help them with decisions that ranged from medical to military, including whether or not to go to war. Some of these experts found themselves embroiled in life or death situations, like the unlucky Kudurru, an imprisoned Babylonian prince deported to Assyria in the seventh century BCE who copied works of cuneiform science while held captive. In a letter to King Esarhaddon, he describes how he was released from captivity, taken to a temple, and forced to drink wine until sunset with several major political players who eventually forced him to perform some divination. They wanted Kudurru to ask the gods a simple question: 'Will the chief eunuch take over the kingship?' The question made clear to poor Kudurru that whether he liked it or not, he was now part of that chief eunuch's plot to overthrow the king. 'The only thing I was thinking,' he writes in a desperate letter to the king, 'was "May he not kill me".' He reassures the king that the extispicy he had been forced to perform was 'a colossal fraud'.[47] The bizarre episode tells us that even a coup needed to be backed by divination, and such divine communication carried high stakes, especially among those who could access, or influence, those trained in the art of reading the divine writing.

Different methods of divination could complement – or contradict – each other, and kings relied on every means at their disposal to interpret the will of the gods and make the right decision. But equally seers could be put under pressure to come up with the 'right' answer to marry up with the king's agenda.

In the ancient city of Mari during the Old Babylonian period, letters and reports attest to the regular use of divination by kings and regents. One report to the king, addressed as 'my lord', by an official whose name unfortunately is lost, stresses the importance of these divine messages.

I have had omens taken about Mari's safety. The diviners have said, 'The omens are mixed. Be attentive about guarding the city and the Bank of the Euphrates. Our omens are not favourable. Give us sheep and tomorrow we will once again take omens for the (same) round.'[48]

Archaeologists have unearthed dozens of unique clay liver models from the palace at Mari that may have been used to train diviners. They bear one or more observations, and many make clear that when such an observation was made, the liver looked just like the model. 'If the enemy plots an attack against any town, yet his plan becomes known; this (liver) would look like this,' one reads.[49] Others also describe situations, including when a king annexed an enemy country and when a ruler planned to attack another, associated with the features moulded into the clay liver model. These remarkable objects preserve more than the appearance of a particular liver on a particular day; they embody popular beliefs about the relationship between human and divine, as well as the complicated expertise that mediated that relationship and its political import. They also open up a clay, liver-shaped window onto what kept people awake at night, like Beltani who worried about illness and kings who hoped to keep their cities safe. Illness and war still worry us. These anxieties reach across the multi-millennia divide and remind us that people still struggle with the same things, dressed up in era-appropriate clothing. Specifics aside, omens show that people worried about the future, and anyone faced with a stressful, uncertain situation can relate to that sometimes desperate need to know what will happen next.

Communicating with the divine was the basis of all knowledge and ways of knowing in ancient Mesopotamia, even knowledge that was gained through empirical observation or mathematical application. Revelation was not at odds with science as it is today. Although it looks like little more than a clay Cornetto, the cone of Kudur-Mabuk is a thread in a tapestry of ongoing communication that helps us understand the very fabric of reality in ancient Mesopotamia. In that reality, supernatural beings, like Shamash, are as real as a reed stylus, a clay tablet, and the people who used them. They were not 'super' natural at all, but as natural as anything else in the world, and they also used that world as a tableau. When astronomers observed the appearance of Mercury or Halley's Comet in the night sky, they were reading what they called the 'heavenly writing', and when diviners interpreted the marks on a sheep's liver, they were reading what they called the 'tablet of the gods'. As our reality is populated with quarks, atoms, and the unimaginably large planets and stars they ultimately make up, so the world of ancient Mesopotamia was populated by divine cuneiform signs and their various natural media.

Gods and goddesses used a metaphorical stylus to draw the movement of Venus across the night sky or to impress a mark on some obscure part of a sheep's liver. Humans had only clay to write their messages on, like the cone of Kudur-Mabuk, but their deities had the whole world. To access those messages meant meticulous observation by those trained to interpret natural phenomena in this specific way. Eventually, centuries of such observation and knowledge production gave way to more exact enterprises like mathematical astronomy. These attempts to make sense of the world in a systematic way are no less than some of the earliest examples of what we today call science.

7

The Boundary Stone

Slaves and Scribes, Weavers and Wives

In the mid-1100s BCE, Elamite soldiers from what is now Iran descended on Babylonia. When the Elamite king Shutruk-Nahhunte conquered the capital Babylon, he looted the city and its temples for *objets d'art*. I can imagine the foreign army spilling through the city's brick gates with spears overhead, weaving between their fellow soldiers on horseback. The clamour of hoofbeats on the paved roads, of battle cries alongside the shrieks of ordinary citizens, and of the even more disturbing bone breaks add a layer of horror to the scene. Babylon formed the epicentre of more than one conflict in the region's history, and this time, Shutruk-Nahhunte might have had vengeance in mind after his father-in-law was killed. Even revenge, however, cannot alone justify political violence, and most wars boil down to nothing more than resources.

Wealth might have given Shutruk-Nahhunte an added incentive, and the armies looted much of the city, taking home with them some of the finest examples of art – contemporary and ancient – that Babylon had to offer.

Among the items seized by the invaders and carted back to their home in what is now Iran were several tombstone-like obelisks called *kudurru* made of expensive stone and carved in exquisite detail. One of these is about 20 inches tall and portrays Gula, a healing goddess almost never seen without her dog. The image in intaglio shows her seated on a square pedestal with her pointy-eared canine at her feet. Engraved with hundreds of hairline grooves, the fabric of her dress ripples in an imaginary wind, and above her float divine symbols and a scorpion whose sternal plates, walking legs, and even pincers are carved so clearly that the creature looks as if it might scuttle off at any moment. The cuneiform text engraved into the obelisk describes how the Kassite king Nazimaruttash gave gifts of land to the god Marduk (or his temple).[1]

Elamite raids meant that some of the most striking and historically significant objects from ancient Mesopotamia were found not among the ruins by the Tigris and Euphrates, but tucked into the archaeological layers of ancient Susa several hundred miles away in modern-day Iran. Before being taken from Babylon, the *kudurru* would have once stood in a temple, bearing perpetual witness to a person's entitlement to land, their authority cemented by carvings of a particular god or goddess bestowing divine power.

The Elamite king Shutruk-Nahhunte must have sensed there was something special about these stone monuments. I can imagine him weaving his way between these thigh-high obelisks in the poorly lit cella of a Babylonian temple, preternaturally quiet in the aftermath of battle. He may have pointed to the ones he wanted to take home to Susa while a scribe at his side made a rushed inventory of the designated contents for transport. Maybe the divine iconography struck a deep chord in him, spiritual or otherwise. He may have quickly grasped the enormous effort involved in creating these objects and assumed that they carried enough importance to warrant taking. Or he may have just thought they were beautiful. Did the king take them from Babylon's temples to display them in his palace as evidence of conquest and exemplars of foreign art?

One of the oldest objects found in Ennigaldi-Nanna's palace was another of these *kudurru* – a curved stone slab, almost as tall as a mini-fridge.[2] Made of the valuable black stone diorite, the tombstone-like object dates to the end of the Kassite period, which pre-dated Ennigaldi-Nanna by hundreds of years. Already an imposing object in dark, heavy stone, its surface is highly decorated with mythological creatures to imbue it with power like Nazimaruttash's *kudurru* shipped to Susa. One side shows an exaggeratedly large cuneiform wedge atop an ornate pedestal, representative of Nabû, the god of writing. Next to the symbol sits a type of dragon who faces a lightning fork, symbol of the storm god. A scorpion crawls above them alongside the head of an eagle, and a snake slithers across the very top. The whole object exudes power.

Time has left much of the surface damaged, but we can still make out the chiselled writing that records the positions and outlines of landed property in an area in Ur. This ancient boundary stone would have belonged to an individual during the Kassite period whose name is now unfortunately too fragmentary to read. Boundary stones like this one usually record land grants, disputes, entitlements, sales, and revenues from kings to those privileged enough to have received such distinctions and the elaborately decorated artefacts to immortalise them. We can perhaps look to Windsor Castle for a regal parallel, where the title deed for Buckingham Palace, purchased from Sir Charles Sheffield for £28,000 in 1763, was displayed in 2014 as part of an exhibition of 'treasures' from the royal archives.[3] Over 20 miles from the land itself, the title deed went on display much like a land grant from ancient Mesopotamia to bear witness to a moment in history.

We have many examples of boundary stones from the region that may hint at something Arab speakers from the Middle East today call *wasta*. It's hard to reduce *wasta* to a straightforward translation, but it is something like using your personal influence, or that of someone close to you, to fast-track pretty much anything that needs fast-tracking – a property purchase, a visa application, admission into a school. 'Clout' comes somewhat close to *wasta*, but there is no stigma against deploying influence this way in parts of the Middle East; it's a normalised part of how privilege operates. Was a similar social lubricant at work in some of the gifts behind the boundary stones from ancient Mesopotamia? Did you have to know the king – or know someone who knew someone who knew the king – to access such a gift?

Boundary stones reveal one mechanism for land ownership in which the king donated land – and by extension, whatever income that land might generate – to a private individual. In one, the Kassite king Meli-Shipak granted arable land with an estimated yield of about 15,000 litres of grain to a man named

Hasardu, the son of one of his servants, in around 1180 BCE.[4] Another one records a dispute over land brought by a man named Nabû-shuma-iddina (not to be confused with the much later Nabû-shuma-iddin, the scribe who wrote the clay drum from Ennigaldi-Nanna's palace) against another named Ekarra-iqisha. In support of his account of the land's boundaries, Nabû-shuma-iddina describes ownership dating back '696 years', secured and protected by the goddess Nanshe, which the king decided to uphold until 'whensoever into the distant future' – a fancy way of saying 'forever'.[5]

I will confess that I find such records, as outwardly beautiful as they may be, difficult to read because, quite frankly, they can be very boring. Few among us crawl into bed at night with a sixteen-page rental agreement for a flat in London in lieu of the latest Stephen King novel. Contracts are not riveting, whether written on paper or clay or expensive stone, but they can tell us a lot about people. That sixteen-page rental agreement would state the name of the person who occupies the flat, their occupation, and the many, often onerous requirements they would have to fulfil. The landlord named in the document might appear in other, contemporary rental contracts or even the odd lawsuit for failing to ensure, for example, that the flat met basic safety standards. As dry as the analogous cuneiform records may be, they have much to teach about the Hasardus and Nabû-shuma-iddinas of ancient Mesopotamia, as well as those born into far less privileged circumstances whose names and likenesses nevertheless survive to tell us something about their lives many millennia ago.

In many ways, boundary stones like these are visual symbols of privilege, monumental records of moments in the lives of those who benefit from the status quo. They throw into relief an important (and frustrating) caveat about almost all cuneiform sources from ancient Mesopotamia. Although the hundreds of thousands of clay tablets that have weathered millennia between then and now tell hundreds of thousands of stories about as many people, they remain silent on as many others.

At the same time, the Mesopotamian penchant for keeping clay records means that the names, and sometimes the stories, of some of the most disenfranchised members of the population *do* still survive. Early administrators, for example, kept close track of enslaved agricultural workers from abroad, and the occasional servant leaves behind their own, sometimes heartbreaking record. Servants occasionally had to commission letters to their masters to update them on their affairs. A letter from around 1800 BCE preserves the plea of a (possibly enslaved) pregnant woman named Dabitum to her master about a devastating loss – that of her unborn baby. Although seven months pregnant, she laments, 'the foetus is dead in my belly', and she begs her master not to let her die too.[6] These exceptions remind us that life in ancient Mesopotamia was not easy for the majority, and that, for the most part, it's the businesspeople, scholars, scribes, generals, doctors, and the like who left their words behind – people who perhaps experienced less of the kinds of hardship faced by the poorest and most disenfranchised.

Generally, those who could afford to or were trained to leave their words behind in clay, did so. Cuneiform, as a result, tends to document the lives of a narrow sector of the population. To commission a scribe and artist to chisel a stone monument that records your right to land, like the boundary stone from Ennigaldi-Nanna's museum, you needed either power or money (or both). Where can we turn to learn about those on the other end of the social and economic spectrum, whose work in many ways made the lives of the wealthy possible? Although they lack the intricate art and monumentality of a *kudurru*, some of the most mundane, everyday records impressed in often rushed handwriting on lumps of clay open up these lives for us – sometimes in even greater detail than any boundary stone might afford.

Long before the Kassites came up with the elaborate stone monuments like the one from Ennigaldi-Nanna's museum, when writing was in its nascent stages, we start to see the first records of people and their lives laid out in administrative documents, including those born into far less lucky circumstances than the later boundary stone owners. Clay tablets from all periods of ancient Mesopotamia reference people in underprivileged circumstances in legal, economic, and administrative contexts, from lists of people captured in war to legal records about fugitive slaves. Because of the nature of these documents and the types of information they preserve – occupations, hours, rations, runaways – there is a limit to how much of a picture we can paint of these individuals. Most of the clay tablets were drafted for a specific reason, such as to provide proof of ownership or some other financial obligation, to record some legal kerfuffle related to an individual, or to list names and payments in food. However, the records do offer a glimpse into these lives, while also reminding us of the limitations of cuneiform sources, no matter how abundant they may be.

Some of the earliest cuneiform texts from two of the oldest Mesopotamian cities, Uruk and Jemdet Nasr, record lists of workers whose sexes were labelled in the same way as those of cattle using signs that resembled genitalia.[7] They were counted and accounted for like animals. These early records also include the ages of named individuals, like 'child in third year' and 'girl, very young'. Other qualifications also appeared alongside people's names, including the combination of the signs for 'head' and 'rope' to refer to a person led by a noose, and one sign that simply means 'yoke'. In other words, tools of physical control and subjugation, used also on animals, appeared with their names, suggesting that the people named in these early texts were enslaved. Some of these people may have been taken from foreign populations by an invading army, but one way or another, their names are difficult to read with certainty because it's difficult to know how to interpret these early cuneiform signs. One name includes the sign for bird in it, and another the sign for heaven, giving precious hints at what the listed workers were actually called, what their parents might have thought sounded beautiful or meaningful.[8] Stripped of their home and humanity, these enslaved people and their tales survive at least in part – their names, their work, and where they ended up – in some of the oldest known examples of writing anywhere in the world.

Slavery is not as clear-cut in ancient Mesopotamia as it was in, for example, nineteenth-century America. The words used to denote slaves in the cuneiform sources can apply to non-slaves, depending on the context, and different categories of labourers with varying levels of independence populate clay tablets from all periods. Some enjoyed limited mobility and freedom, while others did not. Some remained stuck in certain jobs for financial or social reasons, while others could be bought and sold into other forms of servitude. The boundaries between these social categories were 'fluid and poorly defined', writes Dr J. Nicholas Reid, who has dedicated years to understanding slavery in the ancient Middle East.[9] Through his work, he reminds us of the perils of projecting modern ideas about slavery and freedom onto ancient records.[10] Those records suggest that for certain periods, the life of an enslaved person was not necessarily distinguishable from that of other labourers of certain classes. While these nuances may sound pedantic, they are still important to understand and help us fill the gaps in the fragmentary stories of a great number of people in ancient Mesopotamia.

People labelled as 'slaves' in cuneiform tablets worked in a variety of jobs, from making textiles in state-run workshops to managing far-flung pubs on behalf of their wealthy owners. The foreigners named in the early texts from Uruk and Jemdet Nasr may have worked in agricultural roles. In later periods, they participated in factory-style production of everyday goods, like textiles and pots, or domestic work within households or temples, among other occupations. They may have started work as early as toddlerhood, like five-year-old boys attached to the Ebabbar temple in Sippar in the sixth century BCE who joined the agricultural workforce alongside adult and even elderly men.[11]

Occasionally, records hint that some slaves acquired specialised skills for a specific profession, such as writing, baking, or etching with minuscule tools the engravings that cover small stone cylinder seals.[12] In the sixth century BCE, an enslaved woman named Ishunnatu, who belonged to the wealthy Egibi family in Babylon, ran a pub in nearby Kish, and several records show just how much she had to manage. Not only did she receive a sizeable number of items needed to institute and run a drinking establishment – ten chairs, three tables, a lampstand, and a vat for brewing beer, among others – but she also had to pay the rent 'of the house' where she was told to set up shop all by herself.[13] The pressure was therefore very much on. (Curiously, she ordered more beds than tables, raising questions for some about the exact nature of the pub.[14]) Often, the records omit the specific work or profession of a slave, but those that do hint at their jobs show that they worked in as varied occupations as their free counterparts – the major difference being that they had no legal choice in the matter.

People became enslaved and escaped slavery in a number of ways. They could be bartered, born, sold, adopted, or captured into slavery. Prisoners of war and conquest often replenished staff quotas. In the twenty-first century BCE during the reign of Amar-Suen (whose missing brick was also part of Ennigaldi-Nanna's museum), a clay tablet records the arrival of 172 slaves described as 'booty', a Sumerian word composed of three cuneiform signs that together translate, depressingly, to 'the beaten ones' (nam-ra-ak). These 113 women and 59 children were received by the governor of the city of Umma before beginning their lives as slaves, possibly attached to a temple.[15] From the same city, an iPad-sized tablet, so perfectly preserved that it looks almost fake, records barley rations distributed to women and children with names like Ganana and Niana. They were captured as 'booty' and put to work in some of the major state-run industries, families fragmented and full lives reduced to how much flour they could grind in a given month.[16] The fate of their husbands, brothers, and fathers remains unknown. Were they introduced into the workforce elsewhere, or did they perish in whatever battle precipitated the capture of so many women and children?

In some cases, people were kidnapped – or trafficked – into slavery. In the early second millennium BCE, a wet-nurse sold a little Babylonian girl in her charge during a raid on her hometown of Idamaras near what is now Baghdad. Years later, after Hammurabi united the disparate regions of ancient Mesopotamia, the slaver who purchased the young girl became a Babylonian subject and was forced to release her, making this unnamed woman one of the earliest recorded survivors of human trafficking, some 4,000 years ago.[17]

Even in times of peace, financial difficulty could make certain individuals vulnerable to enslavement. Around the same time that the boundary stone from Ennigaldi-Nanna's museum was made, a family fell on hard times in Emar, a city situated on a bend in the Euphrates in what is now Syria. Impressions of tiny feet pressed into clay still survive to record a sombre story of this family. Three lumps of clay, each one just large enough to accommodate a single tiny footprint, preserve the names of three toddlers – a girl named Ba'la-bia who was around two years old, and her twin brothers Ba'al-belu and Ishma'-Dagan who were a year younger.[18] The twins' footprints barely measure the length of a deck of cards. Their names match up to children named in a contemporary contract that, although worded in dry legal lingo, left me in stunned silence. A woman named Ku'e and her husband Zadamma, in a 'year of distress', were forced to sell their four young children into slavery for a mere 60 shekels, a comparatively low price at the time.[19] The youngest, a newborn girl named Ba'la-ummī, was still nursing (no clay footprint survives for her). To imagine a parent having to part with a baby cradled in their arms and their three disoriented toddlers, to imagine that final goodbye, hurts even now, thousands of years later, even if only a few dry records remain of this moment.

The toddlers and baby were sold to the son of a diviner, one of the highly trained scholars who could read the signs from the gods. Amazingly, we can trace the twin boys into adolescence. Clay tablets from the archive and scribal school of the diviner's family preserve the names of the boys later on in their lives. 'Hand of Ishma'-Dagan, novice diviner,' reads the signature section of one such tablet, a school exercise text from the intermediate stages of education. Ba'al-belu also called himself a 'novice diviner' in a tablet found at the same site. The purchaser of all four children was an instructor and diviner at that school, and he bought the young twins to teach them to become scribes. Although still forced into the profession, the twins' tiny footprints eventually lead to a slightly less bleak ending than we might expect, or at least a known ending of some kind.[20] It seems these siblings at least ended up under the same proverbial roof in a highly respected scholarly profession, though tragically separated from their parents and a life of freedom.

Cuneiform sometimes preserves the names and even the details of the lives of people like the twins from Emar and the trafficking survivor from Idamaras. We can learn the who, where, and when, but often *what* we can know remains restricted. It was an administrative imperative to record people's working hours, sex, ages, and even names, but other details of their lives remain lost. Moments in their stories – and sometimes even their footprints – were pressed into clay, but they were not usually the ones who wielded the stylus.[21]

Was it possible to escape one's slave status in ancient Mesopotamia? Enslaved people occasionally did run away – quite literally – at great personal risk to themselves and anyone who might come to their aid. Many of the rules chiselled into the towering diorite stela listing Hammurabi's laws of the 1700s BCE tackle the issue of runaway slaves, and it is thanks to this that we know that anyone who helps a slave escape or harbours a fugitive slave faces none other than the death penalty.[22] Any man who finds an escaped slave without making an effort to return them to their owner was similarly to be put to death.[23] These laws demonstrate that an enslaved person was considered little more than property, so any attempt to help one run away was tantamount to theft.[24] Although we will never know if these laws were applied to the letter (they most likely weren't), they betray contemporary attitudes towards runaways that may have influenced actual practice.

Enslaved people themselves could also face harsh punishments if caught on the run. From the same era as Hammurabi's laws, a man named Abdi-Ishtar fled the city of Larsa where he was forced to work as a weaver. When found, he was handed over to the 'overseer of the prisoners' – in other words, he found himself behind bars.[25] Just a few centuries earlier, slaves who ran away faced mutilation. One person's nostrils were cut after they tried to escape twice, the last time through a hole in the roof of their house.[26] A scarred nose would have immediately marked him as an enslaved person (with unsuccessful escape attempts in his past). Some may have even had ropes attached to their noses, like the 'nose-ropes' from some of the earliest written texts that describe humans bound in the same way as cattle.[27] Bounty hunters would often chase down fugitives for a financial reward, making it hard to evade capture. For some, their circumstances clearly made the risk worth taking.

There were some 'above board' ways an enslaved person could achieve legal emancipation, or manumission. During the twenty-first-century BCE reign of Amar-Suen, a woman named Gudaga purchased the freedom of her two children for 20 shekels of silver.[28] An enslaved person could also take their owner to court over their legal status as a slave. Many centuries after Gudaga freed her children, and just one generation before Ennigaldi-Nanna may have curated her collection in Ur, another mother contested the slave status of her children in court in Babylon. Remarkably, five clay tablets that span over three decades preserve almost every stage of her story. The woman is named as La-Tubashinni, and although her life left her at the mercy of others, she found a way to reclaim some power in the end. The clay tablets tell us that her adoptive mother had sold her into marriage to a man named Dagal-ili in 592 BCE. The marital arrangement was financed by a third party, the Sîn-damaqu family, perhaps to secure access to any children born of the forced union. Through this marriage-by-purchase, La-Tubashinni began her life as a slave, as would each of the six children she ultimately bore with her husband. The family moved from one owner to another, and a rectangular clay tablet records the sale of her two daughters and one son on 5 September 560 BCE. Around that time, La-Tubashinni was emancipated from her slave status for reasons that are missing from the written record.

What did she do with her newfound freedom? She fought for her children. A lawsuit dated to 29 October 560 BCE records her arguing before a minister and the king's judges that, like her, her children should be freed. In the end, the judges ruled that only one son, Ardiya, born after 'her tablet of manumission' – in other words, after the date on the clay tablet that recorded her legal release from slavery – was considered free. The rest would remain enslaved.[29]

Incidentally, one word used to express manumission combines the Sumerian signs *ama*, 'mother', and *gi*, 'return', for a literal and rather moving translation of 'return to the mother'. The cuneiform signs survive into modern Iraqi protest art to mean 'freedom', including in the work of Osama Sadiq whose massive murals cover canvases, walls, pavements, and even car park floors in Baghdad and beyond. Whenever I see those cuneiform signs, I think of women like La-Tubashinni, Gudaga, and even Ku'e in Emar – mothers whose children did and did not return to them, based on the economic gain or legal claim of a complete stranger.

The names, stories, and even the tiny feet preserved in clay help piece together an often bleak picture – a reminder that life was not easy for a lot of people. Their lives survive in moments frozen into the records of those who never had to worry about giving up their nursing daughter with no hope of future reunion, running away into the unforgiving open country to escape a life of servitude, or fighting for their enslaved children in court.

While the lives of enslaved people or those on the lower end of the socio-economic spectrum are played out in fleeting moments on clay, objects like the Babylonian boundary stone from Ennigaldi-Nanna's palace tell completely different stories – ones of wealth and privilege, luxury and royalty. The legal scenario outlined in the boundary stone suggests that the winner in the case, who ends up with the many acres of land in the Bit-Sîn-sheme district of Ur, must have already enjoyed some level of privilege in society for his case to have been heard at all – likely by the king himself – and for such high-value property to have ended up in his portfolio. The object itself speaks directly to a vastly different experience of ancient Mesopotamian life than that of Ku'e who couldn't afford to feed her own children. A highly skilled craftsperson and scribe would have had to combine forces to chisel the monument's many divine icons and hundreds of cuneiform signs. Before committing the message to stone, scribes had to make rough drafts on writing boards, made out of wood and covered in a layer of wax that could easily be 'erased' and reused by smoothing over impressed signs. This draft would have drawn from an official clay tablet belonging to the king himself, a record of his oral pronouncement of the land grant, which triggered a survey and further royal record. It was an extensive process involving the king, local officials, surveyors, and scribes.[30]

The boundary stone was a culmination of many steps and skills. Although precious few signs in the Ennigaldi-Nanna stone remain legible today, the craftsmanship involved in such a production is staggering. The beneficiary whose name is now broken must have had enough disposable income to commission such an obelisk, in lieu of the basic clay record of the king's pronouncements, not to mention the immense tracts of land memorialised in the stone itself. It is an elite object that carves out a chapter in an elite life.

Those who could afford it left behind detailed, deliberate, and sometimes even opulent evidence of their lives. Buried beneath the ground southeast of the ziggurat complex at Ur, a stone's throw from Ennigaldi-Nanna's palace, was the Royal Cemetery, a large burial ground in use for about 1,000 years. Despite its name, the vast majority of the over 2,000 graves found so far are simple burials. In the oldest graves, dated to around 3000 BCE, the dead lie on their sides with knees nearly touching their chins and hands clutching a cup near their face – leaving their earthly life in the same foetal position that preceded their birth.[31] Later graves find the dead wrapped in reed matting or placed in coffins made of wood, wickerwork, or clay at the bottom of a small pit.[32] Accompanied by precious few grave goods, these bodies also lie on their sides, but in a position more reminiscent of sleep than of an unborn foetus. Although the cemetery was mostly made up of such simple graves, the cemetery gets its name from the discovery of sixteen (less than 1 per cent) lavish burials, which are thought to belong to Ur's elite and royalty from the mid-third millennium BCE.

Perhaps most memorable among these is the tomb of Puabi, the Sumerian queen. Within a once vaulted, now crushed chamber lay her remains on a bier, her body blanketed by gemstones and precious metals. Strands of cylindrical beads stretched down from her shoulders to her waist with hints of precious metals throughout.[33] Long gold pins leaned against one of her arms to secure a now disintegrated garment, along with amulets and cylinder seals, one of which identified her by name. An even more luxurious headdress made of gold ribbons and leaves, strung together with more colourful stones from far-flung parts of the globe, covered Puabi's crushed skull. Near her hand lay an undisturbed gold cup. To Ur's excavators in the 1920s, the glint of silver and gold, and the rich blues and reds of the stones would have popped out of the surrounding light brown brick, sand, and soil. We can only imagine the splendour of her burial 4,500 years earlier, and the subterranean darkness after the doors of her tomb were sealed to leave her to rest. She left this world with more luxury items than most of us will even see, let alone own, in one lifetime (unless we visit the museums in Philadelphia and London where some of her grave goods are on display).

She also took with her a tragic entourage. Within her tomb chamber lay the remains of three others, one of whom lay near her head. Just above her tomb chamber was a room that contained the bodies of twenty-one nameless people who may have met their involuntary end by blunt force trauma as part of a grisly funerary ritual to accompany the queen.[34]

Attendants (those possibly forced to accompany another in death) filled several other graves. Another vaulted tomb that abutted Puabi's spanned 33 by 16 feet – a bit bigger than the footprint of a bus – and although its arched entrance had been blocked with brick and stone, grave robbers in antiquity managed to loot the chamber from above. Nothing remained of the main burial, which may have belonged to someone like a king, but as with Puabi, the chamber became the final resting place for three additional people. Arranged in an elaborate scene together with ox-drawn wagons and musical instruments, more bodies lay in the undisturbed pit next to the plundered tomb chamber. Six soldiers with spears and copper helmets lay at the foot of the pit's access ramp and, within the pit itself, bodies lay next to two wagons drawn by oxen. Just beyond them, fifty-four corpses covered the floor of the pit. In all, sixty-three people guarded the pit at the entrance of the looted tomb chamber of the now missing (maybe) king.[35] The Great Death Pit contained the remains of a further seventy-four people, also associated with a tomb that had been plundered.[36] This variation remains something of a mystery. Was the number proportional to a person's importance? Did it depend on the specific ritual carried out at the funeral? Did something like a will make provision for the number, or was it simply random? Whatever the explanation for these death pits, they furnish a distressing metaphor for the lives of a silent majority that died to serve a minority.

Other than their extensive grave goods, we know little more about the identities of those buried in the sixteen lavish tombs at Ur's Royal Cemetery. They are not named in any contemporary clay tablets so far uncovered, and apart from Puabi, their royal identities remain rather murky; but royal or not, they appear to have entered the afterlife with a lot of stuff. They took their stories into death, along with their many privileges, propped up by an economic system that concentrated wealth, for the most part, in the hands of palaces and temples for partial redistribution to a wider population of dependents.

Elsewhere in ancient Mesopotamia's history, others in comparably privileged positions left behind myriad records in clay that help us connect the cuneiform dots of their lives. During the reign of the twenty-first-century BCE king Shulgi of the Third Dynasty of Ur, a man named Lugal-irida worked his way up the social and economic ladder and left behind a sizeable paper (or rather clay) trail in the process. A scribe and administrator, he enjoyed a decades-long career that began as one of several overseers of weavers at a factory in the village of Guabba and ended up heading the entire establishment. Hundreds of people worked at the factory, and at one point its staff numbered around 600, including managers, weavers, assistants, and even sixteen bodyguards. As the superintendent, Lugal-irida received various products from the central administration, like dates and sesame oil, to distribute to workers as their monthly pay. He also received and managed raw materials used in textile production, such as wool, goat hair, and lard. As well as managing staff, he oversaw every stage of production, including quality control.[37] His daily to-do list was extensive, and we might imagine an intimidating, somewhat Dickensian figure touring the 'factory floor' – though in reality it was more likely a network of houses, lit only through small windows, that together formed a 'factory' of sorts. Lugal-irida might have checked on the work of individual weavers and doled out rations at the end of a long day. Or maybe he spent the day budgeting, record-making, and giving orders from behind a mud brick desk with all the social finesse of Michael Scott from *The Office*.

Whatever his management style, what is clear is that Lugal-irida worked a lot, and much of what he did relied on the hard work of others. His modern biographer, Dr Palmiro

Notizia, writes that Lugal-irida was primarily a professional manager whose over twenty years of heading the Third Dynasty's main centre of textile production must have also meant he reached a somewhat high social status.[38] During an era touted for its highly centralised state that concentrated power into the hands of very few, his story might strike us as quite remarkable; then again, that same state power relied on the very factories organised by individuals like Lugal-irida and the thousands of hours of work done by the many people he oversaw.

Contemporary clay tablets show that Lugal-irida owned extensive arable land and orchards that turned their own profits. An entrepreneur, he used his income from his managerial job to gain a foothold in long-distance trade of copper and borax, a salt used in industries like metallurgy and glass-making. Fortunately for posterity, Lugal-irida seems to have been a man who liked to have his affairs in order; a six-column tablet even lists his household assets − a document that reads not unlike a modern portfolio report or an inventory list for a property insurance application − to fill out this picture of his hard work and financial success.[39] Various objects made of metals like silver and bronze, textiles, oils, aromatics, wool, and even farm animals are among his lot, along with 10 shekels (nearly 3 ounces) of silver − a significant amount, given that liquid capital was hard to come by during his era.[40]

Lugal-irida has all the hallmarks of a modern-day capitalist success story − he worked his way up the ladder and was what we might call a 'self-made man'. Trained as an accountant, scribe, and manager, he used his skills and income to expand his own enterprises and enhance his social position. This is also partly down to luck and timing; at the turn of the millennium, in what would become the Babylonian south and Assyrian north of ancient Mesopotamia, the economy transitions into one that leaves a bit more potential for the kind of entrepreneurship and mercantilism shown by Lugal-irida. More potential, however, does not translate to more luck for everyone who worked hard. He was in the right place at the right time with the right set of skills, and his success remains more of an exception than a rule.

What family someone was born into, what training or education they could access, what financial concerns constrained their everyday lives, and other often totally random circumstances could shuffle them forward or backward on their path. People make good choices when they have good choices – then, as now. Precious few had skill and opportunity align in such a way that propelled them to the privileged end of the socio-economic continuum, and even fewer met death with such abundant signs of affluence as Queen Puabi. Far more common was the financial hardship that forced parents in Emar to sell their own children, that found mothers desperate to buy their children back, and locked enslaved individuals into work they never chose. Social mobility remained limited, depending on one's circumstances.

For some, a right by birth or marriage, and for others, a position earned through decades of enterprise, privilege in ancient Mesopotamia came in many shapes and sizes. During the same Kassite era when a scribe and artist worked to carve divine symbols atop land rights on the boundary stone from Ennigaldi-Nanna's museum, others with incredible skill began to chisel at a bright slab of magnesite to preserve the likeness of a king a bit further north. The result is a wide-eyed statue of a seated King Idrimi, about the height of a guitar, made of a dull white stone that looks like unpolished porcelain. Born around 1500 BCE in the city of Halab (now Aleppo, Syria, which is one of the oldest continuously occupied places on earth), the man in the statue sits upon a stone throne and stares into the distance with dark glass eyes. He wears an egg-shaped headdress and moustache-less beard, and he holds his right hand flat across his chest in a gesture that resembles the start of a bow.

Somewhat literally, he wears his heart on his sleeve. Over 100 lines of cuneiform signs cover his garment, his shoulders, arms, and even his cheek. The tale's first words are, 'I am Idrimi, son of Ili-ilimma'. The son of a lord, Idrimi fled his home city with his family after 'a bad thing happened', we are cryptically told. According to the inscription, after his family fled to Emar, he journeyed to Canaan, a region that corresponds to today's southern Levant, and spent 'seven long years' among nomads and refugees before amassing an army. 'I built ships, I loaded soldiers onto the ships,' reads the inscription. It goes on to say that 'in one day, as one man', Idrimi conquered a number of cities in what is now Turkey, including Alalakh – the exaggerated wording a cautious reminder that we are dealing with a royal inscription that leaves out as many details as it includes.

Once established as king, Idrimi carried out the typical tasks of a king. He made peace with his neighbours, expanded his territory, and showed respect for the gods. He made sure his people had comfortable homes, and he housed 'even those who lacked a dwelling'. From riches to rags to riches again, Idrimi went on to rule Alalakh and the surrounding cities for three decades. Although the inscription on the sleeve of his statue is signed by a scribe named Sharruwa, it ends with a blessing by the king in his own words: 'I was king for 30 years. I wrote my labours on myself. May one regularly look upon them [the words on the statue] so that they may call blessings on me regularly.'[41]

Idrimi's inscription may end with a blessing, but his story does not. Almost 3,000 years later in 1939, his statue would be unearthed by none other than Woolley during excavations at Alalakh, which at the time fell within the borders of Hatay, a semi-autonomous state that was about to be incorporated into Turkey. Idrimi's story has since captured the imaginations of historians, and the first-person narrative tattooed across the statue's body makes it a unique find from ancient Mesopotamia. No other statue so far unearthed combines text and image in this way, and even though Woolley deemed it to have 'little artistic value' he fought over the object with representatives of the Hatay Archaeological Museum. Local law mandated that the excavator divide finds into two qualitatively equal lots – no easy feat – and the host country's Director of the Antiquities Service would choose one lot for the national collections and leave the other to the excavating institution. When the choice did not go Woolley's way, he involved a powerful diplomat, Cevat Açıkalın, to help him convince the Hatay authorities to relinquish Idrimi's likeness. Woolley's power play and own privilege paid off. The magnesite statue now sits in a glass display case in the British Museum, while only a hologram of Idrimi glows in the New Hatay Archaeological Museum.[42]

As today, people sought, perpetuated, and protected privilege in ancient Mesopotamia, even if that involved the most convoluted (and occasionally even illegal) of ruses, from smuggling to fraud. A few centuries before Idrimi became a refugee-turned-king, a vast trade network stretched all the way from the Assyrian heartland to what is now Turkey. I can imagine the Assyrian merchants of the early second millennium BCE crowded around the gates of Assur, their capital, in the twilight before dawn with their donkeys, ready to head north with their goods. The sound of their braying pack animals would rise above the tumult of voices – a chorus of goodbyes between family members and haggling between merchants. There, an older man named Ashur-idi once stood with his two black donkeys, laden with bags of tin that weighed a collective 130 pounds, thirty textiles in their waterproof wraps, and another 17 pounds of tin kept separately to pay tolls along the way. Those donkeys would carry these items on their backs all the way to the major trade hub of Kanesh in what is now Turkey, a journey of about five weeks, for the goods to be sold or traded. Although expecting to make the journey himself, he trusted another man named Sharrum-Adad, a professional transporter, to carry it instead at the very last minute. It was not a huge shipment, by any means. The largest ever recorded was carried by 34 donkeys, and included over 600 textiles, 100 gemstones, and 60 litres of saffron.[43] If 1 litre of saffron today weighs 5 ounces and costs about £500, then the saffron alone was worth the equivalent of almost £30,000. Today, such a shipment might warrant something like an armoured van, rather than a drove of donkeys.

Many such merchants and traders even moved to Kanesh to carry out their business, and records preserve letters between far-flung family members, including those between siblings and married couples. In some cases, women stayed in the Assyrian heartland to become the head of their households and manage or produce goods for trade, while men remained in Kanesh semi-permanently – some even married second wives locally.[44] Whatever the arrangement, families and individuals amassed quite a fortune through this trade, and some went to great lengths to protect their holdings (the impetus for this perhaps shared by some people today who find perfectly legal ways to manage their tax obligations).

Around 23,000 tablets composed over a period of a century and a half have helped scholars reconstruct not just the broad elements of this trade network, but also the minutiae of merchants' everyday disputes, transactions, and taxes. Loan documents preserve interest rates, payment plans, and penalties. Alone, each tablet is about as fun to read as watching paint dry. But collectively, they give a picture of the economic and social history of the era in astounding detail. We can follow every stage of a typical transaction, from spinning the wool for textiles to calculating tax on tin. We even learn the names of those who spun that wool into textiles, those who transported them, taxed them, sold them, and sent the money back home to Assur.

Countless letters between business partners and family members fill in many of the blanks, including instructions, arguments, and even the occasional sass. A woman named Ahaha sent seven letters from the Assyrian heartland to her brothers in Kanesh about managing the family estate. Her brother Buzazu writes to another party about a delay in getting silver to Ahaha thanks to a blocked road and hopes word of the reason will reach his sister. 'I suffer from her a great wrath for as long as I am alive!' he complains rather emphatically.[45]

The same Buzazu took steep risks to avoid paying tax on their family's trading enterprise. In one letter, he instructs his trading partners to 'bring the tin via the narrow track', a known smuggling route, if the coast is clear. We should not underestimate the dangers. This route could have crossed the grassy, undulating area of today's Uzunyayla, a region of mountain pasture that at the time was known for its bandits who assaulted travelling caravans. People, their animals, and their cargo would have been vulnerable to thieves – a far higher price to pay than the roughly 5 per cent tax levied on many goods. If the coast is not clear, Buzazu clarifies in the letter, 'let them make small packets of my tin and introduce them gradually into Kanesh, concealed in their underwear'.[46]

He ultimately cancels the smuggling operation, but he is not alone in his attempts at tax evasion. Another merchant named Kunilum instructs his trading partners, who included Buzazu's father Pushu-ken, to mix taxable goods previously cleared by customs with undeclared goods. The goal was to sneak them into Kanesh without paying any import duties. Pushu-ken, it seems, was a node for several smuggling operations, and another letter records a merchant's plea that he aid in further illegal activity. 'Just as you send an order for your own goods to be smuggled,' that merchant writes to Pushu-ken, 'do also send one for my goods.'[47] Pushu-ken ultimately paid a high price for his attempts to keep more of what he made when his home in Kanesh was raided for smuggled goods, and he ended up in prison.

As well as capturing snapshots of Pushu-ken's life as a trader and dedicated tax evader, cuneiform tablets remind us that he was also a father. One son named Sueyya, left behind in Assur, had spent several years learning cuneiform in school, and sent a small clay letter to his father covered in neat handwriting far more legible than most of the records unearthed in Kanesh. In it, the young boy boasts to his father that he has learned cuneiform, demonstrated by the flawless script impressed into the tiny square tablet of clay.[48]

Protecting wealth and privileges wasn't just the pastime of merchants. One of my favourite examples from the many millennia of ancient Mesopotamia's history is a group of priests in the city of Sippar, who were almost contemporary with Ennigaldi-Nanna. These holy men attempted to pull off an overzealous forgery that somehow passed muster at the time; they carved a black stone into the shape of a three-dimensional cross that stood at not quite a foot tall. On the twelve resulting sides and edges, they inscribed statements of the grants and privileges bestowed on them as priests of the temple of Shamash in an archaic-looking script. The language is trying so hard to sound old, as if I were to write a letter in the style of Shakespeare to sound more authoritative. In that faked ancient dialect, the text describes those priestly privileges as going as far back as King Manishtushu who had ruled almost two millennia earlier, from the dynasty founded by Sargon. They even used a sham ancient font – a style of cuneiform known from no other period in Mesopotamian history but that must, at the time, have looked older.[49]

The priests must have buried the small monument in the foundation of the Shamash temple and, not long afterwards, dug it up to play out some kind of staged 'discovery' of the supposedly historic item. The idea was that the 'ancient' object would show the antiquity of their office and thereby justify the continued support of their temple (and salaries) by the king. It would be like typing out an excerpt of the Declaration of Independence in Lucida Blackletter font, burning the printed document's edges, and trying to pass it off as an artefact from Thomas Jefferson's time. However cheesy this all sounds, the artefact gained such traction at the time that copies of it were made in both Sippar and Babylon.[50] 'This is not a lie, it is indeed the truth,' reads one of the cruciform monument's hundreds of lines. (Nothing inspires more confidence than the claim that something is both not a lie, and also the truth, chiselled into stone in a completely fabricated font.)

As privileges remained the domain of the lucky few, it comes as no surprise that people used whatever means at their disposal – from pulling off a forgery to evading tax – to create and preserve their social and economic positions. Even with these less than glamorous sides to their stories, cuneiform texts are skewed in favour of those who could afford to impress their records into clay and other materials. A minority have left behind a disproportionate amount of evidence for their activities and interests, and it's important to remember that, overall, the things that got recorded in this wonderful wedge-shaped writing tend to favour the lives of the privileged. They not only *could* keep records, including elaborate ones on diorite boundary stones, but often *had to* in order to keep their businesses operational. However abundant cuneiform texts might be, whether impressed in clay or chiselled into stone, they preserve but a fraction of the lives and stories from ancient Mesopotamia.

With their copious records, they thankfully also leave behind evidence of the lives of those in their immediate orbit, like Ishunnatu who ran a tavern around the time of Ennigaldi-Nanna, Ganana who survived war thousands of years ago, and the enslaved twin toddlers in Emar who went on to become scribes. Cuneiform preserves the stories of people whose work in many ways made life in ancient Mesopotamia possible. The agricultural labourers who harvested grain, factory workers who made textiles, and the runaway slaves (and perhaps even their bounty hunters) live on in the tiny triangles from ancient Mesopotamia and provide a glimpse of what life might have been like for those whose stories were written down by and for others.

As for the boundary stone found in Ennigaldi-Nanna's museum, the man bestowed with acres upon acres of land along the 'bank of the New Canal' in the Bit-Sîn-sheme area of Ur likely formed part of an elite minority. Although accidents of preservation have all but erased the first column of text, some of the surviving signs hint that the land grant related to a royal adjudication over a land dispute. The king ultimately ruled in favour of the one for whom the boundary stone was then chiselled before it was placed in a temple to bear perpetual witness to his new asset.

But how long, really, did people expect their boundary stones to hold up? Did they expect the Ennigaldi-Nannas of Babylon's future (and our past) to find and display them, or did they imagine that time and the elements would eventually bury them? The boundary stone from Ennigaldi-Nanna's museum lay face down by a doorway where it had slept since some time after Ur was abandoned, only to be roused from its ancient slumber by excavators in the 1920s, extending its life by many thousands of years. By the time it landed in the National Museum of Iraq in Baghdad, it had lived three lives – as the title deed of a man in Ur, as an object in the collection of a Babylonian princess, and as a modern museum object.

Some boundary stones do give hints as to how long their owners hoped such deeds would last. Chiselled into limestone, Nabû-shuma-iddina's dispute over land around 1100 BCE describes a border in place for the previous 696 years. The king instructed that 'descendants of the experts familiar with the neighbouring lands' must be consulted to determine and restore the rightful location of the field's border.[51] Conversely, similar records of land entitlements curse anyone from any point in the future who might contravene the boundary.[52] They had, in other words, both the distant past and an infinite future in mind.[53] They may not have imagined that their objects would be collected for posterity in sizeable museum collections around the globe, but they may have hoped some relic of their lives and entitlements would survive into future generations.

What strikes me about the boundary stone from Ennigaldi-Nanna's museum, though, is that we do not actually know the name of the man who ended up with quite a lot of land in the Bit-Sîn-sheme district in Ur. In fact, we know more about Ba'al-belu and Ishma'-Dagan, the twin enslaved scribes from Emar, than we do about the circumstances of this man's victory over a land dispute in Ur. We know more about the activities of Ishunnatu, the enslaved woman who ran a tavern, than we do about those of Queen Puabi who leaves behind only a few AA battery-sized seals to tell us anything concrete about her identity. We know as little about those buried with jewels and chariots as we do about the tens of attendants killed to follow them into the afterlife. Even if cuneiform tends to privilege certain segments of society, it too must contend with the passage of time and accidents of preservation that erode some stories and leave others perfectly preserved, including the stories of those without boundary stones or magnesite statues with glass eyes.

8

The Mace Head

The Art vs Reality of War

Thousands of years after the Euphrates changed its meandering course, and Ur and its ziggurat were buried under mounds of rubble and desert sand, the land that was once ancient Mesopotamia witnessed occupation, war, and death. In the poem 'The Iraqi Nights' Iraqi-American poet Dunya Mikhail writes of the progression of war, like a game that leaves the so-called winners behind to recall those they lost.

> the winner is the one
> who returns from the journey
> alone
> full of stories of the dead.[1]

By the end of 'The Iraqi Nights', it becomes clear that war has no real winners. Even those who survive must carry their grief into every new sunrise, recalling one of the last things Gilgamesh said to Enkidu: 'The deceased left sorrow to the one who survived.'[2]

The history of warfare in ancient Mesopotamia tells the same stories of violence and loss, making it difficult to find a real winner despite the boasts of victorious kings. How can anyone make sense of something so senseless? Back then, people wrote poetry about war and death too, and a lot of it centres their gods, like Nergal who reigned over the triple threats of death, war, and disease. Although the name Nergal first pops up in texts from around 2100 BCE, he was known as Meslamtaea in earlier periods, which is a name that graces god lists from some of the earliest periods of writings. Within centuries of inventing a way to write things down, people wrote the name of a death god. He represented not the kind of quiet death that visits us naturally at the end of a long life, but *inflicted* death. He accompanied kings into battle, often portrayed with a deadly weapon: a mace with twin lion heads snaking out of the top of the staff to flank either side of the weapon's pear-shaped head.

With a spherical or pear-shaped head, usually made of stone or metal mounted atop a staff, a mace would bear considerable power. One strike with the head of such a weapon could put a devastating crack in someone's skull with relative ease. A Sumerian epic known as *Lugal-e* is testimony to the destruction the mace could unleash. The story recounts a battle between the victory god Ninurta and a creature known as the Asag demon, who was so repulsive in appearance that he later becomes a harbinger of disease. The Asag demon was said to cause fish to boil alive in rivers,[3] but even he was no match for Ninurta and his mace. In battle, the mace took on its own agency, snarling at and setting fire to mountains, devouring the enemy, and smashing skulls.[4]

A mace head was one of the curiosities found by Woolley in Ennigaldi-Nanna's museum. But unlike Nergal's ornate weapon, this mace is entirely plain, like an imperfect concrete sphere bollard. For most of the out-of-place-and-time objects found in the museum, inscriptions that were either chiselled or pressed into the material provide clues about their age. The boundary stone follows the style of mid- to late-second-millennium BCE boundary stones, the clay cone references the historically datable ruler named Kudur-Mabuk, as does the fragment of the statue of King Shulgi. But the stone mace head is the one object from the collection that has no writing on it, so its age must remain a mystery. (To Woolley, it seemed older than any of the objects in the room.) When you handle an ancient artefact, it's natural to think about how its creator made it fit for its purpose. The messiness of a hastily made bowl, for example, might mean it was an everyday kitchen staple rather than a work of art. The teeny tininess of a teeny tiny model chariot might have made it better suited to the hands of a child than an adult, so we might guess it was a toy. The same plainness that makes the mace head hard to date may suggest it was functional, rather than decorative. Whenever it was made, it may well have seen battle and dripped with the blood of fallen enemies.

Unlike the plain one found in Ennigaldi-Nanna's museum, some mace heads were made as ceremonial objects, which served not as weapons but as symbolically powerful pieces of art dedicated to deities. These sometimes bore elaborate designs and were crafted from prized materials unsuitable for war, like glass or lapis lazuli. One mace head from the Sumerian city of Girsu shows a lion-headed eagle dominating six lions, and bears a brief inscription of King Mesilim and his dedication to Ningirsu, a Sumerian god of victory. These ceremonial objects were made to be beautiful, but, as symbols of power and authority, they were also the perfect way of sending a personal message to the divine. The ornate mace heads served as ancient votive offerings not unlike those that still carry deep personal and religious meaning for people today. Catholics, for example, light and leave candles in church for their loved ones, or Eastern Orthodox Christians dedicate *tamata*, or metal plaques that symbolise prayers, and other offerings as signs of devotion to God.

As an object that was both functional and symbolic, it's not surprising that mace heads have often been found when excavating Mesopotamian tombs. People would have wanted this multi-purpose object to accompany them into their lives beyond the grave. In one of the tombs excavated by Woolley and his team in Ur's Royal Cemetery, intricate treasures and weapons were unearthed, including a copper mace head and a gold dagger with a deep-blue lapis lazuli hilt and dazzling gold sheath traced with tiny geometric designs, which must have glinted in the dirt as diggers saw it for the first time since its burial five millennia ago.[5]

Such burials open up a whole can of worms about the afterlife in Mesopotamia. What would weapons have been used for? What did people believe awaited them in the Underworld? *The Death of Ur-Nammu* is a Sumerian poem about King Ur-Nammu's death and journey to the Underworld. En route, he slaughtered animals to feed the otherwise only dust-fed dead. 'The food of the Underworld is bitter; the water of the Underworld is brackish', and the king brought with him offerings for a royal feast. He also brought gifts for the gods. To Nergal, he offered 'a mace, a large bow with quiver and arrows, an artfully made . . . dagger, and a multi-coloured leather bag for wearing at the hilt'. He also offered several weapons to the legendary King Gilgamesh, including a battle-axe, a shield, and a 'heavenly' lion-headed mace.[6] Was the copper mace from the Royal Cemetery – and perhaps even all the weapons that accompanied it – also intended as a gift for the gods who dwelled in the world of the dead?

The power inherent in the mace – as a weapon of war, as a symbol of strength and authority, and as divine armament – might explain its appearance in an otherwise unexpected place, like a medical prescription. As well as a weapon of destruction, the mace also had a role in protecting against illness. In the rich collection of medical textbooks housed in King Ashurbanipal's library at Nineveh, one prescription promises to increase a man's sexual potency if he drinks the iron flakes of a mace mixed with beer.[7] Another ritual to protect a patient from the demons behind an epidemic instructs that a wooden sceptre or mace be placed at his head to 'ward off' the evil.[8] Certain doctors may have even carried a kind of ceremonial mace, called a *gamlu*. Even today, medical experiences are sometimes described in terms better suited to battle. We 'fight' a cold, win a 'battle' against cancer, or see healthcare workers as forming the 'frontline' in the war against a pandemic like Covid-19. What better medical 'weapon' to use than a literal weapon?

The mace head seems to have been ubiquitous throughout Mesopotamian history; a multi-purpose object that could at once represent the authority of leaders, tap into the power of deities, and summon health to sick patients. But while it had other uses, the mace head like the one found in Ennigaldi-Nanna's palace is ultimately a symbol of violence and war. We may never know when the first battles raged between the two rivers, but some of the earliest written sources in Sumerian describe conflicts between cities. There are graphic accounts of corpses piled so high they reach the heavens themselves. But these early inter-city battles look tame compared to the brutality of the later Neo-Assyrian period. Lengthy chronicles of ancient Assyrian kings from the first millennium BCE describe the gory minutiae of acts of violence and military conquests in ways that epitomise the history of war and death, and how people made sense of it all, in ancient Mesopotamia.

The earliest recorded border conflict in the world comes from ancient Mesopotamia, one of the many firsts alongside the wheel and early writing that punctuate the Early Dynastic period. (That era's many innovations seemed to come with some sizeable skeletons in the closet.) This became apparent the first time I saw the delicately carved image of vultures pecking at severed human heads along the top of a fragmentary limestone war memorial. Known today as the Stele of the Vultures, even broken, this striking stone monument has presence. It towers over modern viewers at nearly 6 feet tall and over 4 feet wide. The monument commemorates this border conflict between the ancient city of Lagash and the neighbouring city of Umma in the mid-third millennium

BCE. Like an ancient Hundred Years' War, the conflict spanned several generations, and the stela celebrates the victory of Lagash.

Below the grisly image, columns of a Sumerian script stretch across the stone, describing a momentous victory for the city of Lagash roughly east of Uruk. In a blend of history and mythology, the account tells us that the Lagash king fought the enemy not just with a mortal army, but also with the help of the city's chief god, Ningirsu, a heroic warrior who fought alongside the mortals to bring them to victory. The story culminates in Ningirsu's command that Lagash 'slay' the enemy and his promise that 'their myriad corpses will reach the base of heaven'.[9] Fragments of the broken text provide snapshots of the battle: the king of Lagash is shot with an arrow, he retaliates by summoning a flood, and eventually succeeds in drawing a new boundary line between the enemy cities. One has to wonder, what might generations of kings of Umma have written about the same battle? Did they lament their losses, or did they spin the same story to leave them victorious?

Ningirsu's promise that enemy corpses will be piled so high they will reach the base of heaven introduces a recurring, but not always straightforward, symbol of victory in accounts of warfare from ancient Mesopotamia: the burial mound, or tumulus. The Stele of the Vultures even makes broken reference to the construction of twenty such mounds to honour the enemy's dead. A roughly contemporary account of the same Umma–Lagash border conflict is impressed into a foot-long clay cone. Six columns of cuneiform wrap around the cone like textured bands, which include descriptions of burying the enemy in a handful of mass graves.[10] When the defeated Umman king fled and was killed, he allegedly left behind sixty teams of asses and the bones of his own fallen soldiers. It was the victors instead who took care of the bodies and laid their enemies to rest. In early Mesopotamian history, such burials seem to be a question of principle. If the enemy king can't or won't honour his fallen with a burial, then the victor must. Reading between the lines resurrects a sort of military code from almost 5,000 years ago.

While this may have originally been a matter of honour, inscriptions of much later Assyrian kings suggest that these practices morphed into something altogether different. The Assyrian records show a more macabre practice of corpse abuse, as part of a broader show of military might. 'I made heaps of their corpses like grain piles beside their gates,' reads an inscription of the thirteenth-century BCE Assyrian king Tukulti-Ninurta I.[11] Even more graphic, the later king Tiglath-Pileser I records a campaign in northern Mesopotamia with corpses and heads stacked like piles of grain and blood-soaked battlefields.[12]

Did the victorious Assyrian kings actually carry out these violent post-battle rituals, or are these fictional boasts, made up to add texture to their propaganda? Did the king of Lagash over 1,000 years earlier really bury the enemy dead in multiple mounds as a matter of honour, or did he just say so to add some moral colour to the blood-stained slaughter?

Although all good propaganda uses hyperbole for maximum effect, in this case the descriptions may have some basis in reality – at least for the early periods. A handful of archaeological sites provide evidence of mass burials associated with war.[13] In what is now northeast Syria lie the sprawling remains of one of the world's oldest and largest settlements, Tell Brak.

The site was continuously occupied from at least the seventh millennium BCE for about 5,000 years, possibly thanks to its location in a favourable climate zone and on a number of trade routes.[14] (For comparison, London was established about 2,000 years ago and according to some climate models may be mostly underwater by the end of this century.) From the 2300s BCE, Tell Brak became an outpost of King Sargon's Akkadian empire, and Naram-Sîn, the third king in that dynasty, even had a 'palace' there.[15]

About half a mile from the city, archaeologists have found several mass graves dating to the fourth millennium BCE that held the remains of hundreds of people. In antiquity, in a typical mass grave, the majority of remains would belong to either the very young or very old – in other words the people most vulnerable in an epidemic or natural disaster, events that would require a mass burial. By contrast, in a burial mound that was just a regular cemetery for the nearby city, the demography would match up to that of a typical town, with a variety of age groups represented. The burial mounds outside of Tell Brak matched neither of these scenarios. In fact, most of the bodies belonged to adults and young adults who all seemed to have died at the same time. The demography of the dead reflects neither that of a typical population, nor that most likely to die of disease or disaster.

One of the excavated areas, which revealed the remains of around sixty individuals, showed a number of disarticulated skeletons – bones that were not put back together as discrete individuals, but rather piled together unceremoniously, which was very much at odds with normal burial practices. Looking closely at the bones revealed other hints at something sinister. They were covered in small scratches – the bite marks from animals as small as rats and as large as lions and dogs. The corpses must have laid out in the open, maybe on an abandoned battlefield, for weeks or even months before being brought to the mound for haphazard interment in a single burial event. Some of the skulls even showed signs of post-mortem abuse, marked by abrasions and even polish, telltale signs that they might have been used as trophy heads.[16]

All of these disturbing details add up to suggest that the dead were not from among the local population in the nearby city but were, instead, most likely the bodies of the enemy. The Tell Brak burial comes from the millennium before the Umma–Lagash border conflict recorded on the Stele of the Vultures. Was this an early (or even, the earliest known) version of what would become a regular post-war practice?[17]

On the other hand, there is an example of something like a war memorial from this period too, where features of the burials do far more to honour the dead. In the 1990s, at a site known as Tell Banat, also in Syria, archaeologists excavated a cone-shaped vertical cemetery about six storeys high. It was coated in gypsum, a pale-coloured stone that acted a bit like plaster and gave the site its nickname of 'The White Monument'. Like a conical hill, the monument once rose out of the flat plains just beyond the block-shaped homes of the town of Jebel Bazi. A closer look showed deliberate grooves in parts of the gypsum exterior, as if to mark this ostensible hill as a human-made monument, more than a natural feature of the area's geography.

The mound was built in several phases, and in some of the resulting sections and layers, the incomplete remains of numerous individuals suggest that they were moved from their original resting place to be interred here. Their grave goods had a decidedly military character. Egg-shaped pellets with sharpened ends that would have been used in projectile weapons – sling-shot bullets that would rain down on an opposing army like hail to halt their progress – were found with almost all of the bodies. Buried with these bodies were the remains of several *kunga*, a kind of donkey used for pulling vehicles. A high percentage of the dead, in other words, were buried with weaponry and animals used in war. They may have been members of an organised army made up of soldiers who drove wagons, like early charioteers, as well as foot soldiers.[18] Given the great care with which the remains were relaid, it seems likely that these fallen soldiers were laid to rest by those they left behind – those who grieved them.

It would make sense for there to be different outcomes for the victims of different battles during different time periods; some were left behind, some were further brutalised or buried helter skelter by the enemy, and some were carefully buried by their own people. Tell Banat's vertical cemetery is a unique find among the dearth of archaeological evidence for post-battle burial mounds. But this remarkable exception shows there was a need collectively to remember, maybe even to thank, those who fell while protecting their fellow citizens, and Tell Banat may be one of, if not *the* first surviving example of that need. Tragically, under President Hafez Al-Assad, the construction of the Tishreen Dam in Syria led this unique site to be flooded in the 1990s, and what might be the earliest known war memorial in history now lies submerged beneath the redirected waters of Lake Assad.

Ancient kings seemed to have a kind of monopoly on violence, all in the name of protecting their people and expanding their realms.[19] Shaped like the craggy peak of a mountain, an ancient stone stela stands at 6 feet 7 inches tall, showing an oversized King Naram-Sîn, who ruled the Akkadian empire from 2254 to 2218 BCE. He stands with his bow and arrow atop a chaotic pile of his fallen enemies, the Lullubi people from the Zagros Mountains, and an impaled soldier kneels at his feet, while another appears to beg for mercy. Today, this 'Naram-Sîn Victory Stele' is considered one of the most important relics from ancient Mesopotamia, but like any work of art, it gives only a snapshot of a moment in time – the very end of a battle. Ancient monuments like these capture some of the most memorable and often hideous moments of battle in what would have once been vibrant colours. Day-to-day clay tablets, on the other hand, paint a less striking picture of war and its minutiae – from distributing 400 cloaks during a siege to confirming the king's actual location at the end of a battle (spoiler alert: he was sometimes at home).[20] To understand ancient Mesopotamia's military history, we have to look both at the showy accounts of kings and the dry daily records of the many people who worked at their beck and call.

There is no better era to mine for military history than that of unprecedented power and might under ancient Assyrian rule from around 900 to 600 BCE, known as the Neo-Assyrian period. The empire during this period swelled to such proportions that it became the largest that the world had yet seen in antiquity. No king expands an empire to that extent without some, or even a lot of, bloodshed. Arguably, the most striking accounts of this state-sanctioned violence and war come from this period, as well as some of the most detailed (and sometimes dull) letters back and forth between kings and their magnates to keep that very war machine oiled.

Stone reliefs from the palaces of Neo-Assyrian kings leave behind disturbing images of brutality, and their written chronologies detail vivid acts of violence, including the flayed skins of enemies and their severed heads on stakes. It's likely that much of what they leave behind are exaggerated accounts, meant to prop up their power and make enemies think twice before testing the battle readiness of an Assyrian king. Either way, thanks to the immense stone reliefs and lengthy cuneiform chronicles left behind by its kings, perhaps no era in ancient Mesopotamia's long history gets more closely associated with war than the Neo-Assyrian period.[21]

To me, the king that exemplifies this is Ashurbanipal, who ruled the empire at the height of its power in the seventh century BCE. He appears in stone reliefs as a towering figure with muscular calves and forearms, long curly hair, and an equally long beard. In one image from his palace in Nineveh, he grasps a lion by the tail with one hand and, in the other, brandishes a mace. Above the scene is a brief inscription: 'I seized a lion of the steppe by its tail, and at the command of Ninurta and Nergal, the gods whom I trust, I smashed its skull with my own mace.'[22] From his place on a grand chariot, the king impales a lion in one panel, and in others, dying lions lie contorted on the ground. Some vomit in the final moments of their lives. These scenes freeze moments of agony into stone in such exquisite detail that it is hard to look away. Anyone taking in these images can feel the Assyrian king's raw power, his strength and, more specifically, his ability to conquer the chaotic forces of nature, including the chaos of the enemy in the foreign lands outside the empire's borders. The mace, tellingly, is one of the king's weapons of choice in palace reliefs, especially in scenes designed to memorialise his power over chaos, and reminds us of the symbolic power of this weapon. The reliefs feature processions of mythological creatures in profile, mid-step, richly carved down to the curls in their beards and the veins in their features. These protective beings include demons who sometimes bear maces. In a palace that once sprawled across the northern part of Nineveh, a demon is frozen into a tall stone panel, his leonine jaw agape with a roar. Although his body is human, he has huge talons in the place of feet and the head of a lion with two curved horns that jut out of his forehead. In one hand he brandishes a dagger, and in the other a mace.

As historians, we can only piece together pictures of the past from the surviving sources, but not all sources are created equal. In trying to reconstruct the history of American military intervention in Iraq, a historian 3,000 years from now might stumble upon nothing more than President George W. Bush's speeches. References to weapons of mass destruction, a war on the entire concept of terror, and the liberation of a monolithic Iraqi population make for a rousing piece of wartime propaganda, but pluck very few details from reality. That future historian might even be forgiven for thinking that 'Dubya' decided to go to war all on his own and that no one else, including the thousands of anti-war protesters on his own country's soil, had anything to say about it. (I was one of those protesters in Columbia University's quad alongside hundreds of others who opposed the invasion, including a friend who held up a cardboard sign that read, 'My bush would make a better president'.) I am absolutely not comparing Assyrian kings to President Bush. Rather, I am comparing the *types* of sources for political history that we must interrogate to try to get at what actually happened three millennia ago when the Assyrian empire grew to be the largest empire the world had yet seen. That empire was far more than Ashurbanipal, his forebears, and the sum of their battles chronicled in royal sources. It was also a testament to political acumen, scholarship, and ingenuity.

I am fundamentally a historian of ancient science, and most of the cuneiform tablets I research come from the Assyrian heartland in the first millennium BCE. They have nothing to do with war. A circular clay tablet from the Library of Ashurbanipal divided into sections like a pie draws the constellations, including the Pleiades, and mathematical figures. This clay star map transports us back in time, showing the night sky over Nineveh on 3 January 650 BCE. Chapters from the *Epic of Gilgamesh* and medical treatments for depression and fevers once filled the library's proverbial shelves. Clay letters preserve profoundly human moments among royalty, from a queen reprimanding a princess for not doing her homework to the king lamenting the loss of a child. I love these tablets to bits, and even though they only preserve a fraction of a fraction of human experience in ancient Mesopotamia, they tell us something about what life was like, what kings thought worth defending and expanding so many millennia ago, and even what knowledge they used to make military decisions. Tens of thousands of such tablets remind us that there was far more to ancient Assyria than bloodshed.[23]

The empire was also far more than the king alone, and the monumental art and inscriptions commissioned to record his (alleged) wartime valour. It had so many moving parts that it is difficult to follow them all in the thousands of surviving clay records that lack the bombast of royal inscriptions, but instead include everyday details that make for a more accurate history.[24] To enable those parts to function in unison, the king also relied on long-distance communication, served by a royal road dotted with road stations in strategic positions so the king could correspond with his widespread officials quickly and securely, a sort of ancient DHL network.[25]

I will not for a moment pretend the combined force of these administrative records can take as much of my breath away as a single square inch of a palatial relief bearing the image of a king alongside a dying lion. As historians of ancient Mesopotamia, though, we are lucky to have both the (sometimes boring) day-to-day letters and the monumental art, the complaints about cloaks for soldiers and the elephantine images of kings and their maces. It is an *embarras de richesses* of sources, and I will never forget that this was the thing that really struck me the day cuneiform re-entered my life in London almost two decades ago – the sheer volume of written things that survive from ancient Mesopotamia. A big chunk of that summer morning involved the Library of Ashurbanipal with its Gilgamesh tablets and star maps, but it also involved slow walking through a wide hallway guarded by two winged human-lion *lamassu* and lined with limestone slabs from a Neo-Assyrian palace that showed violence on an unimaginable scale.

The mace-wielding Ashurbanipal came to the throne after the death of his father, Esarhaddon. Because he was neither the eldest nor the second (or even third) eldest son, his father drafted a succession treaty in 672 BCE to ensure that his chosen heir would rule Assyria while one of his other sons, Shamash-shumu-ukin, would become king of Babylon (Babylonia at the time needed a separate ruler to manage such a large territory often riddled with conflict and unrest of a population unhappy with Assyrian rule). But two decades after the succession treaty, and perhaps somewhat inevitably, tensions would rise between the brothers and co-kings – one in Assyria to the north and one in Babylonia to the south – that escalated into a full-blown civil war. It only ended with the suspicious death of Shamash-shumu-ukin in 648 BCE.[26] Did he die in battle? Did an assassin carry out a clandestine attack? Or did Ashurbanipal quietly execute him? To kill one's own brother, even among royalty, was a big no-no, so it makes sense that Ashurbanipal's own accounts of his brother's death almost gloss over it in an attempt to distance himself from the event. Some accounts simply describe his death as 'cruel', while others blame the gods who 'consigned him to fire and destroyed his life'.[27] Only the outcome is clear: Ashurbanipal takes control over the whole of the Assyrian realm, including the coveted ruling seat of the south, Babylon.

Time and again, Ashurbanipal proved to be an astute leader who led a powerful army that, like a trusted mace head, crushed the empire's enemies. Under his forty years of rule, Assyria stretched all the way from what is now Cyprus in the west and Turkey in the north to Iran in the east and Egypt in the south. He waged costly but successful wars with Egypt, Elam (now Iran), and Babylonia. Interestingly, however, the prosaic administrative texts suggest that he did not actually get his hands dirty. The mighty, muscular, mace-wielding

Ashurbanipal who could supposedly wrestle a lion with his bare hands did not even accompany his army into battle or even on campaign. As Professor Eckart Frahm writes in his recent book on Assyria's imperial age, the king 'simply stayed home, recited some prayers – and enjoyed himself'.[28]

This discrepancy, I have to admit, makes me chuckle. Much of what the Assyrian kings themselves left behind give the impression that they did nothing but go to war (and fight lions) and that they uniquely revelled in violence. They paint pictures of war at a level of detail that I could quite frankly do without, from heads hanging from trees to bodies impaled on posts.

Unlike accounts from earlier epochs, the royal inscriptions of the Neo-Assyrian period give lengthy narratives with precise chronological accounts of military events with clear, yearly divisions, often called annals because of their length and detail.[29] The sheer variety of media and volume of text is mind-blowing, with thousands of lines impressed and engraved across thousands of objects. The royal inscriptions of Assyrian kings are impressed or engraved onto artefacts made of clay, metal, and stone. Scribes shaped clay into the somewhat standard mobile-phone-sized tablets, and they also made tall multi-sided prisms, barrel-shaped cylinders, cones, and, of course, bricks before impressing or stamping them with tens, hundreds, and even thousands of little wedges. Large limestone wall panels, statues, mace heads, and stone sculptures of mythical creatures also bear these royal messages and narratives.

One depiction that crops up frequently is that of a *lamassu*; with the body of a bull or lion, wings of an eagle, and a human head, these creatures were protective deities who flanked the entrances to palaces and cities. A pair once stood at the entrance to the sweeping palace of the eighth century BCE king Ashurnasirpal II at Nimrud, ancient Kalhu, near modern-day Mosul. Once the capital city of the ancient Assyrians, the extraordinary ruins of Nimrud were targeted by Daesh in 2016 for systematic, large-scale destruction. 'When I heard about Nimrud,' said Hiba Hazim Hamad, professor of archaeology at the University of Mosul who often took her students to the site, 'my heart wept before my eyes did.'[30]

When I first visited the British Museum in the summer of 2008, I met one such pair of *lamassu* that flanked the entrance not to a palace, but to a long hallway lined with gypsum and limestone reliefs excavated from Iraq. I can only imagine the impact the divine beings would have had in their original setting, but even in a hallway far away from their ninth-century BCE throne room in Nimrud, I walked in a daze between the dizzying images that look beige now but would have once popped with colour. As I took my first steps into the gallery to peer at the tall reliefs, I could not help but marvel at the beauty of the perfectly geometrical cuneiform characters amid busy scenes of battle. On one tableau, a protective genie, standing in profile, is mid-stride with a brawny calf poking out from under a tasselled garment. The genie has the body of a human and the face and wings of an eagle, and a close look at one wing reveals a delicate dance of the feather's lines with the perfect triangles of cuneiform writing. Expert scribes and artisans overlaid the cuneiform onto these larger-than-life images, or set them apart like captions for some of the busier battle scenes. I couldn't read them at the time, but I would later learn that their meaning doesn't always tally with their beauty.

Scenes of battle and their aftermath tell the story of Assyrian might and may have served as a deterrent to any foreign dignitaries who enjoyed an audience with the 'king of the world', the title the Assyrian ruler took to emphasise his dominion over such a massive empire. Anyone who beheld such images might think twice before entering into any kind of conflict with the empire. In a special exhibition on Ashurbanipal at the British Museum that spotlighted many of these reliefs, Jonathan Jones of the *Guardian* called them 'some of the most appalling images ever created'.[31] When I first saw the battle scenes on the reliefs with my own eyes, I struggled to parse the subject matter from the swirling scenes. I found the artistry so breathtaking that I only grasped the horrors of it once the initial impression of the craft itself had begun to fade.

Intricately carved, these scenes show battles, sieges, weaponry, armour, and the brutal punishment of fallen enemies. Hundreds of soldiers wear protective helmets and shields. They brandish long spears, daggers, axes, and even maces much like the one from Ennigaldi-Nanna's palace, though these would have been mass-produced from iron rather than the older bronze or stone. Ancient Assyria was one of the first empires to take full advantage of the use of iron in weaponry and its devastating consequences on the human body. Many scenes capture the chaos of battle, a clamour of bodies, bows and arrows, spears, and horses, interspersed with elements of local landscape and wildlife. A fish swims alongside a dying horse in the Tigris, and enemy dead pile up amid the river's reed beds. The impact of these images might have struck an even deeper chord when the panels were coloured in, as they were in antiquity. Although precious little paint survives on the stone, the reliefs once boasted an array of reds, greens, purples, blues, whites, and more to animate the death scenes.

Amid the battle mêlée, defining moments of the war are sometimes accompanied by cuneiform captions like an enormous, gory stone comic book. One such sequence appears in a relief from Ashurbanipal's palace at Nimrud that shows the battle of Til-Tuba, where the Assyrian army clashed with Elamite armies from what is now Iran. The stone canvas is so densely packed with horses, asses, weapons, people, and chariots, which move in all directions with no perspective or focal point, that it almost feels like the artist was allergic to the idea of a single square inch of empty space in the scene.[32] Armed with spears, battle-axes, and maces, Assyrian warriors fight the enemy, while vultures feast on the remains of the dead. Near the centre of the panel is the crashed chariot that carries Teumman, the Elamite king, who dons a conical royal hat. His story resumes elsewhere in the panel where separate scenes show Teumman fleeing with his son who gets executed first, the king's submission before an Assyrian soldier, and his eventual decapitation. The largest caption amid these various scenes reads:

Teumman, king of Elam, was wounded in fierce battle. Tammaritu, his eldest son, took him by the hand and they fled to save their lives. They hid in the midst of a forest. With the encouragement of Assur and Ishtar, I killed them. I cut off their heads before one another.[33]

Teumman's head itself becomes a motif, repeated across this relief and others, including one that may have come from a passageway in the same palace of Ashurbanipal. The reclining king feasts amid vines and conifers next to the enthroned queen Liballi-sharrat. Behind her, suspended from a tree, hangs the disembodied head of Teumman.

It's important not to fall under the spell cast by these overwhelming scenes. The military triumphs and violence detailed in royal inscriptions and displayed in palace reliefs do not necessarily tally with an accurate history of warfare in this era. It's unlikely they battled as often or as brutally as these royal sources suggest, and these scenes tell us more about how the Assyrian king wanted to be seen and remembered than about ancient Assyrian history.

The actual reality of war and its aftermath would have been very ugly indeed in this era of iron weaponry, millennia before Alexander Fleming discovered penicillin. Without antibiotics, any war wound could be a death sentence, even if one managed to survive an individual battle. Perhaps in light of this, for nearly all periods of Mesopotamian history, archaeological evidence for the effects of war is sparse. Evidence for the deliberate and violent destruction of buildings, for example, is actually quite unusual.[34] Skeletons, similarly, rarely show signs of battlefield violence, and archaeologists have yet to find a single mound of decapitated skulls (or of headless bodies) to match up to Neo-Assyrian accounts. Who, after all, would it serve to destroy the infrastructure of a newly conquered city and murder every last member of robust segments of its population?

There are a few exceptions, of course. Several skeletons excavated at one of Nineveh's defensive gates show signs of burning and battle injuries, including one of a young teenage boy with knife wounds above his eyes and a fractured skull.[35] At Lachish, a fortress town protecting the city of Jerusalem where the kingdom of Judah lost a major battle to the

Assyrians, a few mass burials date to the period of these campaigns. Lachish may also provide a notable exception to the overall absence of evidence for the deliberate destruction of architecture. The city was burned to the ground, leaving behind piles of burnt bricks, over 6 feet high and scarred red from the conflagration's heat.[36]

For the logistics and realities of war, we let the less polished sources – the clay rough drafts of history that record elements of everyday administration in the Assyrian empire – complement the royal accounts. These tablets are not trying to be historical, they do not want to be remembered, and as a result, they tell a history in the words of those who were there to create and witness it. Thousands of people went on campaign with the king. Foot soldiers, cavalry, and charioteers with their heavy weapons, shields, leather armour, and other equipment made long treks from the Assyrian heartland to battle sites. Diviners also accompanied the king and his army into war, and some remained behind in the royal court to help with war-related enquiries, like whether or not to carry out an attack on a specific city.[37]

War was an undertaking as epic as the royal inscriptions made it sound. To move thousands of people and animals across long distances, including treacherous terrain like mountains, to keep them fed, and to protect them against infection, random ambushes, and even the weather took precise planning and a lot of luck.

Troops would have had to carry their own provisions too. We learn this from the letters that several magnates wrote to King Sargon II to inform him that troops near the border with Elam had no food other than 'the travel provisions which they carry with them'.[38] Villages and garrisons within Assyrian territory could also supply food to troops on the move.[39] Once in enemy territory, they might have also raided the food stores of enemy encampments and of villages in enemy territories. Aside from the challenge of staying fed, armies faced all manner of non-battle dangers on their journeys, from random attacks to epidemics. One letter to Sargon II told of an attack by Arabs under the leadership of one named Ammili'ti, son of Amiri. With 300 she-camels, he descended on Assyrian personnel who had been transporting post-battle booty all the way from Damascus to the empire's heartland. The group was ambushed from behind, and although a large tranche of the clay letter is broken, it seems that the Assyrians tried to pursue the Arabs to no avail. The terrain 'was too difficult, it was not fit for horses or for chariots', are the last surviving words.[40]

Such descriptions remind us that war wasn't waged by the stone figures in the Neo-Assyrian reliefs or even the Stele of the Vultures 2,000 years earlier, but by flesh and blood people who must have suffered immensely in the service of their kings – but hopefully not as frequently as royal sources would have us believe. The history of warfare in ancient Mesopotamia has many faces, including the polished, perfect mask that kings wanted us (and the gods) to see. Behind that mask lies a fragmented face. Historians must piece together its mismatched features from everyday clay tablets impressed with the exhausted messages of people on the frontlines, or from the remains of fallen soldiers laid to rest with their weapons. Far from sensationalised royal sources from any era, war was ugly and scary and sad. It left loved ones behind. It inspired myths and gods to help make sense of such suffering. It may have had victors who wanted to be remembered, but it had no real winners.

9

Ennigaldi-Nanna

Princess, Priestess, and Curator?

I have always had something of a soft spot for Ennigaldi-Nanna's father, Nabonidus, the last Babylonian king. This might be because I see in him the same love of history that I too feel, millennia later. So embedded was the importance of history in his reign that he resurrected from a bygone era an entire palace and the role of high priestess for his own daughter. Although this move would have had the intended effect of shoring up power and legitimising his kingship, I like to think he was also motivated by a fascination with his own past, which he shared with the kings of his era — from Nabopolassar who founded the Neo-Babylonian dynasty in 626 BCE to Nabonidus himself, whose last living hours might have witnessed the fall of Babylon to the Persians in 539 BCE.

One of the first cuneiform artefacts I ever saw was a slab shaped like a cartoon tombstone with a rounded top that shows King Nabonidus on the left in profile. He faces the right half of the stela, which is densely packed with eroded cuneiform signs. Above the cuneiform text hover three divine symbols that pop out as if not a millennium has passed since they were first chiselled into the grey stone: the crescent moon of Sîn, the winged sun of Shamash, and the seven-sided star of Ishtar. At the time, I had no idea what (or who) those three symbols stood for and barely noticed the faded tetrahedron signs below them. But something about the solemn king in a conical crown stuck with me.

Since then, I have read, translated, held, or just generally stared at thousands of other artefacts. I have held school tablets with fingerprints so clear you can see each individual crease, a beige-coloured clay letter from King Hammurabi, and the cross-shaped ancient fake forged by Sippar's priesthood. I have stared at the swirling battle scenes on Neo-Assyrian reliefs and towering *lamassu*, the protective deities with human heads but the bodies of winged lions or bulls. I have studied and marvelled at countless ancient objects, but after well over a decade, it's Nabonidus's stela that remains etched into my memory as clearly as those three divine symbols in stone.

In the early 2000s, a nearly identical, but far more eroded, stela was found in a city called Tayma, which lies about 200 miles from my hometown of Ha'il in Saudi Arabia. A major trade outpost on the incense route in the first millennium BCE, Tayma was home to a diverse population and, for about a decade, to Nabonidus himself. The site boasts 7,000 years of occupation with a modern town today built atop part of the ancient settlement. Rocky outcroppings that dot the desert landscape of the city's hinterlands are covered in graffiti that is thousands of years old, mostly written in the alphabetic scripts of the ancient Arabian peninsula by semi-literate people who passed through the area en route from one oasis to another. Much of the graffiti reads like the ancient North Arabian equivalent of 'Moudhy was here', occasionally with added details like one by 'Wdd son of Rhm' that notes that he camped at the boulder during a time of conflict. Some invoke gods, like a brief couplet, tucked among a jumble of other letters and tribal signs, by B'rl who writes, 'May (the god) Slm be pleased'. Others are rather graphic, including ones that describe love, sex, and possibly murder.[1]

A handful of far more mundane messages name the king of Babylon. Everyday snippets by his staff have, against all odds, survived from the distant past. Written in the local script of Tayma and its environs, known as Taymanitic, one inscription etched into a dark boulder surrounded by yellow sand mentions the king by name:

I am Mrdn, servant of Nabonidus, king of Babylon.
I came with the Chief Officer Kyt
in the waterless wilderness beyond the desert of L'q.[2]

Closer to my tribal home, a large rock face amid the reddish dunes outside of Ha'il shows an image of the king himself in profile, much like the Tayma stela, with a badly damaged cuneiform inscription that names him.[3] I think his time in Saudi Arabia, with his name and likeness etched onto desert rocks not far from the mud brick house where my father was born, helps explain my soft spot for this last Babylonian king and his love of history, and eventually for his daughter and her museum.

It was more or less just after Nabonidus returned to Babylon from Tayma that the city fell to the Persians. The Cyrus Cylinder, a barrel-shaped clay document excavated from Babylon by the archaeologist Hormuzd Rassam, gives an account of the Persian conquest in cuneiform that paints Nabonidus as a tyrant and religious zealot. Among other things, readers are told the Persian king Cyrus 'freed' the Babylonians from their bonds after the cruelty wrought by Nabonidus, described as 'an incompetent person who was put in charge of his country'. Like all royal inscriptions, the account is the product of politically motivated decisions about what historical details to include (and exclude). Whatever transpired in Babylon on that fateful day in 539 BCE, Cyrus's arrival was the death knell of the last independent Babylonian dynasty, and the fate of Nabonidus and his descendants, including Ennigaldi-Nanna, remains unknown.[4]

If Nabonidus seems to form a motif in my own life – from his stela that I saw the day cuneiform re-entered my life in my twenties to its replica found close to my home – his daughter Ennigaldi-Nanna has become far more than that. Together with her still puzzling collection of ancient arte-facts, she inspired this book. It is not impossible to imagine that her dynasty's passion for the past left some sort of impres-sion on the princess. Her role as high priestess to the moon god at Ur certainly tapped into a long history that she would have understood – she would have known she was one of many in a long line of women who occupied this position and may have even known their names. Is it possible that her historic role could have inspired her to curate this collection of ancient objects?

We know precious little about Ennigaldi-Nanna herself; we don't even know her real name, only that she got *renamed* as such when she was christened high priestess. Ennigaldi-Nanna means 'the high priestess requested by the god Nanna', a reference to the Sumerian name for Sîn. Grammatically, the name is a sentence modelled on the names of the high priestesses who preceded her, like Enheduanna and Enanedu. Even without knowing any Sumerian, at least one shared element emerges: the names begin with *en*, the Sumerian word for the role of high priestess that they each fulfilled.

Most of the information we have about Ennigaldi-Nanna comes from second-hand accounts that are more concerned with her father. Documents from the time relay the story of how Ennigaldi-Nanna was elevated to her role in Ur with an emphasis on the king's attentiveness to the request for a high priestess by Sîn, which allegedly took the form of a partial lunar eclipse on the night of 26 September 554 BCE.[5] Even a clay record known today as the Ennigaldi-Nanna Cylinder is more about the antiquity of the site of her palace at Ur and the king's renovation works.[6] All of these accounts tell us much more about the king's self-presentation than about Ennigaldi-Nanna herself.

Only two far more mundane records from the Neo-Babylonian period exist that actually say something about Ennigaldi-Nanna herself. These are the only direct biographical sources for the princess. A slightly mottled but otherwise perfectly preserved clay tablet from Uruk hints at her having originally held a post in the city's Eanna temple. It lists nine instructions to the letter's recipient relating to that temple, including 'plaster the double gates of the Eanna just as it was of old, in the time of Nebuchadnezzar' and 'give the regular offerings to the brewers and bakers'.[7] The final one instructs that food allotments for the king's daughter be deposited in 'the box of the king', an order so terse it requires a bit of imagination to make sense of it.[8] Originally, 'the king's daughter', likely Ennigaldi-Nanna, had received rations at the Eanna temple in Uruk, which according to this order needed to be redirected to a royal cash-box instead. Her time at the Eanna must have come to an abrupt end when the king gave the order to effectively cancel her rations before, presumably, transferring her to Ur.

About six years later, another equally terse text mentions the household of the high priestess at Ur, but does not name Ennigaldi-Nanna directly. From a private family archive in the city of Larsa just north of Ur, the small clay tablet covered in somewhat sloppy signs describes a man's responsibility for a team of workers attached to the priestess's household in Ur.[9] These workers carry out that labour in lieu of paying tax, or 'corvée labour', levied to maintain Ennigaldi-Nanna's household. This confirms that by this point in Nabonidus's reign there was a household for the high priestess who cannot have been anyone but Ennigaldi-Nanna. These two texts are our clearest direct window onto the princess found so far. They confirm that she existed and that she was high priestess at Ur, but they are woefully insufficient. To try to piece together what her day-to-day life looked like, and whether or not it included a curatorial role in relation to her 'museum', we must instead look to the long line of priestesses who came before her.

The technical term for Ennigaldi-Nanna's role was the *en* in Sumerian or *entu* in Akkadian, a word that must remain untranslated because no modern equivalent can capture the unique constellation of responsibilities involved in the job. We know its history reaches all the way back to the third millennium BCE and Enheduanna's time, and possibly even earlier to a woman named Ninmetabarri. She may be the earliest *en*-priestess to leave behind her name – in this case, on a dedicatory cup shaped a bit like a (broken) gin glass made of cream-coloured calcite.[10] Every high priestess to the moon god had to hail from royal stock, and they also had to be chosen by an omen.[11] A handful of such priestesses leave behind enough traces of their tenure for us to understand just how important this role was and just how much was expected of these royal women.

Enheduanna might just be the most famous of them given her status as the first named author in history. A lot of her surviving poetry was written in praise of the power of the goddess Inana. Enheduanna subjugates even the most powerful gods in a male-dominated pantheon (a mantheon, perhaps) to the will of this goddess. Her roar makes the gods tremble with fear, and her fury makes mortals quake. With a bit less gravity, her poetry also hints at the responsibilities of the *entu*, including one that describes a simple ritual:

I, Enheduanna, the *en*-priestess,
Entered my sacred *giparu*, in your service.
I carried the ritual basket and intoned the song of joy.
My ritual meal was brought to me as if I had never lived
    there.[12]

These lines fill in precious few details, but they do tell us that she participated in certain rituals within the temple complex. Not just a symbolic head of the moon god's cult, Enheduanna 'got her hands dirty', or as dirty as they can get while carrying a basket, singing, and eating a meal made by someone else. We can guess from her hymns that temple staff did enough food prep to rival even the most famous chefs in today's Michelin-starred restaurants. Those in charge of milling grain, for example, 'did not rest in her abode'.[13] Enheduanna's food sampling role in the ritual might not sound like much, but rituals held together the relations between human and divine; they kept deities happy, which kept people safe. This task she carried out was therefore of immense, cosmic importance.

Only a single image of Enheduanna has managed to traverse the thousands of years between her life in the 2300s BCE and today. Fragments of a 3-inch-thick alabaster disc that bears her image would have stood out to archaeologists amid the dusty rubble of the palace in Ur for its bright, almost translucent hue. Reconstructed, this stone disc is about the size of a regular frisbee, and on one side is traced a rectangle, populated with thirteen neat but damaged lines of archaic cuneiform characters. Thankfully, during the Old Babylonian period just before Hammurabi rose to power, someone in Ur made a complete copy of it on a clay tablet, which was found intact in a residential house that excavators dubbed 'No. 7 Quiet Street', making it sound like an address in a children's book. Despite the damage to the original disc, the clay copy confirms that it names Enheduanna, the 'wife of the god Nanna' and 'daughter of Sargon'.[14]

On the other side of the disc appears the image of several figures who look as if they're walking towards a pedestal and a miniature ziggurat, which is so stylised it looks a bit like a wedding cake. The figures are in profile, and a nude man pours some kind of libation from a vessel into the pedestal at the foot of a temple. Behind him stands a towering woman in a headdress and flowing, layered gown with her arm bent in a gesture that looks like a pious greeting.[15] She can be none other than Enheduanna. Interestingly, she is not the one who performs the actual ritual in the image. She simply stands in worship, more of a symbolic figure or an overseer of the rites. With very little text and imagery, the disc of Enheduanna still manages to hint at some of her responsibilities as the high priestess to the moon god at Ur. She participated in and over-saw rituals; she was public-facing and may have performed the nitty-gritty of some religious rites at different temples.

A few centuries later, in the 1800s BCE, another princess named Enanedu occupies the post. Although she authored no hymns, she self-styles her own power in the sources left behind. Much like kings sometimes bill themselves as chosen for their royal roles before birth, Enanedu introduces herself as destined 'from the holy womb (for) the great fate' of her office.[16] Like a king, she stressed that fate led her to her posi-tion and she even carried out renovations. On a clay cone found at Ur, two columns of cuneiform preserve the story of Enanedu's own renovation of the same palace that Nabonidus would also rebuild over 1,000 years later.

In Enanedu's version of events, the *en*-priestess was like a deputy of the Babylonian king, an extension of his political might in a major city of his realm. The purpose of her role was to serve as an important instrument of royal authority, akin to that of a bishop in seventeenth-century England. Enanedu might even be the only non-reigning royal to have a section of a praise hymn devoted to her, celebrating her 'rejoicing heart' and wishing her 'years of joy'.[17] Some inscriptions even call her the 'son' of the king, which is highly unusual in ancient Mesopotamia and likely a sign of the power she wielded.

Part of the *en*-priestess's power drew not just from her royal lineage, but from her relationship to the moon god. Enheduanna, Enanedu, Ennigaldi-Nanna, and all the others in between also served as the symbolic earthly wives of the moon god, alongside (or perhaps even in some way representing) his divine wife Ningal.[18] In this divine-human throuple, as it were, the priestesses had to care for Ningal and make sure she had everything a real person might need, but of the kind of quality we imagine a deity would come to expect. Enanedu, for example, gave Ningal several combs made of gold and silver to tame her long divine locks. For all the goddess's dining needs, Enanedu also gave her silver cutlery and a silver flask for oil. In ancient Mesopotamia, the statue of a deity literally embodied them, and Enanedu dutifully fed Ningal's statue monthly offerings of bread, beer, and meat.[19]

As the co-wife, the priestess also wanted to make the goddess feel special, and what better way to do that than with a gold-encrusted bed and accessories to rival those of today's celebrities?[20] For Ningal's statue, Enanedu commissioned a resplendent collar described as a 'disc of red gold' that weighed almost a pound, 'shining like the sun at her throat'.[21] Undoubtedly, Ennigaldi-Nanna had to care for her divine co-wife in similar ways. Even without written records of her daily life we can imagine that at least part of it was occupied with making sure Ningal's needs – from the basics to the luxuries – were met.

As the moon god's wife, the priestesses also had to participate in the sacred marriage, a yearly wedding ritual to help ensure the fertility of the harvest. Although little evidence remains of what this ceremony looked like in Ur, we might hazard a guess based on parallel rituals from other cities. A public parade followed the god, possibly represented by a priest, to meet his wife, the priestess, at the door to her palace or to the temple before the two entered a bedchamber to symbolically consummate the marriage. It was a union of the divine and human to ensure food security. '(My) hands are no longer stretched out on the fruitful bed,' reads a hymn by Enheduanna, a possible allusion to a completed sexual act in the service of a 'fruitful' harvest.[22] In truth, what happened behind closed doors between the two mortals, re-enacting the marriage night of two deities, remains a mystery. To us, this parade that culminates in fake or real sex between religious leaders may seem awkward at best, violent at worst, but we nevertheless cannot underestimate the importance of the symbolic union. In a region where the weather oscillated between torrential storms and scorching heat, a successful harvest was not guaranteed. As carbon emissions today begin to hasten climate breakdown, we may soon appreciate the psychological impact of a ritual to usher in a good harvest.[23]

Alongside such ritual responsibilities, the high priestess at Ur had to manage large swathes of rural land owned by the temple. Contemporary clay tablets tell us that the same Enanedu who had to renovate the *giparu*, care for the goddess Ningal (and her statue), and ritually ensure a successful harvest also had to restore various meadows, farmland, dams, and reservoirs in and around Ur.[24] It's

possible that Ennigaldi-Nanna had a similar set of responsibilities, much like the manager of a sprawling estate
complete with agricultural land and livestock in early
modern England. At the time of Ennigaldi-Nanna's tenure,
Nabonidus mentions a lengthy list of domestic staff, fields,
orchards, cattle, sheep, and goats, all attached to the temple
that Ennigaldi-Nanna served.[25] The priestess, in effect, was
the head of an extensive, wealthy household that needed
daily maintenance and administration. Given the extent of
the temple's holdings, it is easy to imagine that she had a
full schedule, especially if she had to meet the same ritual
expectations as her forebears like Enheduanna and Enanedu.
Although her father may have elevated her to the priestess-
hood for political or ideological reasons, her role was far
from just titular.

Indeed, royal women from all periods of ancient
Mesopotamian history exercised vast administrative powers,
sometimes equivalent to those of the king. In the northern-
most reaches of modern Iraq lies a site known as Tell al-Rimah,
home to a huge palace that was in use for centuries. In a
bathroom, of all places, archaeologists found a number of clay
tablets belonging to the archive of a queen named Iltani,
whose husband, Aqba-hammu, ruled in the early second
millennium BCE. Other tablets and fragments from the archive
were found scattered in an antechamber near the palace
courtyard and wedged into a gap between two walls.
Presumably, these clay documents had been discarded by
those in search of more exciting finds than pieces of clay
covered in cuneiform when, or after, the palace was demol-
ished and abandoned in antiquity. Once the disparate parts of
the archive were reunited, archaeologists found they had

about 200 tablets outlining the queen's daily role in running palace industries, such as textile production, and in managing staff.[26]

Textile production was an important economic industry during this era, and even a staple of contemporary trade hubs further afield. Remember the Old Assyrian traders like Ashur-idi at the city gates with his two black donkeys and Buzazu's 'narrow track' smuggling operation? They and their fellow merchants carried many tons of textiles from the Assyrian heartland into what is now Turkey to trade, and would have been near contemporaries with Iltani. Weaving a textile was also about as relaxing as anything else that causes tendonitis and chronic inflammation. A single garment took months to complete, which King Aqba-hammu sometimes gave away as diplomatic gifts, or even as tribute to the capital city of Babylon.[27]

Around the same time, further south in the city of Mari, Queen Shiptu similarly held extensive powers and responsibilities, especially in the absence of her husband, King Zimri-Lim. Letters show that she managed access to confidential clay tablets kept in sealed containers, devised a more rigorous way to carry out omens for royal decision-making, and even took measures to deal with an epidemic. Her husband once wrote to her about a woman named Nanna who suffered from an infectious disease. 'Since she is often at the palace,' he worried, 'it will infect the many women who are with her.' His concerns are followed, in effect, by a highly personalised lockdown order. 'No one is to drink from the cup she uses; no one is to sit on the seat she takes; no one is to lie on the bed she uses, lest it infect the many women who are with her. This is a very contagious infection!' Aside from showing an awareness for how infections spread, this letter suggests Queen Shiptu had a lot to juggle.[28]

It wasn't just royal women who exercised such wide powers. During the era of Enanedu and Queen Shiptu, in the city of Sippar over 100 miles up the Euphrates from Ur, groups of unmarried women from privileged families came together in something like a cloister connected to the temple of the sun god Shamash. These women were the same *naditum* who employed female scribes. As a type of votary to the sun god, the *naditum* were not allowed to bear children. They could and did, however, adopt them. During the reign of Hammurabi in the eighteenth century BCE, one *naditum* named Huzalatum gave her adopted daughter to a wet-nurse named Dubabatum for a period of three years to nurse.

This may initially strike a modern reader as bizarre: why adopt a baby girl only to hand her over to another woman for (arguably) the most adorable period in that baby's life, which is also the period when 80 per cent of her brain develops? In an era without baby formula, sterilisation, or even reliably clean water, women had to rely on each other for breastmilk if a newborn's mother perished in childbirth or if the baby was adopted. When Dubabatum agreed to breastfeed Huzalatum's daughter, she was paid 4 shekels to cover 'food and clothing' for the three-year period.[29] (For comparison, during the same period, a slave could earn 4 shekels per year for their work, and an independent hired labourer could earn around 8.[30]) This three-year fee, which functions more like a ration than a salary, pales in comparison to the amount a parent would owe if they failed to provide for the standard three-year nursing period. According to a law collection from the same period, a man who fails to provide 'food, oil, and clothing rations' to the wet-nurse in charge of his infant must pay her 10 shekels of silver to cover the costs of child-rearing and, on top of that, must take his child back.[31]

The *naditum* women used their private funds to participate in business activities, like buying, selling, and leasing property. One woman named Ribatum, who lived around 1900 BCE, owned several houses and leased at least one shop out on a yearly basis for just over 1 shekel.[32] She also rented out a wing of her house and a room on the second floor, and is named in no fewer than nine house rentals – a professional landlord from 4,000 years ago.[33] *Naditum* also owned arable land and fields, which they leased to tenant farmers in return for a percentage of yields. As might be expected of business-minded people, several *naditum* also found themselves embroiled in lawsuits, including with their own family members and even with each other.[34]

Given such complex business arrangements, they naturally needed scribes to keep tabs on things, and many of them were women, sometimes even *naditum* themselves.[35] Like these *naditum*, might Ennigaldi-Nanna have been trained to read and write in order to enable her to access or even make records of her day-to-day administrative dealings as an *en*-priestess? Given that women in temple contexts served as scribes during other periods, the answer might well have been yes. With all the responsibilities of past *en*-priestesses and other women entrenched in temple life, Ennigaldi-Nanna must have worn more than one hat – an estate manager, a political figurehead, a religious authority, a leader of rituals, and the earthly wife of a god. If we look at the lives of women in Mesopotamia more generally, it becomes clear that they took on such a diverse range of professions that, perhaps, even adding curator or collector to the list doesn't seem outside the realm of possibility.

There might be a tendency to look back on women of the ancient past as little more than incubators, silent and invisible in the sources that otherwise spotlight the stories of men. As we have already seen, this is far from the truth. Queens, princesses, and priestesses wore many professional hats, but this is just a narrow segment of society – royals and cloistered women – whose identities and positions overlap with those of Ennigaldi-Nanna in a way that may shed some light on her life. What about the other women, the majority? In fact, women in all periods of ancient Mesopotamian history played a significant role in the workforce, from midwives to weavers and a great many things in between. They were the backbone of the textile and milling industries, and in some cities also worked in farming, at irrigation systems, and in transportation and boat towing on canals.[36] This doesn't mean they received equal pay for their work. As oil-pressers in the city of Umma, female workers were paid rations in barley and oil equivalent to less than half of the rations of their male counterparts.[37] The pay gap, it seems, has an incredibly long history.

Around the same time period as the *naditum* in Sippar, women of ancient Assyria further north were part of a far-reaching international trade network, centred on the trading quarter in the city of Kanesh (in Turkey). Donkeys in trade caravans carried tin and textiles for weeks at a time from Assur to Kanesh, a distance of 620 miles, where those goods would be sold or traded, and they returned to the Assyrian heartland with silver and gold. The same trade caravans also carried clay letters back and forth between business partners and family members, including husbands and wives who worked together. The exchanges between one woman named Lamassi and her husband, Pushu-ken (the same man who did time for dodging tax), show the perils of mixing professional and married life. In an exasperated letter, she asks why Pushu-ken constantly accuses her of sending sub-par textiles:

> Who is this man who lives in your house and who is criticizing the textiles when they get to him? As for me, in order that from each caravan trip at least 10 shekels of silver accrue to your house, I try my best to make and send textiles to you![38]

She ends her letter here, without so much as a final sign-off. In another letter, she complains that she is struggling to make enough cloth for her family's trade in Kanesh, for her children, and for other household personnel, on top of her daily responsibilities like making beer and fielding an annoying neighbour – the trials of a working mother 4,000 years ago.[39]

Even in ancient Assyria, mothers were expected to work like they didn't have children and raise children like they didn't have work. Lamassi may have had seven children – five boys and at least one but possibly two girls. Not including her husband's prison sentence, she would have raised them alone for years at a time. One of her letters contains a heartfelt plea for him to come home: 'Be an honourable man, break your obligations, and come here!' In the same letter, she also asks that he finally pay the export duty he owes so that the tax man will stop badgering her to fork up the silver for it.[40]

Women like Lamassi often got paid for their textiles independently of their husbands – about 10 to 12 shekels a piece after tax.[41] Considering that they were responsible for every stage of production – from sourcing wool and weaving the textiles to sometimes arranging their donkey DHL to Kanesh – this financial outcome is only fair. They even knew what prices their work should fetch in the markets of Kanesh, and sometimes even gave instructions to relatives on the ground not to sell particular pieces for anything less than the market value. A woman named Taram-Kubi, for example, complains that she was underpaid for previous products and instructs her brother not to sell the next lot of textiles she has sent him for anything less than a third of a mina per textile (about 20 shekels).[42] Many of these women also learned enough cuneiform to be able to write their own letters to remote family members and business partners without relying on professional scribes. They acted as producers, traders, and scribes, in addition to running their households and raising their kids.

Aside from international trade, Assyrian women of the early second millennium BCE also carried out business transactions on their home turf, sometimes from the money they made through their work in the textile trade. They bought properties, invested in international enterprise, and even gave out interest-bearing loans. A woman named Bazaya entrusted a man named Adad-Rabi with selling an impressive list of goods she had accumulated, including refined copper, three black donkeys, and a large amount of wool and textiles.[43] Her ability to purchase and resell such an extensive list of commodities shows serious business acumen. A woman named Waqqurtum, on the other hand, invested in a failed enterprise and begged her brother to help her recover the silver she invested, as she had 'come out empty-handed'.[44]

Women continued to take on important roles in business and enterprise well into the first millennium BCE, including contemporaries of Ennigaldi-Nanna. Archives of documents from private homes tell us that women from wealthy urban families could buy and sell land, give loans, rent their properties out, or enter into business partnerships with some level of autonomy.[45] A woman named Ina-Esagil-ramat managed fields in her own name that her father gave her when she got married. In one convoluted case I had to reread several times to understand, a woman named Tabatu loaned money to two people, a man and his mother. Those two people then sold an enslaved person to Tabatu's husband, but instead of paying them for the transaction, he gave the money to his wife. This was just the most efficient way of moving the money around – rather than Tabatu paying the people who owed her money, her husband paid off their loan to her.[46] The money flowed through fewer hands this way. But it's interesting that in such cases, women like Ina-Esagil-ramat and Tabatu were seen as separate financial entities to their husbands. Although many of these women carried these transactions out on behalf of husbands, fathers, brothers, or even sons, they still played an active enough role that their input got written down.

Beyond the world of temple and trade, women also helped other women through one of the most difficult (and dangerous) medical experiences of the ancient world: childbirth and its aftermath. During the pandemic, I spent the loneliest night of my life in Oxford's John Radcliffe Hospital next to a transparent plastic crib on wheels, where my newborn baby slept. Across the bottom of my belly stretched a 10-inch scar where my obstetric surgeon had sliced through seven layers of my muscle, flesh, and organs to pull my little girl out of my body. The pain of trying to sit up after a Caesarean section felt a thousand times worse than any of my strongest contractions, but my husband had been asked to leave my side within forty-five minutes of the procedure because of lockdown-inspired policies. Who helped me stand up for the first time post-op while I carried a bag of my own urine? Who helped my baby latch onto my breast to feed almost hourly throughout that first night? Who checked my wound for signs of infection and reassured me, through sheets of postpartum tears, that everything would be okay?

In cuneiform, the word 'midwife' is written with three logographic signs – or signs that stand for whole words – meaning 'woman', 'inside' or 'womb', and 'to know'. Midwives, in other words, were women who knew the inside. Their role had both medical and mythological import. Clay tablets that record medical instructions often feature midwives, like one reddish tablet unearthed from an ancient library in Assur written down in the early first millennium BCE. A lengthy collection of prescriptions for a challenging birth combines spells and medicine. It reads like an instruction manual, explaining how to mix and apply salves and oils, and how to massage the pregnant woman's abdomen to help move labour along. These practical instructions almost get interrupted part way through the tablet by, of all things, a myth about a cow. 'I am pregnant and ready to gore,' the cow says somewhat relatably, but the 'boat' is stuck at the 'quay of death'. It is a metaphor for labour that won't progress; the baby, like a trapped boat, is stuck in the birth canal, and the prayer asks that the boat be freed. The cow at the centre of this myth is not just any cow, but the cow of the moon god Sîn, and she lets out such blood-curdling labour cries that he summons two protective deities to administer treatments just like those listed throughout the tablet. Those deities, in other words, played the role of a midwife.

A myth initially seems out of place in the middle of a medical text, but it is rather like hypnobirthing in today's world, a guided visualisation to help manage fear and move things along. In the same way, the myth in this ancient medical text manifests the desired outcome – a speedy birth – for the patient. As Sîn's cow 'gave birth straightaway' with the aid of the protective deities, so may the woman 'who is having difficulty giving birth' with a midwife at her side. 'May the midwife not be kept waiting,' reads a last line of this mythological digression, 'may the pregnant woman give birth.'[47]

Women didn't just treat illnesses and processes specific to other women; they also served as ancient GPs. Some of the earliest records of female physicians appear in clay tablets from the third millennium BCE, including even their names. Dubildamu may not have used a stethoscope 4,500 years ago, but she is listed in an accounting tablet as an *azu munus*, which in Sumerian means 'female physician'. A few centuries later, a woman called Ubartum also carried her proverbial medical bag to visit so many patients that her name appears in no fewer than fifty documents. (Incidentally, Ubartum's brother was also a physician who was married to a princess, the daughter of King Shulgi.) Women continued to work as physicians throughout the region's long history, and they may have even composed and used medical texts, including one clay tablet written in the early second millennium BCE to assist with childbirth.[48]

Far from being limited to a handful of professional or commercial roles, though, women could also be artists. In the same era when Enanedu was acting as high priestess, the *naditum* women were conducting business, and Lamassi was battling through life as a working mother in ancient Assyria, there lived a young blind girl named Shinunutum. Her name refers to a small mountain bird (or possibly the constellation that looks like it), and she was brought from her hometown in the northern reaches of the Babylonian empire to the city of Kish to begin her life as a musician.[49] On the tiny square tablet that mentions her existence we read: 'On the 18th day of the month of Tebitum', a chilly month that fell sometime around December and January, 'they brought Shinunutum the blind girl here before me to learn the art of music.' Like so many clay records, it raises more questions than it answers. Who are 'they'? Who is 'me'? And why was Shinunutum taken away from her home to some sort of ancient school of music? As the scholar Dr Eric J. Harvey writes in his study of this young Babylonian songbird, the thousands upon thousands of daily records – from receipts and ration lists to letters and legal cases – give incomplete details like these, 'isolated moments from the lives of real people unchanged and unedited for thousands of years'.[50]

Although it can be unreliable to identify gender from visual imagery, women playing instruments also appear in art throughout ancient Mesopotamian history. A clay plaque from Ur from the same period as Shinunutum's lifetime seems to show a woman holding a drum against her chest.[51] Over 1,000 years later, Neo-Assyrian palace reliefs show women playing a special kind of harp.

Isolated moments in the lives of women and girls like Shinunutum the musician, Ubartum the ancient GP, and the working mothers of ancient Assyria are clay snapshots of real lives – it feels important to remind ourselves that these women lived and breathed just as we do. What these stories show is that women's lives in the ancient past were just as complex and rich as ours today. Women were more than the wives, mothers, and sisters of men. They did more than marry and bear children (which is already a lot today, let alone during an era without painkillers, antibiotics, or formula), and a great many did neither of those things while also undertaking a range of other meaningful activities. These priestesses, weavers, oil-pressers, businesswomen, doctors, wet-nurses, musicians, midwives, and scribes give only a small sampling of the kinds of roles women filled in ancient Mesopotamia.

Clay tablets from ancient Mesopotamia are far from silent on the lives of women but, as with nearly all of what cuneiform preserves, the sources allow only certain segments of ancient Mesopotamia to speak. Those who could afford to leave records behind, like the priestesses in Sippar and the businesswomen in Assur, somewhat skew the record in their favour. Others who do make it into the written record as brief mentions, like Dubabatum the wet-nurse or Shinunutum the musician, hint at the myriad lives lost to time. Cuneiform only captures a narrow subset of society throughout all periods of the region's history, preserving hundreds of thousands of stories, but leaving even more forgotten below the sandy mounds of Iraq, Syria and beyond.

The stories of these women offer us a vast backdrop to Ennigaldi-Nanna's busy life in Ur and allow us to imagine the versatility, and credibility, of her working life as princess, priestess, divine wife, and administrator. But what about her role as curator? Could she have been the visionary behind the 'museum' of ancient objects? There is no way to prove that Ennigaldi-Nanna deliberately curated the collection because there is no single source that definitively tells us this. The clay drum – the smoking gun – that supports the museum hypothesis was composed almost a century before her father ascended the throne and renovated the palace. But the clay drum, along with the other older things, were found on the unbroken brick floor of her home, which makes it hard to dismiss her role completely in bringing these old things together in some way. The collection of artefacts under one roof – if perhaps not in a single room – also fits nicely with the academic and political interest in the distant past shared by Neo-Babylonian kings and scholars. Digging up the past was an essential element of her dynasty's strategy for royal legitimation, and Ennigaldi-Nanna's presence in Ur was an extension of that strategy. Her life was an embodiment of her past.

For many people in ancient Mesopotamia, the evidence for that past was *right there*. They had complete collections of ancient clay tablets from previous generations. They described events, like the arrival of kingship, so far back that their original eras are unknowable. They described building foundations as being laid 700 years before already ancient kings, and land rights as dating back 696 years. They walked among the ruin mounds outside of their own cities. They carried out their own digs and composed records of their shared past. The objects in Ennigaldi-Nanna's museum give us some insights not just into the history of ancient Mesopotamia, but the history of doing history.

Today, hundreds of thousands of clay tablets remain to be translated, and an undoubtedly larger number still lie buried beneath the untouched tells that swell over the rich landscapes around the Tigris and Euphrates rivers. Assyriology is a tiny field; there are far more tablets than scholars to translate them, and there are far more sites than archaeologists to unearth the stories still hidden. Perhaps one day we will know more about Ennigaldi–Nanna and her relationship to these objects. Women in ancient Mesopotamia, after all, did many things, and the past was all around them – could something like 'archaeologist' or 'museum curator' be added to the repertoire?

To me, the questions are more interesting than the answers. It doesn't really matter if the objects from Ennigaldi–Nanna's palace form a coherent collection, or if Ennigaldi–Nanna herself curated it. What we learn from them is so much more than just one story in a single era of ancient Mesopotamia's multi-millennia history. The questions these objects raise lead us on journeys through the hundreds of thousands of surviving clay tablets, impressed with the millions of tiny triangles of cuneiform that allow ancient Mesopotamians to speak to us across time in their own words.

Epilogue

Between Us and Them

There is nothing like holding an ancient clay tablet in your hands, tilting it this way and that to let an overhead light hit its eroded wedges in just the right way to reveal messages from the past. As a three-dimensional script cuneiform needs just the right combination of shadows and lighting to be readable. How can it be that I get to cradle a clay tablet from the cradle of civilisation? It is an experience that still leaves me winded – before the stress kicks in of having to copy out the signs as quickly as possible before museum doors close.

To me, cuneiform is not just a breathtaking array of tiny triangles, but each one carries layers of meaning that preserve leaps in human ingenuity, or capture historical turning points like the arrival of Akkadian-speakers to Mesopotamia, or

253

embody an ancient love affair with dead languages. Like a ruin that preserves levels of occupation from major periods in ancient Mesopotamia, each sign's layers of meaning capture whole worlds within it.

The hundreds of thousands of clay tablets from ancient Mesopotamia have also filled major gaps in our knowledge of global history. So many firsts come from this region – from the development of writing itself and the first (potter's) wheel to the first use of advanced maths to calculate the trajectory of Jupiter across the night sky. But to me, these leaps, turning points, and firsts are not as interesting as the thousands of glimpses into the lives of people that cuneiform tablets have given us.

I have spent almost two decades immersed in the stories of those who lived along the Tigris and Euphrates. For every difficult or beautiful moment in my life over the course of those years, I managed to find someone from thousands of years ago who could relate. There's some comfort in knowing that so many of the things we go through, so many of the things we feel, are timeless. Preparing (or more accurately, procrastinating any semblance of preparation) for my Akkadian language exams, I came across a seventh-century BCE woman named Sherua-etirat who scolded her sister-in-law – at the time, the crown princess – Libbali-sharrat for failing to practise her cuneiform. The questions she asks the young princess feel eternally relatable. 'Why don't you write your tablet,' she demands, 'and do your homework?'

When I became a mother after so many years of trying, I saw glimpses of myself in the Babylonian lullabies, and my first attempts at breastfeeding made me obsessed with wet-nursing contracts from the time of Hammurabi. Four lousy shekels for three years of nursing? That was equivalent to over 5,000 hours of work for less than the lowest annual wages. After my many pregnancy losses, I wept – I mean really *wept* – with Dabitum who had stopped feeling her baby kick seven months into a pregnancy 4,000 years ago.

When I spot Venus and even Mercury in the night sky, I think of the Assyrian astronomers in the court of Esarhaddon who wrote their nightly reports to the king (and called each other 'ignoramuses') and of the people who watched the heavens to compile the many hundreds of Astronomical Diaries in Babylon.

In the late summer of 87 BCE, scholars wrote about the return of Halley's Comet, whose appearance had also been recorded in a much earlier Astronomical Diary from 164 BCE. What remains of the later record is so fragmentary that we are lucky to have the unbroken word for 'comet' (*ṣallammû*), with the observation that the comet moved 'one cubit' per day. At the same time, halfway across the world in China, people recorded the very same comet. 'A star appeared fuzzy in the east,' reads the brief record made under the rule of Emperor Zhao of the Han Dynasty.[1]

Intellectually, I know the astronomers in 87 BCE were just doing their jobs, but I cannot help but assume they felt a similar awe, along with anyone else who looked up at night during those summer weeks. Without realising it, the Babylonians were having a shared experience with people halfway across the world, who also felt the need to write about the same 'fuzzy' star pelting through the night sky.[2]

In my life, I've been lucky enough to see two comets. I stared nightly at Comet NEOWISE in 2020, and as a child I saw Hale-Bopp Comet in the 1990s from an aeroplane window at twilight. I will never forget the overwhelming sense of awe that silenced me for the rest of the flight and followed me into adulthood. Both times I knew I was looking at nothing more than a ball of dust and ice, but these glimpses still felt surreal, even unreal, and otherworldly.

With Halley's Comet every seventy-five or so years, countless people have shared these cosmic, cometary connections with a ball of dust and ice millions of miles away. For me, something about this closes the vast gap between then and now, between here and there, between us and them, and you and me.

The history of ancient Mesopotamia is not just about the milestones or the monumental temples. It's about the people who looked at comets, cradled their babies, and procrastinated their homework. It's about you, your loved ones, and even your loathed ones because there are some things that we all share, and it is hard not to find those things in cuneiform. That is really what moves me about this writing system from so long ago, and the many things it was written on – from clay drums and mud bricks to boundary stones and basic, half-broken tablets. They tell us about life thousands of years ago between two rivers, and about what it means to live.

Even if cuneiform came to a gradual end, life between and around the life-giving rivers continued. The Persians ousted the Babylonians in the sixth century BCE, but were ousted themselves by the Seleucids, who then lost to the Parthians, who then ruled the region until the third century CE. Somewhere along the way, in 79–80 CE, an ancient astronomer impressed the very last known cuneiform wedge in the very same Uruk that saw the birth of writing. This final vestige of cuneiform is broken, of course, and in such a way that it looks like a triangle – a *sattakku* in Akkadian, the same word scribes used to refer to the cuneiform writing system itself. The astronomer's words document observations of the year's planetary movements, the moon's visibility, a partial solar eclipse, and more, that have allowed modern scholars to date the tablet. Its final semi-legible word seems to be the cuneiform sign for 'king'.

Although this almanac is the latest datable tablet so far found, it may not be the last bit of clay ever impressed with a wedge-shaped sign in antiquity. We don't know how much longer cuneiform continued to be used or to what extent, but we know that life in the region continued long after the last wedge. The Sasanians defeated the Parthians, and the seventh century CE saw the rise of Islam with Baghdad eventually a centre of Islamic power and learning.

While people outlived the cuneiform of their ancestors, the histories it preserves still shape life in the region today. The street art of Osama Sadiq harks back to cuneiform's wedges, enlarged to cover walls and car parks, spelling out Sumerian words like 'freedom' (literally translated, 'return to the mother'), or modified to write words in Arabic like 'love'. Figures including Sargon of Akkad and Hammurabi graced murals during the protests in Iraq that began in late 2019. As for Gilgamesh – he remains as popular as ever, as he intended to be. He is present in modern Middle Eastern poetry, he faces digital adversaries in a side-scrolling video game, and stands guard in stone in various locations in Baghdad. He and so many others from ancient Mesopotamia's past are ever-present.

There is something to be said for things that have survived from so long ago, for the clay and mud that tell such a long history that they give some hope for the future. If something ancient is still here, then maybe some part of us will also be here thousands of years hence.

The objects in Ennigaldi-Nanna's museum give us some insights not just into the history of ancient Mesopotamia, but the history of doing history. The objects provide us with a way into the birth of writing, physical and mythical architecture, leadership, education, science, warfare, poverty and privilege, and the lives of women and children. Each topic has, in its own way, also shown how people in ancient Mesopotamia related to their own, even more ancient past. They used it to write, to cement power, to keep their jobs, to beautify the courtyards of their palaces, and to connect with those who came before them. By revering their own history, the people of this land between two great rivers have ensured snapshots of what was important to them were preserved and that something of themselves would live on.

Acknowledgements

I set out to write a thematic history of ancient Mesopotamia through the objects unearthed in what early excavators thought was an ancient museum in Ur. Given the vast temporal landscape of the region, scarred with cultural, linguistic, and even civilisational shifts, this was no easy feat. The resulting work, to me, feels almost like an ancient clay tablet, put together from multiple fragments and criss-crossed with cracks. Pulling the fragments together wouldn't have been possible without my incredible publishers and editors, Anna Baty and Izzy Everington at Hodder & Stoughton, and Alane Mason at W.W. Norton. They faced countless iterations of this book and helped me find a new joy in some very old material. I'm so grateful for their guidance, patience and care throughout this whole process.

I am so grateful to my incredible agent, Doug Young, for taking a chance on me. I didn't know that our handful of Twitter messages, followed by a coffee in Marylebone, would change the course of my life, and I'm so thankful.

Much of my research was made possible by Wolfson College, Oxford, my academic home for the last fifteen years, where my fellowship allowed me the freedom to write this book (and afforded me pretty much the only hot meals

I got to enjoy from 2021 to 2024). I'm indebted to my former supervisor, Jacob L. Dahl, for his help with various tablets and references throughout this book and for reading some early drafts, as well as my incredible colleagues and friends in Oxford, including Émilie Pagé-Perron, Christie Carr and Troels Pank Arbøll, who were always generous with their time and knowledge (and PDFs). I am also grateful to Heather Baker, Ulrike Steinert, Klaus Wagensonner, M. Willis Monroe, Lynn-Salammbô Zimmerman and many others who helped with obscure questions or references. Special thanks are due to William B. Hafford, who helped me complicate the question of the 'museum' and whose open access research on Ur has been invaluable. This book would not have been possible without the high-quality research of countless Assyriologists throughout the world who have dedicated their lives to this subject. In this book I have tried to digest some of their hard work for a wider audience, but it goes without saying that any errors are my own.

I'm indebted to the handful of people who read early drafts of various chapters, including Iain Purdue, Cameron Brockmann and Salman Al-Rashid. Your insights and constructive criticism helped steer my approach. Thank you for poring over every word and inspiring me to work even harder to get things right. No one has read my work with as much attention to detail in the later editorial stages as the brilliant Tamsin Shelton and Ian Allen, and I owe them both my deepest gratitude.

Writing a book is so much fun but also kind of terrible, and I'm grateful to Greg Jenner for helping me through the moments when, between a newborn baby and a new round of edits, I was ready to give up. Thank you for always taking the time to listen to me and to share your wisdom with me, and for your kindness throughout the years.

There is no way I could have written this book without childcare, and I cannot express my gratitude in enough words to those who supported us, particularly the incredible carers and teachers at our children's nursery. It really takes a village, and you were our village when we had no other. You were our family when we lost ours. Thank you to all of you.

I wrote most of this book with a toddler at home during a pandemic while I was also pregnant, and I edited it often one-handed during maternity leave with a baby at my breast after many sleepless nights. I wouldn't have traded that timing for the world, and I'm grateful to my tiny children for inspiring me every day, for asking weird and hard questions, and for reminding me how much joy there is to be found in things I used to take for granted, like a slow-moving snail on the sidewalk and a full moon. I'm thankful to my husband, David, for keeping me sane and cheering me on. Thank you for being my bedrock through every emotional wobble as we both did all the hardest things we've ever done before. I could fill another book with my gratitude to him and our little ones. If there is one thing I have learned from ancient Mesopotamia, it is that love is and always has been the most important thing of all. The three of you make everything worth doing.

Selected Artefacts Cited

Below is a list of some of the artefacts referenced in this book with identifiers for further reading or research. For most of these, the number reflects the museum collection number. 'IM', for example, is the abbreviation for the Iraq Museum, and 'SB' for the Louvre Museum. Some artefacts have only been assigned an excavation number, which is the label given at the time of excavation, and for Ur, these numbers are preceded simply by the letter 'U'. All artefacts appear in the online *Cuneiform Digital Library Initiative* with additional information, including publication data and photos.

Accounting record from Uruk	Ashm 1926-602
Astronomical almanac, last datable cuneiform tablet	W22340a
Astronomical Diary for Halley's Comet	BM 41941
Babylonian map of the world	BM 92687
Boundary stone from Ennigaldi-Nanna's museum	U 2758
Brick with dog paw prints	BM 137495
Clay drum from Ennigaldi-Nanna's museum	BM 119014
Complete brick of Amar-Suen from Ur	BM 90036
Complete statue of King Shulgi	OIM A03700
Cone of Enanedu	BM 130729
Cone of Kudur-Mabuk from Ennigaldi-Nanna's museum	BM 119022
Contract with Ishunnatu	Camb 330
Cylinder seal for Puabi	CBS 16728
Cylinder seal with reed structure, or mudhif	Ashm 1964-744
Disc of Enheduanna	CBS 16665

Drawing of a ghost	BM 47817
Ennigaldi-Nanna Cylinder	YBC 2182
Enuma Anu Enlil, Tablet 63	K 160
Epic of Gilgamesh, Tablet XI or 'Flood Tablet', copy from Library of Ashurbanipal	K 3375
Footprint in clay	Msk 74340
Fragment of Neo-Babylonian boys' school tablet from Ur	U 2815
Hammurabi's law stele	SB 8
Jupiter tablet	BM 40054
Lamassu from Northwest Palace at Nineveh	BM 118801
Lamentation over the Destruction of Sumer and Ur, copy from Nippur	CBS 2307
Letter from Balasî to Esarhaddon	K 1169
Letter from Lamassi to Pushu-ken about textiles	NBC 3658
List of vessels and garments from Uruk, fragment	Ashm 1928-445b
Mace head from Ennigaldi-Nanna's museum	U 2760
Naram-Sîn Victory Stele	SB 4
Old Babylonian list of Pythagorean triples	Plimpton 322
Old Babylonian lullaby	BM 122691
Queen Naqia's building inscription	K 2745
Schooldays (or Eduba A), copy from Nippur	SC 4, 9
School tablet signed by Belti-reminni	VAT 6574
School tablet with approximation of pi	YBC 7302
School tablet with bite mark	N5326B
Statue fragment of King Shulgi from Ennigaldi-Nanna's museum	IM 939
Stele of the Vultures	AO 50
Sumerian King List, copy	Ashm 1923-444

A Timeline of Ancient Mesopotamian History

Dates (BCE)	Period	Major Figures and Milestones
c. 3500–2900	Late Uruk and Jemdet Nasr	• Development of early cuneiform writing system • Early urbanism and the first cities • Kushim, administrator and beer brewer
c. 2900–2340	Early Dynastic	• Rise of city-states and inter-city conflict • Development of kingship as separate political institution • Plano-Convex Building of Kish and early palace architecture • Puabi, Sumerian queen buried in Ur's Royal Cemetery • Ku-Bau, bartender-turned-queen • Era of legendary kings like Gilgamesh
c. 2340–2200	Sargonic (Old Akkadian)	• Enheduanna, the first named poet and high priestess to the moon god at Ur • Sargon, who founds the empire • Naram-Sîn, grandson of Sargon with Victory Stele and brick stamp
c. 2200–2112	Gutian	(Not mentioned in this book)
c. 2112–2004	Third Dynasty of Ur (Ur III)	• Ur-Nammu, who begins construction of ziggurat at Ur • Shulgi, who ruled for almost 50 years • Ubartum, physician named in c. 50 documents • Lugal-irida, superintendent of weavers in Guabba • *Brick of Amar-Suen and statue fragment of Shulgi*

c. 2000–1600	Old Babylonian (c. 2004–1595)	• Enanedu, high priestess to the moon god at Ur • Kudur-Mabuk, tribal leader with clay cone • Hammurabi, first complete law collection from antiquity • Shinunutum, the songbird • *Naditum* women in Sippar and their scribes • Evidence of Pythagorean theorem and earliest approximation of pi • *Clay cone of Kudur-Mabuk*
	Old Assyrian (c. 2020–1591)	• Major international trade network established • Rise of the god Ashur to the top of the Assyrian pantheon • Ahaha, Lamassi, Taram-Kubi, Bazaya, and other businesswomen
c. 1500–1000	Kassite (c. 1475–1155)	• Amarna letters between Great Powers • Flourishing of scholarship • King Agum-Kakrime returns Marduk statue to Babylon • *Boundary stone*
	Middle Assyrian (1350–1000)	(Not mentioned in this book)
c. 900–612	Neo-Assyrian	• Neo-Assyrian empire becomes world's largest empire to date under Ashurbanipal • Sammu-ramat, Assyrian queen who inspires Semiramis legend • Library of Ashurbanipal
c. 626–539	Neo-Babylonian	• Ennigaldi-Nanna, high priestess to the moon god at Ur • Nabonidus, last independent Babylonian king • Ishunnatu, enslaved woman and pub manager in Kish • Nabû-shuma-iddin, author of the 'clay drum' • Earliest Astronomical Diaries set stage for later scientific leaps • *Clay drum and school tablets*

Bibliography

Abusch, Tzvi, and Daniel Schwemer. 2016. *Corpus of Mesopotamian Anti -Witchcraft Rituals*. Vol. 2. Ancient Magic and Divination 8. Leiden/ Boston: Brill.

Ackerman, Susan. 2005. *When Heroes Love: The Ambiguity of Eros in the Stories of Gilgamesh and David*. New York: Columbia University Press.

Agha, Rand Hazim Mahmood. 2016. 'The role of intelligent systems in traditional courtyard houses in Baghdad, Iraq', PhD Dissertation, Newcastle University.

Anastasio, Stefano. 2020. *Building between the Two Rivers: An Introduction to the Building Archaeology of Ancient Mesopotamia*. Oxford: Archaeopress.

Anonymous. 2015. 'Two Babylonian Lullabies (BM 122691 and OECT 11 002)'. Tumblr. *Slightly Alive Translations* (blog). 3 December 2015. https://mostlydeadlanguages.tumblr.com/post/134484418018/two-babylonian-lullabies-bm-122691-and-oect-11

Arbøll, Troels Pank, et al. 2023. 'Revealing the Secrets of a 2900-Year-Old Clay Brick, Discovering a Time Capsule of Ancient DNA'. *Nature: Scientific Reports* 13 (Article 13092).

Baadsgaard, Aubrey, et al. 2011. 'Human Sacrifice and Intentional Corpse Preservation in the Royal Cemetery of Ur'. *Antiquity* 85: 27–42.

Bahrani, Zainab. 2004. 'The King's Head'. *Iraq*, Papers of the 49th Rencontre Assyriologique Internationale, Part One, 66: 115–19.

Baker, Heather D. 2001. 'Degrees of Freedom: Slavery in Mid-First Millennium BC Babylonia'. *World Archaeology* 33 (1): 18–26.

Baldi, Johnny. 2021. 'How the Uruk Potters Used the Wheel. New Data on Modalities and Conditions of Emergence of the Potter's Wheel in the Uruk World'. *Interdisciplinaria Archaeologica* 12 (2): 181–99.

Beaulieu, Paul-Alain. 1989. *The Reign of Nabonidus, King of Babylon 556–539 B.C.* New Haven/London: Yale University Press.

———. 2003. 'Nabopolassar and the Antiquity of Babylon'. In *Hayim and Miriam Tadmor Volume*, edited by Israel Eph'al et al., 1-9. Jerusalem: The Israel Exploration Society.

———. 2021. 'The City of Ur and the Neo-Babylonian Empire'. In *Ur in the Twenty-First Century CE: Proceedings of the 62nd Rencontre Assyriologique Internationale at Philadelphia, July 11–15, 2016*, edited by Grant Frame et al., 153–70. University Park, PA: Penn State University Press.

Bennison-Chapman, Lucy. 2018. 'Reconsidering "Tokens": The Neolithic Origins of Accounting or Multifunctional, Utilitarian Tools?' *Cambridge Archaeological Journal* 29 (2): 233–59.

Black, Jeremy A., et al. 1998–. 'Proverbs: Collection 2+6'. In *The Electronic Text Corpus of Sumerian Literature*. https://etcsl.orinst.ox.ac.uk/proverbs/t.6.1.02.html

———. 'Proverbs: Collection 5'. In *The Electronic Text Corpus of Sumerian Literature*. https://etcsl.orinst.ox.ac.uk/proverbs/t.6.1.05.html

———. 'A Praise Poem of Shulgi (Shulgi A): Translation'. In *The Electronic Text Corpus of Sumerian Literature*. https://etcsl.orinst.ox.ac.uk/section2/tr24201.htm

———. 'The Death of Ur-Namma (Ur-Namma A): A Version from Nippur'. In *The Electronic Text Corpus of Sumerian Literature*. https://etcsl.orinst.ox.ac.uk/section2/tr2411.htm

———. 'Enki and Ninmah'. In *The Electronic Text Corpus of Sumerian Literature*. https://etcsl.orinst.ox.ac.uk/section1/tr112.htm

———. 'The Exploits of Ninurta'. In *The Electronic Text Corpus of Sumerian Literature*. https://etcsl.orinst.ox.ac.uk/section1/tr162.htm

———. 'Hymn to Nisaba A'. In *The Electronic Text Corpus of Sumerian Literature*. https://etcsl.orinst.ox.ac.uk/section4/b4161.htm

———. 'Iddin-Dagan A'. In *The Electronic Text Corpus of Sumerian Literature*. https://etcsl.orinst.ox.ac.uk/section2/tr2531.htm

Black, Jeremy, and Anthony Green. 2004. *Gods, Demons, and Symbols of*

Ancient Mesopotamia. Second Edition. London: The British Museum Press.

Bondar, Maria. 2024. 'Prehistoric Innovations: Wheels and Wheeled Vehicles'. *Acta Archaeologica* 69 (2): 271–97.

Brack-Bernsen, Lis, and John M. Steele. 2005. 'Eclipse Prediction and the Length of the Saros Cycle in Babylonian Astronomy'. *Centaurus* 47: 181–206.

Brisch, Nicole. 2006. 'The Priestess and the King: The Divine Kingship of Su-Sîn of Ur'. *Journal of the American Oriental Society* 126 (2): 161–76.

Britton, John P,. et al. 2011. 'Plimpton 322: A Review and a Different Perspective'. *Archive for History of Exact Sciences* 65: 519–66.

Burke, Aaron A. 2020. *The Amorites and the Bronze Age Near East: The Making of a Regional Identity*. Cambridge: Cambridge University Press.

Burmeister, Stefan, et al. 2019. 'Some Notes on Pictograms Interpreted as Sledges and Wheeled Vehicles in the Archaic Texts from Uruk'. In *Equids and Wheeled Vehicles in the Ancient World*, edited by Peter Raulwing, Katheryn M. Linduff, and Joost H. Crouwel, 49–70. BAR International Series 2923. Oxford: BAR Publishing.

Cathcart, Kevin. 2011. 'The Earliest Contributions to the Decipherment of Sumerian and Akkadian'. *Cuneiform Digital Library Journal* 2011 (1). https://cdli.ucla.edu/pubs/cdlj/2011/cdlj2011_001.html

'CDLI Literary 000754 (*Edubba* A) Composite Artifact Entry'. 2014. In *Cuneiform Digital Library Initiative (CDLI)*. https://cdli.ucla.edu/P464238

'CDLI Literary Descent of Ishtar (Composite) Artifact Entry'. 2016. In *Cuneiform Digital Library Initiative (CDLI)*. https://cdli.ucla.edu/P497322

'Clay Bricks for the Ziggurat of Uruk (Iraq)'. 2018. *Cultural Heritage News* (blog). 13 November 2018. https://www.culthernews.de/clay-bricks-for-the-ziggurat-of-uruk/

Cohen, Yoram. 2005. 'Feet of Clay at Emar: A Happy End?' *Orientalia, Nova Series* 74 (2): 165–70.

Cooper, Jerrold S. 2002. *Reconstructing History from Ancient Inscriptions: The Lagash-Umma Border Conflict*. Revised Third Printing. Malibu: Undena Publications.

———. 2016. 'The Job of Sex: The Social and Economic Role of

Prostitutes in Ancient Mesopotamia'. In *The Role of Women in Work and Society in the Ancient Near East*, edited by Brigitte Lion and Cécile Michel, 13:209–27. Studies in Ancient Near Eastern Records. Boston /Berlin: De Gruyter.

Crisostomo, C. Jay. 2018. 'Language, Translation, and Commentary in Cuneiform Scribal Practice'. *Journal of Ancient Near Eastern History* 5 (1–2): 41–56.

———. 2019. *Translation as Scholarship: Language, Writing, and Bilingual Education in Ancient Babylonia*. Vol. 22. Studies in Ancient Near Eastern Records. Boston/Berlin: De Gruyter.

Da Riva, Roció. 2008. *The Neo-Babylonian Royal Inscriptions: An Introduction*. Guides for the Mesopotamian Textual Records 4. Münster: Ugarit-Verlag.

Dalley, Stephanie. 2017. 'Assyrian Warfare'. In *A Companion to Assyria*, edited by Eckart Frahm, 522–33. Hoboken: Wiley Blackwell.

Dalley, Stephanie, et al. 1976. *The Old Babylonian Tablets from Tell al Rimah*. London: British School of Archaeology in Iraq.

Damdamayev, M.A. 2002. 'Review of *Schulunterricht in Babylonien im Ersten Jahrtausend v. Chr. Alter Orient Und Altes Testament, 275* by Petra D. Gesche'. *Orientalia, Nova Series* 71 (4): 462–5.

Delnero, Paul. 2018. 'A Land with No Borders: A New Interpretation of the Babylonian "Map of the World"'. *Journal of Ancient Near Eastern History* 4 (1–2): 19–37.

Démare-Lafont, Sophie. 2016. 'Women at Work in Mesopotamia: An Attempt at a Legal Perspective'. In *The Role of Women in Work and Society in the Ancient Near East*, edited by Brigitte Lion and Cécile Michel, 13:310–27. Studies in Ancient Near Eastern Records. Boston /Berlin: De Gruyter.

Dietrich, Manfried. 2003. *The Babylonian Correspondence of Sargon and Sennacherib*. Translated by Inka Parpola and Ronald Mayer-Opificus. Vol. 17. State Archives of Assyria. Helsinki: Helsinki University Press.

Dyson, Robert H. 1977. 'Archival Glimpses of the Ur Expedition in the Years 1920–1926'. *Expedition Magazine* 20 (1): 5–23.

Edzard, Sibylle. 1997. *Gudea and His Dynasty*. Vol. 3/1. The Royal Inscriptions of Mesopotamia: Early Periods. Toronto: University of Toronto Press.

Eichmann, Ricardo. 2019. 'Uruk's Early Monumental Architecture'. In *Uruk: First City of the Ancient World*, edited by Nicola Crüsemann et al., 97–109. Los Angeles: The J. Paul Getty Museum.

Englund, Robert K. 1998. 'Texts from the Late Uruk Period'. In *Annäherungen 1: Mesopotamien. Späturuk-Zeit Und Frühdynastische Zeit*, 160/1:13–233. Orbis Biblicus et Orientalis. Freiburg Schweiz: Universitätsverlag.

———. 2009. 'The Smell of the Cage'. *Cuneiform Digital Library Journal* 4. https://cdli.mpiwg-berlin.mpg.de/articles/cdlj/2009-4

———. 2011. 'Accounting in Proto-Cuneiform'. In *The Oxford Handbook of Cuneiform Culture*, edited by Karen Radner and Eleanor Robson, 32–50. Oxford: Oxford University Press.

Englund, Robert K., et al. 1991. *The Proto-Cuneiform Texts from Jemdet Nasr. I: Copies, Transliterations and Glossary*. Vol. 1. Materialien Zu Den Frühen Schriftzeugnissen Des Vorderen Orients. Berlin: Gebr. Mann.

Ess, Margarete van. 2019. 'Observations on Construction Techniques in Uruk'. In *Uruk: First City of the Ancient World*, edited by Nicola Crüsemann et al., 212–13. Los Angeles: The J. Paul Getty Museum.

Farber, Howard. 2021. 'An Examination of Prices and Wages in Babylonia – ca. 2000–1600 B.C.E.' PhD Dissertation, University of Chicago.

Farber, W. 1990. 'Magic at the Cradle: Babylonian and Assyrian Lullabies'. *Anthropos* 85: 139–48.

Farber, Walter. 2014. *Lamaštu: An Edition of the Canonical Series of Lamaštu Incantations and Rituals and Related Texts from the Second and First Millennia B.C.* Mesopotamian Civilisations 17. Winona Lake: Eisenbrauns.

Fattori, Anita. 2021. 'Anatolian Women: Who Were the Secondary Wives of the Assyrian Merchants?' *Ancient History from Below* (blog). 25 October 2021. https://en.subalternosblog.com/post/anatolian-women-who-were-the-secondary-wes-of-the-assyrian-merchants

Feliu, Lluís. 2010. 'A New Fragment of Nisaba A'. *Altorientalische Forschungen* 37 (1): 27–37.

Fiette, Baptiste. 2020. '"King" Kudur-Mabuk: A Study on the Identity of a Mesopotamian Ruler Without a Crown'. In *The Construction of Identity in the Ancient World*, edited by Sebastian Grätz et al., 50/

2:275–94. Die Welt Des Orients. Göttingen: Vandenhoeck & Ruprecht GmbH & Co.

Finkel, Irving, ed. 2013. *The Cyrus Cylinder: The King of Persia's Proclamation from Ancient Babylon*. London/New York: I.B. Tauris.

Finkel, Irving, and Alexandra Fletcher. 2016. 'Thinking Outside the Box: The Case of the Sun-God Tablet and the Cruciform Monument'. *Bulletin of the American Schools of Oriental Research* 375: 215–48.

Finkel, Irving, and Jonathan Taylor. 2015. *Cuneiform*. London: The British Museum.

Finkelstein, J.J. 1976. 'Šilip Rēmim and Related Matters'. In *Kramer Anniversary Volume: Cuneiform Studies in Honor of Samuel Noah Kramer*, edited by Barry L. Eichler et al. Vol. 25. Alter Orient Und Altes Testament. Butzon & Bercker.

Foster, Benjamin R. 2005. *Before the Muses: An Anthology of Akkadian Literature*. Third Edition. 2 vols. Bethesda: CDL Press.

Frahm, Eckart. 2011. 'Keeping Company with Men of Learning: The King as Scholar'. In *The Oxford Handbook of Cuneiform Culture*, edited by Karen Radner and Eleanor Robson, 508–32. Oxford: Oxford University Press.

———. 2019. 'The Neo-Assyrian Royal Inscriptions as Text: History, Ideology, and Intertextuality'. In *Writing Neo-Assyrian History: Sources, Problems, and Approaches*, edited by Giovanni Battista Lanfranchi et al., 24:139–59. State Archives of Assyria Studies. Helsinki: Neo-Assyrian Text Corpus Project.

———. 2023. *Assyria: The Rise and Fall of the World's First Empire*. London/Dublin: Bloomsbury.

Frame, Grant, and A.R. George. 2005. 'The Royal Libraries of Nineveh: New Evidence for King Ashurbanipal's Tablet Collecting'. *Iraq* 67 (1): 265–84.

Frayne, Douglas R. 1990. *Old Babylonian Period (2003–1595 BC)*. Vol. 4. The Royal Inscriptions of Mesopotamia. Toronto: University of Toronto Press.

———. 1993. *Sargonic and Gutian Periods (2234–2113 BC)*. Vol. 2. The Royal Inscriptions of Mesopotamia: Early Periods. Toronto: University of Toronto Press.

———. 1997. *Ur III Period (2112–2004 BC)*. Vol. 3/2. The Royal

Inscriptions of Mesopotamia: Early Periods. Toronto: University of Toronto Press.

———. 2008. *Presargonic Period (2700–2350 BC)*. Vol. 1. The Royal Inscriptions of Mesopotamia: Early Periods. Toronto: University of Toronto Press.

Freedman, Sally. 2017. *If a City Is Set on a Height: The Akkadian Omen Series Šumma Alu Ina Mele Šakin*. Vol. 3. Winona Lake: Eisenbrauns.

Gadd, Cyril J., and Léon Legrain. 1928. *Royal Inscriptions*. Vol. 1. Ur Excavations, Texts. London: The Trustees of the British Museum.

Gadotti, Alhena. 2016. 'Mesopotamian Women's Cultic Roles in Late 3rd–Early 2nd Millennia BCE'. In *Women in Antiquity: Real Women across the Ancient World*, edited by Stephanie Lynn Budin and Jean Macintosh Turfa, 64–76. London: Routledge.

Gadotti, Alhena, and Alexandra Kleinerman. 2017. 'The Rules of the School'. *Journal of the American Oriental Society* 137 (1): 89–116.

Gannon, Megan, and Livescience. 2016. 'Babylonians Tracked Jupiter with Fancy Math, Tablet Reveals'. *Scientific American*, 2016. https://www.scientificamerican.com/article/babylonians-tracked-jupiter-with-fancy-math-tablet-reveals/

Garfinkel, Yosef, et al. 2019. 'Lachish Fortifications and State Formation in the Biblical Kingdom of Judah in Light of Radiometric Datings'. *Radiocarbon* 61 (3): 695–712.

Garfinkle, Steven. 2020. 'Violence and State Power in Early Mesopotamia'. In *The Cambridge World History of Violence*, edited by Garrett G. Fagan et al., Volume 1: The Prehistoric and Ancient Worlds: 219–37. Cambridge: Cambridge University Press.

Geller, Markham. 2016. *Healing Magic and Evil Demons: Udug-Hul Incantations*. Vol. 8. Die Babylonisch-Assyrische Medizin in Texten Und Untersuchungen. Boston/Berlin: De Gruyter.

George, A.R. 2003. *The Babylonian Gilgamesh Epic: Introduction, Critical Edition and Cuneiform Texts*. 2 vols. Oxford: Oxford University Press.

Gertoux, Gérard. 2019. 'Mesopotamian Chronology over the Period 2340–539 BCE through Astronomically Dated Synchronisms and Comparison with Carbon-14 Dating'. In *ASOR 2019 Session 3B Archaeology and Biblical Studies*. San Diego, California.

Gesche, Petra D. 2000. *Schulunterricht in Babylonien im ersten Jahrtausend v.*

Chr. Vol. 275. Alter Orient Und Altes Testament. Münster: Ugarit
-Verlag.

Gibson, McGuire. 2023. 'The First Actual Stratigraphic Profile of the
Y Trench'. In *Where Kingship Descended from Heaven: Studies on
Ancient Kish*, edited by Karen L. Wilson and Deborah Bekken,
57–104. Studies in Ancient Cultures 1. Chicago: The University of
Chicago.

Grayson, A. Kirk. 1987. *Assyrian Rulers of the Third and Second Millennia
BC (to 1115 BC)*. Vol. 1. The Royal Inscriptions of Mesopotamia,
Assyrian Periods. Toronto: University of Toronto Press.

———. 1991. *Assyrian Rulers of the Early First Millennium BC (1114–859
BC)*. Vol. 2. The Royal Inscriptions of Mesopotamia, Assyrian
Periods. Toronto: University of Toronto Press.

Grayson, A. Kirk, and Jamie Novotny. 2012. *The Royal Inscriptions of
Sennacherib, King of Assyria (704–681 BC), Part 1*. Vol. 3/1. The Royal
Inscriptions of the Neo-Assyrian Period. Winona Lake: Eisenbrauns.

Grégoire, Jean-Pierre. 1996. *Archives Administratives et Inscriptions
Cunéiformes Ashmolean Museum*. Vol. 1/1. Paris: Librairie orientaliste
Paul Geuthner.

Guinan, Ann, and Erle Leichty. 2010. 'Tasteless Tablets'. In *Gazing on the
Deep: Ancient Near Eastern and Other Studies in Honor of Tsvi Abusch*,
edited by Jeffrey Stackert et al., 49–50. Bethesda: CDL Press.

Hafford, William B. 2015. 'Magnificent with Jewels: Puabi Queen of
Ur'. In *From Ancient to Modern: Archaeology and Aesthetics*, edited by
Jennifer Y. Chi and Pedro Azara, 87–101. Princeton: Princeton
University Press.

———. 2019. 'The Royal Cemetery of Ur'. In *Journey to the City: A
Companion to the Middle East Galleries at the Penn Museum*, edited by
Steve Tinney and Karen Sonik, 195–234. Philadelphia: University of
Pennsylvania Museum of Archaeology and Anthropology.

Hammer, Emily. 2022. 'Multi-Centric, Marsh-Based Urbanism at the
Early Mesopotamian City of Lagash (Tell al-Hiba, Iraq)'. *Journal of
Anthropological Archaeology* 68 (101458).

———. 2019. 'The City and Landscape of Ur: An Aerial, Satellite, and
Ground Assessment'. *Iraq* 81: 173–206.

Hammer, Emily, et al. 2022. 'The Structure and Hydrology of the Early

Dynastic City of Lagash (Tell Al-Hiba) from Satellite and Aerial Images'. *Iraq* 84: 103–27.

Hansen, Donald P. 2003. 'Art of the Early City-States'. In *Art of the First Cities: The Third Millennium B.C. from the Mediterranean to the Indus*, edited by Joan Aruz, 21–42. New York: The Metropolitan Museum of Art.

Harris, Rivkah. 1962. 'Biographical Notes on the *Nadītu* Women of Sippar'. *Journal of Cuneiform Studies* 16 (1): 1–12.

———. 1963. 'The Organization and Administration of the Cloister in Ancient Babylonia'. *Journal of the Economic and Social History of the Orient* 6 (2): 121–57.

———. 1975. *Ancient Sippar: A Demographic Study of an Old-Babylonian City (1894–1595 B.C.)*. Vol. 36. Publications de l'Institut Historique et Archeologique Neerlandais de Stamboul. Nederlands Instituut voor het Nabije Oosten.

Harvey, Eric J. 2020. 'The Songbird: Linking Music and Blindness in Ancient Babylonia'. *All of Us* (blog). 11 May 2020. https://allofusdha. org/research/the-songbird-linking-music-and-blindness-in-ancient-babylonia/#_edn1

Hausleiter, Arnulf, and Hanspeter Schaudig. 2016. 'Rock Relief and Cuneiform Inscription of King Nabonidus at Al-Ḥāʾiṭ (Province of Ḥāʾil, Saudi Arabia), Ancient Padakku'. *Zeitschrift Für Orient-Archäologie* 9:224–40.

Heeßel, Nils P. 2009. 'The Babylonian Physician Rabâ-Ša-Marduk: Another Look at Physicians and Exorcists in the Ancient Near East'. In *Advances in Mesopotamian Medicine from Hammurabi to Hippocrates: Proceedings of the International Conference "Oeil Malade et Mauvais Oeil," Collège de France, Paris, 23rd June 2006*, edited by Annie Attia and Gilles Buisson, 13–28. Cuneiform Monographs 37. Leiden/Boston: Brill.

———. 2018. 'Dating EAE. When Was the Astrological Series *Enūma Anu Ellil* Created?' In *The Scaffolding of Our Thoughts. Essays on Assyriology and the History of Science in Honor of Francesca Rochberg*, edited by C. Jay Crisostomo et al., 253–63. Ancient Magic and Divination 13. Leiden/Boston: Brill.

Helle, Sophus. 2023. *Enheduana: The Complete Poems of the World's First Author*. New Haven/London: Yale University Press.

Herodotus. 1920. *Herodotus, with an English Translation by A.D. Godley*.

Vol. 1. 4 vols. Loeb Classical Library Edition. Cambridge: Harvard University Press.

Hinnant, Lori. 2016. 'Turning Iraq History to Rubble, Leaving the Mess to Looters'. *AP News*, 31 December 2016. https://apnews.com/article/53c801647e084059bc4cbe3fb0237a75

Holtz, Shalom E. 2014. *Neo-Babylonian Trial Records*. Atlanta: Society of Biblical Literature.

Hritz, Carrie. 2021. 'The Umma-Lagash Border Conflict: A View from Above'. In *From Sherds to Landscapes: Studies on the Ancient Near East in Honor of McGuire Gibson*, edited by Mark Altaweel and Carrie Hritz, 71:109–30. Studies in Ancient Oriental Civilization. Chicago: The Oriental Institute of the University of Chicago.

Hughes, Bettany, and Irving Finkel. 2021. Bettany Hughes and Irving Finkel discuss 'The First Ghosts', YouTube. https://www.youtube.com/watch?v=UwS61Y3Jz-s

Hunger, Hermann. 1992. *Astrological Reports to Assyrian Kings*. Vol. 8. State Archives of Assyria. Helsinki: Helsinki University Press.

Hunger, Hermann, and Teije de Jong. 2014. 'Almanac W22340a From Uruk: The Latest Datable Cuneiform Tablet'. *Zeitschrift Für Assyriologie Und Vorderasiatische Archäologie* 104 (2): 182–94.

Hurowitz, Victor Avigdor. 2000. 'Literary Observations on "In Praise of the Scribal Art"'. *Journal of Ancient Near Eastern Studies* 27:49–56.

Izre'el, Shlomo. 1997. *The Amarna Scholarly Tablets*. Cuneiform Monographs 9. Groningen: Styx.

Jeffers, Joshua and Jamie Novotny. 2023. *The Royal Inscriptions of Ashurbanipal (668–631 BC), Aššur-Etel-Ilāni (630–627 BC), and Sîn-Šarra-Iškun (626–612 BC), Kings of Assyria, Part 2*. Vol. 5/2. The Royal Inscriptions of the Neo-Assyrian Period. Winona Lake: Eisenbrauns.

Jones, Jonathan. 2018. '"Some of the Most Appalling Images Ever Created" – I Am Ashurbanipal Review'. *The Guardian*, 6 November 2018. https://www.theguardian.com/artanddesign/2018/nov/06/i-am-ashurbanipal-review-british-museum

Jong, T. de. 2013. 'Astronomical Fine-Tuning of the Chronology of the Hammurabi Age.' *Jaarbericht van Het Vooraziatisch-Egyptisch Genootschap 'Ex Oriente Lux'* 44:147–67.

Jursa, Michael. 2011. 'Cuneiform Writing in Neo-Babylonian Temple Communities'. In *The Oxford Handbook of Cuneiform Culture*, edited by Karen Radner and Eleanor Robson, 184–204. Oxford: Oxford University Press.

Khadr, Ali. 2019. 'Iraq: "Women Are the Backbone of the Marsh Arab Community – as the Effects of Climate Change Are Becoming More Visible, It Is Becoming Clearer That Women Are the First to Suffer"'. Minority and Indigenous Trends 2019 – Focus on Climate Justice. https://minorityrights.org/trends2019/iraq/

Koch, Ulla Susanne. 2015. *Mesopotamian Divination Texts: Conversing with the Gods. Sources from the First Millennium BCE*. Vol. 7. Guides to the Mesopotamian Textual Record. Münster: Ugarit-Verlag.

Koch-Westenholz, Ulla. 2000. *Babylonian Liver Omens: The Chapters Manzāzu, Padānu and Pān tākalti of the Babylonian Extispicy Series Mainly from Aššurbanipal's Library*. The Carsten Neibuhr Institute of Near Eastern Studies 25. Copenhagen: Museum Tusculanum Press.

———. 2002. 'Old Babylonian Extispicy Reports'. In *Mining the Archives: Festschrift for Christopher Walker on the Occasion of His 60th Birthday, 4 October 2002*, edited by Cornelia Wunsch, 131–46. Dresden: Islet.

Lafont, Bertrand. 2016. 'Women at Work and Women in Economy and Society during the Neo-Sumerian Period'. In *The Role of Women in Work and Society in the Ancient Near East*, edited by Brigitte Lion and Cécile Michel, 13:149–73. Studies in Ancient Near Eastern Records. Boston/Berlin: De Gruyter.

Lambert, W.G., and Alan R. Millard. 1969. *Atra-Hasis: The Babylonian Story of the Flood*. Oxford: Oxford University Press.

Larsen, Morgens Trolle. 1988. 'Old Assyrian Texts'. In *Cuneiform Texts in The Metropolitan Museum of Art. Volume I: Tablets, Cones, and Bricks of the Third and Second Millennia B.C.*, edited by Ira Spar, 92–143. New York: The Metropolitan Museum of Art.

———. 2015. *Ancient Kanesh: A Merchant Colony in Bronze Age Anatolia*. Cambridge: Cambridge University Press.

Lauinger, Jacob. 2020. 'The Electronic Idrimi'. In *The Open Richly Annotated Cuneiform Corpus*. http://oracc.iaas.upenn.edu/aemw/alalakh/idrimi/P500443/html

Leick, Gwendolyn. 1988. *A Dictionary of Ancient Near Eastern Architecture*. London/New York: Routledge.

Lenzi, Alan. 2015. 'Mesopotamian Scholarship: Kassite to Late Babylonian Periods'. *Journal of Ancient Near Eastern History* 2 (2): 145–201.

Lion, Brigitte. 2001. 'Dame Inanna-Ama-Mu, Scribe à Sippar'. *Revue d'assyriologie et d'archéologie Orientale* 93 (1): 7–32.

Liu, Changyu. 2021. *The Ur III Administrative Texts from Puzrish-Dagan Kept in the Harvard Museum of the Ancient Near East*. Vol. 68. Harvard Semitic Studies. Leiden/Boston: Brill.

Luukko, Mikko, and Greta Van Buylaere. 2002. *The Political Correspondence of Esarhaddon*. Vol. 16. State Archives of Assyria. Helsinki: Helsinki University Press.

Malko, Helen. 2020. 'The Kassites of Babylonia: A Re-Examination of an Ethnic Identity'. In *Babylonia under the Sealand and Kassite Dynasties*, edited by Susanne Paulus and Tim Clayden, 177–89. Berlin/Boston: De Gruyter.

Maloigne, Hélène. 2017. 'How Idrimi Came to London: Diplomacy and the Division of Archaeological Finds in the 1930s'. *Museum History Journal* 10 (2): 200–16.

Marchesi, Gianni. 2010. 'The Sumerian King List and the Early History of Mesopotamia'. In *Ana Turri Gimilli. Studi Dedicati al Padre Werner R. Mayer, S.J. Da Amici e Allievi*, edited by M.G. Biga and M. Liverani, 231–48. Quaderni Di Vicino Oriente 5. Rome: Sapienza Università di Roma.

Mattila, Raija. 2000. *The King's Magnates: A Study of the Highest Officials of the Neo-Assyrian Empire*. Vol. 11. State Archives of Assyria Studies. Helsinki: Neo-Assyrian Text Corpus Project.

May, Natalie Naomi. 2018. 'Female Scholars in Mesopotamia?' In *Gender and Methodology in the Ancient Near East: Approaches from Assyriology and Beyond*, edited by Stephanie Lynn Budin et al., 100:149–62. BARCINO MONOGRAPHICA ORIENTALIA. Barcelona: Edicions de la Universitat de Barcelona.

McCown, Donald. 1951. 'Nippur: The Holy City'. *University Museum Bulletin* 16 (2): 5–19.

McMahon, Augusta. 2013. 'Tell Brak: Early Northern Mesopotamian

Urbanism, Economic Complexity and Social Stress, Fifth–Fourth Millennia BC'. In *100 Jahre Archäologische Feldforschungen in Nordost-Syrien – Eine Bilanz: Internationales Symposium Des Instituts Für Vorderasiatische Archäologie Der Freien Universität Berlin Und Des Vorderasiatischen Museums Der Staatlichen Museen Zu Berlin Vom 21. Juli Bis 23. Juli 2011 Im Pergamonmuseum*, edited by Dominik Bonatz and Lutz Martin, 67–80. Schriften Der Max Freiherr von Oppenheim-Stiftung 18. Wiesbaden: Harrassowitz.

———. 2015. 'Waste Management in Early Urban Southern Mesopotamia'. In *Sanitation, Latrines and Intestinal Parasites in Past Populations*, edited by Piers D. Mitchell. Farnham/Burlington: Ashgate.

McMahon, Augusta, et al. 2011. 'Late Chalcolithic Mass Graves at Tell Brak, Syria, and Violent Conflict during the Growth of Early City-States'. *Journal of Field Archaeology* 36 (3): 201–20.

Menosky, Joe, and Philip LaZebnik. 1991. 'Darmok'. *Star Trek: The Next Generation* Season 5 (Episode 2).

Michalowski, Piotr. 1989. *The Lamentation over the Destruction of Sumer and Ur*. Winona Lake: Eisenbrauns.

———. 2008. 'The Mortal Kings of Ur: A Short Century of Divine Rule in Ancient Mesopotamia'. In *Religion and Power: Divine Kingship in the Ancient World and Beyond*, edited by Nicole Brisch, 33–45. OIS 4. Chicago: The Oriental Institute of the University of Chicago.

Michel, Cécile. 2016. 'Estimating an Old Assyrian Household Textile Production with the Help of Experimental Archaeology: Feasibility and Limitations'. In *Traditional Textile Craft – an Intangible Cultural Heritage? Workshop Amman, Jordan, March 2014*, edited by Camilla Ebert et al., 126–36. Copenhagen: Centre for Textile Research, University of Copenhagen.

———. 2020a. *Women of Assur and Kanesh: Texts from the Archives of Assyrian Merchants*. Vol. 42. Writings from the Ancient World. Atlanta: SBL Press.

———. 2020b. 'Wool Trade in Upper Mesopotamia and Syria According to Old Babylonian and Old Assyrian Texts'. In *Wool Economy in the Ancient Near East and The Aegean: From the Beginnings of Sheep*

Husbandry to Institutional Textile Industry, edited by Catherine Breniquet and Cécile Michel, 232–54. Oxford/Philadelphia: Oxbow Books.

Middeke-Conlin, Robert. 2023. *Knowledge, Literacy, and Elementary Education in the Old Babylonian Period*. Cham: SpringerBriefs in the History of Science and Technology.

Mikhail, Dunya. 2014. *The Iraqi Nights*. Translated by Kareem James Abu-Zeid. New York: New Directions.

Millerman, Alison Jean. 2015. 'The "Spinning of Ur": How Sir Leonard Woolley, James R. Ogden and the British Museum Interpreted and Represented the Past to Generate Funding for the Excavation of Ur in the 1920's and 1930's'. PhD Dissertation, University of Manchester.

Mirelman, Sam. 2010. 'The Gala Musician Dada and the Si-Im Instrument'. *Nouvelles Assyriologiques Brèves et Utilitaires* 2010 (2): 40–41.

Molina, Manuel, and Marcos Such-Gutiérrez. 2004. 'On Terms for Cutting Plants and Noses in Ancient Sumer'. *Journal of Near Eastern Studies* 63 (1): 1–16.

Monroe, M. Willis. 2022. 'Astronomical and Astrological Diagrams from Cuneiform Sources'. *Journal for the History of Astronomy* 53 (3): 338–61.

Moorey, P.R.S. 1964. 'The "Plano-Convex Building" at Kish and Early Mesopotamian Palaces'. *Iraq* 26 (2): 83–98.

———. 1978. *Kish Excavations, 1923–1933*. Oxford: Clarendon Press.

Nett, Seraina. 2023. 'The Office and Responsibilities of the En Priestess of Nanna'. In *Women and Religion in the Ancient Near East and Asia*, edited by Nicole Maria Brisch and Fumi Karahashi, 93–120. Studies in Ancient Near Eastern Records 30. Berlin/Boston: De Gruyter.

Nissen, Hans J. 2019. 'The Invention and Early Uses of Writing in Mesopotamia'. In *Uruk: First City of the Ancient World*, edited by Nicola Crüsemann et al., 149–53. Los Angeles: The J. Paul Getty Museum.

Nissen, Hans J., et al. 1993. *Archaic Bookkeeping: Early Writing and Techniques of Economic Administration in the Ancient Near East*. Chicago/London: The University of Chicago Press.

Notizia, Palmiro. 2020. 'Wealth and Status in 3rd Millennium Babylonia: The Household Inventory RTC 304 and the Career of Lugal-irida,

Superintendent of Weavers'. In *Working at Home in the Ancient Near East: New Insights and Avenues of Research*, edited by Juliette Was and Palmiro Notizia, 83–106. Archaeopress Ancient Near Eastern Archaeology 7. Oxford: Archaeopress.

Novotny, Jamie, and Joshua Jeffers, 2018. *The Royal Inscriptions of Ashurbanipal (668–631 BC), Aššur-Etel-Ilāni (630–627 BC), and Sîn-Šarra-Iškun (626–612 BC), Kings of Assyria, Part 1.* Vol. 5/1. The Royal Inscriptions of the Neo-Assyrian Period. Winona Lake: Eisenbrauns.

Oates, David. 1990. 'Innovations in Mud-Brick: Decorative and Structural Techniques in Ancient Mesopotamia'. *World Archaeology* 21 (3): 388–406.

Oates, David, and Joan Oates. 1989. 'Akkadian Buildings at Tell Brak'. *Iraq* 51:193–211.

Online Corpus of the Inscriptions of Ancient North Arabia. 2013. Oxford: The Khalili Research Centre for the Art and Material Culture of the Middle East. http://krc.orient.ox.ac.uk/ociana/

Oshima, Takayoshi. 2012. 'Another Attempt at Two Kassite Royal Inscriptions: The Agum-Kakrime Inscription and the Inscription of Kurigalzu the Son of Kadashmanharbe'. In *Babel Und Bibel*, edited by Leonid E. Kogan et al., 6:225–68. Winona Lake: Eisenbrauns for The Russian State University for the Humanities.

Ossendrijver, Mathieu. 2016. 'Ancient Babylonian Astronomers Calculated Jupiter's Position from the Area under a Time-Velocity Graph'. *Science* 351 (6272): 482–4.

Parpola, Simo. 1987. *The Correspondence of Sargon II, Part I: Letters from Assyria and the West.* Vol. 1. State Archives of Assyria. Helsinki: Helsinki University Press.

———. 1993. *Letters from Assyrian and Babylonian Scholars.* Vol. 10. State Archives of Assyria. Winona Lake: Eisenbrauns.

———. 1997. *Assyrian Prophecies.* Vol. 8. State Archives of Assyria. Helsinki: Helsinki University Press.

Paulus, S. 2014. *Die Babylonischen Kudurru-Inschriften von Der Kassitischen Bis Zur Frühneuba-Bylonischen Zeit. Untersucht Unter Besonderer Berücksichtigung Gesellschafts Und Rechtshistorischer Fragestellungen.* Vol. 51. Alter Orient Und Altes Testament. Münster: Ugarit-Verlag.

Petersen, Jeremiah. 2015. 'Examenstext A: Composite Translation and

Line Bibliography'. In *Cuneiform Digital Library Initiative (CDLI)*. https://cdli.mpiwg-berlin.mpg.de/dl/pdf/P481748.pdf

Peterson, Jeremiah, ed. 2014. 'Bilinguals in Late Mesopotamian Scholarship, K. 5688'. In *The Open Richly Annotated Cuneiform Corpus*. http://oracc.org/blms/P396094

———. 2016. 'The Literary Corpus of the Old Babylonian Larsa Dynasties: New Texts, New Readings, and Commentary'. In *Studia Mesopotamica*, edited by Manfried Dietrich et al., 3:1–89. Ugarit-Verlag.

Pickworth, Diana. 2005. 'Excavations at Nineveh: The Halzi Gate'. *Iraq* 67 (1): 295–316.

Porter, Anne, et al. 2021. '"Their Corpses Will Reach the Base of Heaven": A Third-Millennium BC War Memorial in Northern Mesopotamia?' *Antiquity* 95 (382): 900–918.

Postgate, J.N. 1992. *Early Mesopotamia: Society and Economy at the Dawn of History*. London/New York: Routledge.

Powell, M.A. 1984. 'Late-Babylonian Surface Mensuration'. *Archiv Für Orientforschung* 31: 32–66.

Prest, David. 2014. 'Royal Archive Documents Revealed at Windsor Castle'. *BBC News*, 16 May 2014. https://www.bbc.co.uk/news/uk-27426863

Proust, Christine. 2019. 'A Mathematical Collection Found in the "House of the Āšipus". The Art of Metrology in Achaemenid Uruk'. In *Scholars and Scholarship in Late Babylonian Uruk*, edited by Christine Proust and John Steele, 2:89–146. Why the Sciences of the Ancient World Matter. Cham: Springer Nature.

Proust, Christine, and John Steele. 2019. 'Introduction: Scholars, Scholarly Archives and the Practice of Scholarship in Late Babylonian Uruk'. In *Scholars and Scholarship in Late Babylonian Uruk*, edited by Christine Proust and John Steele, 2:1–52. Why the Sciences of the Ancient World Matter. Cham: Springer Nature.

Radner, Karen. 2011. 'Royal Decision-Making: Kings, Magnates, and Scholars'. In *The Oxford Handbook of Cuneiform Culture*, edited by Karen Radner and Eleanor Robson, 358–79. Oxford: Oxford University Press.

———. 2014. 'An Imperial Communication Network: The State Correspondence of the Neo-Assyrian Empire'. In *State Correspondence in the Ancient World: From New Kingdom Egypt to the Roman Empire*, edited by Karen Radner, 64–93. Oxford: Oxford University Press.

Reid, J.N. 2014. 'Slavery in Early Mesopotamia from Late Uruk until the Fall of Babylon in the *Longue Durée*'. DPhil thesis, Oxford: University of Oxford.

———. 2015. 'Runaways and Fugitive-Catchers during the Third Dynasty of Ur'. *Journal of the Economic and Social History of the Orient* 58: 576–605.

———. 2020. 'Prisoners of War: Collated Edition of TCL 5, 6039'. *NABU* 4: 215–18.

Reiner, Erica, and David Pingree. 1998. *Babylonian Planetary Omens: Part Three*. Vol. 11. Cuneiform Monographs. Groningen: Styx.

Renn, Jürgen. 2019. 'Learning from Kushim about the Origins of Writing and Farming'. In *Culture and Cognition: Essays in Honor of Peter Damerow*, edited by Jürgen Renn and Matthias Schemmel, 11–28. Max Planck Research Library for the History and Development of Knowledge Proceedings 11. Berlin: Max Planck Institute for the History of Science.

Richardson, Seth. 2002. 'Ewe Should Be So Lucky: Extispicy Reports and Everyday Life'. In *Mining the Archives: Festschrift for Christopher Walker on the Occasion of His 60th Birthday, 4 October 2002*, edited by Cornelia Wunsch. Dresden: Islet.

Robson, Eleanor. 2001. 'The Tablet House: A scribal school in old Babylonian Nippur', *Revue d'assyriologie et d'archéologie orientale* 93: 39 -66.

———. 2008. *Mathematics in Ancient Iraq: A Social History*. Princeton/Oxford: Princeton University Press.

———. 2019. *Ancient Knowledge Networks: A Social Geography of Cuneiform Scholarship in First-Millennium Assyria and Babylonia*. London: UCL Press.

Ross, Jennifer C. 2014. 'Art's Role in the Origins of Writing: The Seal-Carver, the Scribe, and the Earliest Lexical Texts'. In *Critical Approaches to Ancient Near Eastern Art*, edited by Brian A. Brown and Marian H. Feldman, 295–317. Boston/Berlin: De Gruyter.

Roth, Martha T. 1997. *Law Collections from Mesopotamia and Asia Minor*. Second Edition. Vol. 6. SBL Writings from the Ancient World Series. Atlanta: Scholars Press.

Russell, John Malcolm. 1999. *The Writing on the Wall: Studies in the*

Architectural Context of Late Assyrian Palace Inscriptions. Mesopotamian Civilisations 9. Winona Lake: Eisenbrauns.

Rutz, Matthew T. 2016. 'Astral Knowledge in an International Age: Transmission of the Cuneiform Tradition, ca. 1500–1000 B.C.' In *The Circulation of Astronomical Knowledge in the Ancient Near East*, edited by John M. Steele, 18–54. Leiden/Boston: Brill.

Sachs, A. 1952. 'Babylonian Horoscopes'. *Journal of Cuneiform Studies* 6 (2): 49–75.

Sachs, Abraham J. 1996. *Astronomical Diaries and Related Texts from Babylonia*. Edited by Hermann Hunger. Vol. 3. Wien: Verlag der Österreichischen Akademie der Wissenschaften.

Sachs, Abraham J., and Hermann Hunger. 1988. *Astronomical Diaries and Related Texts from Babylonia*. Vol. 1. Wien: Verlag der Österreichischen Akademie der Wissenschaften.

Sanders, Seth L. 2019. 'Hammurabi, King of the Dead'. *Sethlsanders* (blog). 14 November 2019. https://sethlsanders.wordpress.com/2019/11/14/hammurapi-king-of-the-dead/

Sasson, Jack M. 2015. *From the Mari Archives: An Anthology of Old Babylonian Letters*. Winona Lake: Eisenbrauns.

Sauvage, Martin. 2020. 'Mathematical Computations in the Management of Public Construction Work in Mesopotamia (End of the Third and Beginning of the Second Millennium BCE)'. In *Mathematics, Administrative and Economic Activities in Ancient Worlds*, edited by Cécile Michel and Karine Chemla, 5:201–37. Why the Sciences of the Ancient World Matter. Cham: Springer Nature.

Schaudig, Hanspeter. 2010. 'The Restoration of Temples in the Neo- and Late Babylonian Periods: A Royal Prerogative as the Setting for Political Argument'. In *From the Foundations to the Crenellations: Essays on Temple Building in the Ancient Near East and Hebrew Bible*, edited by Mark J. Boda and Jamie Novotny, 141–64. Alter Orient Und Altes Testament 366. Münster: Ugarit-Verlag.

Schmandt-Besserat, Denise. 1992. *Before Writing: From Counting to Cuneiform*. Vol. 1. Austin: The University of Texas Press.

Schneider, Bernard. 2022. 'Nippur: City of Enlil and Ninurta'. In *Naming and Mapping the Gods in the Ancient Mediterranean:*

Spaces, Mobilities, Imaginaries, 1:745–62. Berlin/Boston: De Gruyter.

Schwartz, Glenn M., et al. 'A Third-Millennium B.C. Elite Mortuary Complex at Umm El-Marra, Syria: 2002 and 2004 Excavations'. *American Journal of Archaeology* 110 (4): 603–41.

Schwartzstein. 2015. 'Iraq's Famed Marshes Are Disappearing – Again'. *National Geographic*, July 2015. https://www.nationalgeographic.com /science/article/150709-iraq-marsh-arabs-middle-east-water-environment-world

Scurlock, JoAnn. 2014. *Sourcebook for Ancient Mesopotamian Medicine*. Vol. 36. Writings from the Ancient World. Atlanta: SBL Press.

Selz, Gebhard J., et al. 2017. 'The Question of Sumerian "Determinatives"'. *Lingua Aegyptia – Journal of Egyptian Language Studies* 25:281–344.

Shepperson, Mary. 2018. 'Sunlight and Shade in the First Cities – A Sensory Archaeology of Early Iraq'. *The Ancient Near East Today* (blog). November 2018. https://www.asor.org/anetoday/2017/08/sunlight-shade

Slanski, Kathryn E. 2003. *The Babylonian Entitlement* narûs *(*kudurrus*): A Study in Their Form and Function*. Vol. 9. ASOR Books. Boston: American Schools of Oriental Research.

Snell, Daniel C. 1974. 'The Mari Livers and the Omen Tradition'. *Journal of the Ancient Near East Society* 6: 117–23.

Steele, John M. 2011. 'Making Sense of Time: Observational and Theoretical Calendars'. In *The Oxford Handbook of Cuneiform Culture*, edited by Karen Radner and Eleanor Robson, 470–85. Oxford: Oxford University Press.

———. 2018. 'The Development of the Babylonian Zodiac: Some Preliminary Observations'. *Mediterranean Archaeology and Archaeometry* 18 (4): 97–105.

———. 2019. 'The Early History of the Astronomical Diaries'. In *Keeping Watch in Babylon: The Astronomical Diaries in Context*, edited by Johannes Haubold et al., 100:19–52. Culture and History of the Ancient Near East. Leiden/Boston: Brill.

Steele, John, and Srishti Ganguli. 2022. 'Babylonian records of transient astronomical phenomena', *Astronomische Nachrichten* 343:6–7, e20220031.

Steinkeller, P. 1999. 'On Rulers, Priests, and Sacred Marriage: Tracing the Evolution of Early Sumerian Kingship'. In *Priests and Officials in the Ancient Near East. Papers of the Second Colloquium on the Ancient Near East — The City and Its Life Held at the Middle Eastern Culture Center in Japan (Mitaka, Tokyo)*, edited by K. Watanabe, 103–37. Heidelberg: Universitätsverlag C. Winter.

Stol, Marten. 2000. *Birth in Babylonia and the Bible: Its Mediterranean Setting*. Vol. 14. Cuneiform Monographs. Groningen: Styx.

———. 2012. 'Bitumen in Ancient Mesopotamia: The Textual Evidence'. *Bibliotheca Orientalis* 69 (1–2): 48–60.

Stone, Elizabeth. 1981. 'Texts, Architecture and Ethnographic Analogy: Patterns of Residence in Old Babylonian Nippur'. *Iraq* 43 (1): 19–33.

Stronk, Jan. 2017. *Semiramis' Legacy: The History of Persia According to Diodorus of Sicily*. Edinburgh: Edinburgh University Press.

Svärd, Saana. 2016. 'Neo-Assyrian Elite Women'. In *Women in Antiquity: Real Women across the Ancient World*, edited by Stephanie Lynn Budin and Jean Macintosh Turfa, 126–37. London/New York: Routledge.

Taylor, Jonathan. 2021. 'Sîn City: New Light from Old Excavations at Ur'. In *Ur in the Twenty-First Century CE: Proceedings of the 62nd Rencontre Assyriologique Internationale at Philadelphia, July 11–15, 2016*, edited by Grant Frame et al,. 35–48. University Park, PA: Penn State University Press.

Taylor, Jonathan, and Markham Geller. n.d. 'The Nineveh Medical Project'. In *The Open Richly Annotated Cuneiform Corpus*. http://oracc.ub.uni-muenchen.de/asbp/ninmed/index.html

Tolini, Gauthier. 2013. 'The Economic Activities of Isḫunnatu, a Slave Woman of the Egibi Family (Sixth Century BC)'. *REFEMA – The Economic Role of Women in the Public Sphere in Mesopotamia*. http://refema.hypotheses.org/766

Touillon-Ricci, Mathilde. 2018. 'Trade and Contraband in Ancient Assyria'. *The British Museum Blog* (blog). 2 April 2018. https://www.britishmuseum.org/blog/trade-and-contraband-ancient-assyria

Tsouparopoulou, Christina. 2014. 'Hidden Messages under the Temple: Foundation Deposits and the Restricted Presence of Writing in 3rd Millennium BCE Mesopotamia'. In *Verborgen, Unsichtbar, Unlesbar*

– *Zur Problematik Restringierter Schriftpräsenz*, edited by Tobias Frese et al., 2:17–31. Materiale Textkulturen. Berlin/Boston: De Gruyter.

———. 2016. 'Deconstructing Textuality, Reconstructing Materiality'. In *Materiality of Early Writing in Early Mesopotamia*, edited by Thomas E. Balke and Christina Tsouparopoulou, 257–76. Materiale Textkulturen 13. Berlin/Boston: De Gruyter.

Tsouparopoulou, Christina, and Laerke Recht. 2021. 'Dogs and Equids in War in Third Millennium BC Mesopotamia'. In *Fierce Lions, Angry Mice and Fat-Tailed Sheep: Animal Encounters in the Ancient Near East*, edited by Laerke Recht and Christina Tsouparopoulou, 279–89. Cambridge: McDonald Institute for Archaeological Research.

Tuplin, Christopher. 2019. 'Logging History in Achaemenid, Hellenistic and Parthian Babylonia: Historical Entries in Dated Astronomical Diaries'. In *Keeping Watch in Babylon: The Astronomical Diaries in Context*, edited by Johannes Haubold et al., 100:79–119. Culture and History of the Ancient Near East. Leiden/Boston: Brill.

Ur, Jason. 2013. 'Patterns of Settlement in Sumer and Akkad'. In *The Sumerian World*, edited by Harriet Crawford, 131–55. Abingdon/New York: Routledge.

Van De Mieroop, Marc. 1989. 'Women in the Economy of Sumer'. In *Women's Earliest Records from Ancient Egypt and Western Asia: Proceedings of the Conference on Women in the Ancient Near East, Brown University, Providence, Rhode Island November 5–7, 1987*, edited by Barbara S. Lesko, 53–66. Atlanta: Scholars Press.

———. 2015. *Philosophy before the Greeks: The Pursuit of Truth in Ancient Babylonia*. Princeton: Princeton University Press.

Vanstiphout, Herman L.J. 2003. *Epics of Sumerian Kings: The Matter of Aratta*. Vol. 20. Writings from the Ancient World. Atlanta: Society of Biblical Literature.

Vidale, Massimo. 2011. 'PG 1237, Royal Cemetery of Ur: Patterns in Death'. *Cambridge Archaeological Journal* 21 (3): 427–51.

Volpi, Luca. 2020. 'The Royal Cemetery at Ur During the Second Half of the Third Millennium B.C.: Pottery Analysis through the Use of Archival Data, a Case Study'. *Iraq* 82:227–57.

Watai, Yoko. 2016. 'Economic Activities of Women in 1st Millennium Babylonia'. In *The Role of Women in Work and Society in the Ancient*

Near East, edited by Brigitte Lion and Cécile Michel, 13:494–511. Studies in Ancient Near Eastern Records. Berlin/Boston: De Gruyter.

Weadock, Penelope N. 1975. 'The Giparu at Ur'. *Iraq* 37 (2): 101–28.

Weadock, Penelope Nesta. 1958. 'The Giparu at Ur: A Study of the Archaeological Remains and Related Textual Material'. PhD Dissertation, Chicago: University of Chicago.

Weiershäuser, Frauke, and Jamie Novotny. 2020. *The Royal Inscriptions of Amēl-Marduk (561–560 BC), Neriglissar (559–556 BC), and Nabonidus (555–539 BC), Kings of Babylon.* Vol. 2. The Royal Inscriptions of the Neo-Babylonian Empire. University Park, PA: Eisenbrauns.

Westbrook, Raymond. 1995. 'Slave and Master in Ancient Near Eastern Law'. *Chicago-Kent Law Review* 70:1631–76.

Westenholz, Joan Goodnick. 1989. 'Enheduanna, En-Priestess, Hen of Nanna, Spouse of Nanna'. In *DUMU E2-DUB-BA-A: Studies in Honor of Åke Sjöberg*, edited by Hermann Behrens et al., 539–56. Philadelphia: The University Museum.

Winter, Irene J. 1993. '"Seat of Kingship"/"Wonder to Behold": The Palace as Construct in the Ancient Near East'. *Ars Orientalis* 23:27–55.

———. 2010. *On Art in the Ancient Near East.* Vol. 2. Leiden/Boston: Brill.

Woolley, C. Leonard. 1925. 'The Excavations at Ur, 1924–1925'. *The Antiquaries Journal* 5 (4): 347–402.

———. 1929. *Ur of the Chaldees: A Record of Seven Years of Excavation.* [London]: Ernest Benn Limited.

———. 1934. *Ur Excavations: The Royal Cemetery, A Report on the Predynastic and Sargonid Graves Excavated between 1926 and 1931.* Vol. 2. Ur Excavations. London: The British Museum.

———. 1962. *Ur Excavations: The Neo-Babylonian and Persian Periods.* Vol. 9. Ur Excavations. London: The Trustees of the British Museum.

Woolley, C. Leonard, and Max Mallowan. 1976. *Ur Excavations: The Old Babylonian Period.* Vol. 7. Ur Excavations. London: British Museum Publications Limited.

Wunsch, Cornelia. 1997. 'Und Die Richter Berieten . . . Streitfalle in Babylon Aus Der Zeit Neriglissars Und Nabonids'. *Archiv Für Orientforschung* 44/45:59–100.

———. 2003. 'Women's Property and the Law of Inheritance in the Neo-Babylonian Period'. In *Women and Property in Ancient Near Eastern and Mediterranean Societies*, edited by D. Lyons and Raymond Westbrook. Cambridge: Harvard University Center for Hellenic Studies. https://classics-at.chs.harvard.edu/wp-content/uploads/2021/05/ca1.2-wunsch.pdf

Zaia, Shana. 2019. 'My Brother's Keeper: Assurbanipal versus Šamaš-Šuma-Ukīn'. *Journal of Ancient Near Eastern History* 6 (1): 19–52.

———. 2021. 'Divine Foundations: Religion and Assyrian Capital Cities'. In *As Above, So Below: Religion and Geography*, edited by Gina Konstantopoulos and Shana Zaia. University Park, PA: Eisenbrauns.

Zaina, Federico. 2015. 'Craft, Administration, and Power in Early Dynastic Mesopotamian Public Buildings: Recovering the Plano-Convex Building at Kish, Iraq'. *Paléorient* 41 (1): 177–97.

Zettler, Richard. 1997. 'Nippur'. In *The Oxford Encyclopaedia of Archaeology in the Near East*, edited by Eric M. Myers, 4:148–52. Oxford: Oxford University Press.

———. 2021. 'Woolley's Excavations at Ur: New Perspectives from Artifact Inventories, Field Records, and Archival Documentation'. In *Ur in the Twenty-First Century CE: Proceedings of the 62nd Rencontre Assyriologique Internationale at Philadelphia, July 11–15, 2016*, edited by Grant Frame et al, 7–34. University Park, PA: Penn State University Press.

Zettler, Richard, and Paul C. Zimmerman. 2021. 'Two Tombs or Three? PG 789 and PG 800 Again!' In *From Sherds to Landscapes: Studies on the Ancient Near East in Honor of McGuire Gibson*, edited by Mark Altaweel and Carrie Hritz, 71:283–96. Studies in Ancient Oriental Civilization. Chicago: The Oriental Institute of the University of Chicago.

Zimmerman, Lynn-Salammbô. 2023. 'Wooden Wax-Covered Writing Boards as Vorlage for Kudurru Inscriptions in the Middle Babylonian Period'. *Journal of Ancient Near Eastern History* 10 (1): 53–106.

Zólyomi, Gábor, et al. 2008. 'The Electronic Text Corpus of Sumerian Royal Inscriptions'. In *The Openly Richly Annotated Cuneiform Corpus*. http://oracc.museum.upenn.edu/etcsri/index.html

Notes

Introduction: Mesopotamia Matters

1 C. Leonard Woolley, 1929, *Ur of the Chaldees*, pp. 202–4.

2 Emily Hammer, 2019, 'The City and Landscape of Ur', p. 173.

3 The horoscope for the little boy begins in rather bleak terms, describing a life of financial ruin and a philandering wife 'whom people will seduce in his presence', but at the age of thirty-six, things take a turn for the better. See A. Sachs, 1952, 'Babylonian Horoscopes', pp. 57–8.

4 This loose and absolutely lovely translation comes from Anonymous, 'Two Babylonian Lullabies', *Slightly Alive Translations* (blog), 3 December 2015, https://mostlydeadlanguages.tumblr.com/post/134484418018/two-babylonian-lullabies-bm-122691-and-oect-11. For a more literal translation and a discussion of language and context, see Walter Farber, 1990, 'Magic at the Cradle', p. 140.

5 Jeremiah Peterson, 2015, 'Examenstext A', *Cuneiform Digital Library Initiative (CDLI)*.

6 For a recent interpretation of this map, see Paul Delnero, 2018, 'A Land with No Borders'.

1: An Ancient Museum and the History of History

1 C. Leonard Woolley, 1929, *Ur of the Chaldees*, p. 203.

2 C. Leonard Woolley, 1962, *Ur Excavations*, vol. 9, p. 16.

3 C. Leonard Woolley, 1929, *Ur of the Chaldees*, p. 203.

4 See Alison Jean Millerman, 2015, *The 'Spinning of Ur'*.

5 Richard Zettler, 2021, 'Woolley's Excavations at Ur', p. 7. For a history of surveys and excavations before the one led by Woolley, sponsored by the University of Pennsylvania Museum of Archaeology and the British Museum, see Jonathan Taylor, 2021, 'Sîn-City'.

6 Richard Zettler, 2021, 'Woolley's Excavations at Ur', p. 7.

7 Although often remembered as simply Woolley's wife, Katharine Woolley actually joined the excavation as a field assistant in 1925 after her illustration skills attracted the attention of the team. At the time, she still carried her dead husband's last name, Keeling. She only married Woolley to remain at the site and continue her work, as the presence of an unmarried woman had apparently ruffled some feathers in London. In a letter dated 8 July 1926, Gordon, one of the excavation's distant overseers, wrote to Woolley that 'the presence of a lone woman with four men in camp makes a more interesting figure for some of them than the outline of the ziggurats'. Woolley's multi-page response made clear that Mrs Keeling's work was integral to the excavation, and that she was hurt to find herself the subject of gossip almost 3,000 miles away in London. 'You know,' Woolley adds with a hint of annoyance, 'it's quite difficult to believe that such gossip can exist when one's in this atmosphere of scientific work, with lots of women . . . when everyone takes the circumstances of the work as a matter of course and is keenly interested in what she is doing.' Katharine played a critical role in digging up, recording, and publishing finds from Ur, and in fundraising for the excavations. See Robert H. Dyson, 1977, 'Archival Glimpses of the Ur Expedition in the Years 1920–1926'.

8 C. Leonard Woolley, 1934, *Ur Excavations*, vol. 2, p. 8.

9 The location of this find is given as 'ES 7' in his field notes, 'Room ES 2' in the initial archaeological report published in the *Antiquaries Journal* in October 1925 ('The Excavations at Ur', p. 383), and 'Room ES 4' in the final and official archaeological report published almost 40 years later (*Ur Excavations*, vol. 9, p. 17). We should keep in mind that over the course of excavations, the internal layout of a building may also change according to new information unearthed, like part of a wall or courtyard. Such shifting borders within a building can make pinpointing an object's findspot even more confusing.

10 Richard Zettler, 2021, 'Woolley's Excavations at Ur', p. 7.

11 Or, at least, the sources from this era are in both Akkadian and Sumerian, and those who wrote things down would have known both languages.

12 Barring a brief period in the seventh century BCE of expansion and conquest by their Assyrian neighbours to the north.

13 Piotr Michalowski, 1989, *The Lamentation over the Destruction of Sumer and Ur*, p. 61.

14 Ibid., p. 59.

15 Frauke Weiershäuser and Jamie Novotny, 2020, *The Royal Inscriptions of Amēl-Marduk (561–560 BC), Neriglissar (559–556 BC), and Nabonidus (555–539 BC), Kings of Babylon*, p. 168.

16 Seraina Nett, 2023, 'The Office and Responsibilities of the En Priestess of Nanna', p. 103.

17 Douglas Frayne, 1990, *Old Babylonian Period (2003–1595 BC)*, pp. 299–301.

18 As well as tapping into his image as the harbinger of Assyria's downfall. See Paul-Alain Beaulieu, 2003, 'Nabopolassar and the Antiquity of Babylon'.

19 Roció Da Riva, 2008, *The Neo-Babylonian Royal Inscriptions*, p. 120. Instead of altering the name on this 'ancient foundation document', Nebuchadnezzar II allegedly inserted his 'written name' alongside it and laid the temple's foundations anew atop the ancient clay or stone foundation tablet. Not exactly good archaeological practice today, but at the time it forged a literal connection to a distant royal ancestor.

20 See Paul-Alain Beaulieu, 2003, 'Nabopolassar and the Antiquity of Babylon', pp. 5–6.

2: The Clay Drum

1 Robert K. Englund et al., 1991, *The Proto-Cuneiform Texts from Jemdet Nasr*, Text 184. Technically, the text is an account of objects counted in the sexagesimal system, but our limited understanding of the signs make it hard to know anything more about the specific reason for making this record. I'm grateful to Dr Jacob L. Dahl for explaining the otherwise impenetrable signs to me.

2 'Copy of a baked brick from the debris of Ur,' reads the first line of the Babylonian column, which goes on to describe the circumstances of the brick's discovery – in other words, its archaeological context. Readers are told that 'Sîn-balassu-iqbi, viceroy of Ur, had discovered while looking for the groundplan of the Egishnugal', the name given to the entire temple complex. The final lines of the column give the scribe's name and reason for making the record: 'Nabû-shuma-iddin, son of Iddin-Papsukkal, the lamentation priest of the god Sîn, saw it and wrote it down for display.' The words 'for display' make us wonder if the original, ancient brick had an audience. Was it actually on display, rather than tucked away in a storeroom? See Douglas R. Frayne, 1997, *The Ur III Period (2112–2004 BC)*, pp. 256–7. See also H. Schaudig, 2010, 'The Restoration of Temples in the Neo- and Late Babylonian Periods'.

3 Hans J. Nissen et al., 1993, *Archaic Bookkeeping*, p. 36. Kushim could have been the name of a person, of an institution, or a title. The reading of the two signs, *ku* and *shim*, that comprise this name are also impossible to confirm, but based on the context of its use and later cuneiform sign readings, it is plausible to suggest that this name refers to an individual and may have been pronounced this way.

4 Ibid.

5 See Robert K. Englund, 1998, 'Texts from the Late Uruk Period', p. 182, and Jürgen Renn, 2019, 'Learning from Kushim about the Origins of Writing and Farming', p. 12.

6 J.N. Postgate, 1994, *Early Mesopotamia,* pp. 109–54; cf. Michael Jursa, 2011, 'Cuneiform Writing in Neo-Babylonian Temple Communities', p. 186.

7 See Robert K. Englund, 2011, 'Accounting in Proto-Cuneiform', and Denise Schmandt-Besserat, 1992, *Before Writing,* vol. 1. See also Lucy E. Bennison-Chapman, 2018, 'Reconsidering "Tokens"'.

8 Hans J. Nissen et al., 1993, *Archaic Bookkeeping*, pp. 12–13.

9 Ibid., pp. 25–9.

10 Jeremy A. Black et al. (eds), 1998–, 'Hymn to Nisaba A', *The Electronic Text Corpus of Sumerian Literature*, https://etcsl.orinst.ox.ac.uk/section4/tr4161.htm. See also Lluís Feliu, 2010, 'A New Fragment of Nisaba A', p. 34.

11 Jennifer C. Ross, 2014, 'Art's Role in the Origins of Writing', p. 295.

12 Andrew George, 2003, *The Babylonian Gilgamesh Epic*, vol. 1, pp. 672–3.

13 This object is currently held in the collections of the British Museum with the identifier BM 116729.

14 This object is currently held in an anonymous private collection, documented in the online *Cuneiform Digital Library Initiative (CDLI)* with the identifier P539341.

15 R. Eichmann, 2019, 'Uruk's Early Monumental Architecture', p. 101.

16 Hans J. Nissen, 2019, 'The Invention and Early Uses of Writing in Mesopotamia', p. 149.

17 The Sumerian god Enki was later known as Ea (pronounced AY, like play, and UH, like love) in Babylonian traditions, where he is the somewhat mischievous god of wisdom and incantations. After learning of divine plans to create a storm to destroy humankind, Ea instructs a man named Atra-hasis, the name of the Uta-napishti figure in the older story, to abandon his home and build a boat. Because the gods had agreed not to divulge the plans for humanity's destruction to any mortal, Ea had to pretend to talk to a reed wall while Atra-hasis simply overheard his words. 'Reed wall, observe all my words!' he called out before reciting detailed instructions to build the ark that would rescue humanity and other living things from total annihilation (W.G. Lambert and Alan R. Millard, 1969, *Atra-hasis*, p. 89). On metrology, see M.A. Powell, 1984, 'Late-Babylonian Surface Mensuration', and Christine Proust, 2019, 'A Mathematical Collection Found in the "House of the *āšipus*"', pp. 118–22.

18 Some of the forcibly displaced survivors escaped to nearby towns, and others fled to refugee camps in Iran. Neighbouring Iran, Turkey, and Syria built a dam at the headwaters of the Tigris and Euphrates, rendering waterflow unsteady and leaving the marshes' freshwater vulnerable to tidal saltwater from the Persian, or Arabian, Gulf. Pollution has clogged once life-giving waterways with rubbish, and climate change has further reduced water levels. See Ali Khadr, 2019, 'Iraq'. See also Peter Schwartzstein, July 2015, 'Iraq's Famed Marshes are Disappearing – Again'.

19 Donald P. Hansen, 2003, 'Art of the Early City States', p. 40.

20 In fact, the word for stylus in Sumerian was *gi-dubba*, which combines the words *gi*, 'reed', and *dub*, 'tablet' – in other words, a 'tablet reed' (although scribes may have also used wood and metal styluses).

21 This number is roughly according to today's count, but it may grow as we learn more.

22 Marc Van De Mieroop, 2015, *Philosophy before the Greeks*, p. 43.

23 Irving L. Finkel and Jonathan Taylor, 2015, *Cuneiform*, p. 6.

24 These are called 'determinatives'. For a recent look at these, see Gebhard J. Selz et al., 2017, 'The Question of Sumerian "Determinatives"'.

25 A masterpiece in explaining this use of analogy in the expansion and exploitation of the cuneiform writing system by scribes and scholars appears in a book on bilingual education in ancient Babylonia by C. Jay Crisostomo, in which he uses the English word 'deer' to generate a modern example. See C. Jay Crisostomo, 2019, *Translation as Scholarship*, p. 144, n92.

26 These objects are currently held in the collections of the Penn Museum with the identifiers CBS 10436 and N 2822, respectively.

27 Herman L J. Vanstiphout, 2003, *Epics of Sumerian Kings*, p. 49.

28 For a full translation of the myth, see Herman L.J. Vanstiphout, 2003, *Epics of Sumerian Kings*.

29 All excerpts are from Jeremy A. Black et al. (eds.), 1998–, 'Enki and Ninmah', *The Electronic Text Corpus of Sumerian Literature*.

30 On the decipherment of cuneiform, see Kevin Cathcart, 2011, 'The Earliest Contributions to the Decipherment of Sumerian and Akkadian'.

31 C. Leonard Woolley, 1934, *Ur of the Chaldees*, p. 204.

32 Frauke Weiershäuser and Jamie Novotny, 2020, *The Royal Inscriptions of Amēl-Marduk (561–560 BC), Nergilassar (559–556 BC), and Nabonidus (555–539 BC), Kings of Babylon*, p. 100.

33 Gerard Gertoux, 2021, 'Mesopotamian chronology over the period 2340–539 BCE through astronomically dated synchronisms and comparison with carbon-14 dating', p. 2 n5.

3: The Brick of Amar-Suen

1 Margaret van Ess, 2019, 'Observations on Construction Techniques in Uruk', p. 213.

2 See Stefano Anastasio, 2020, *Building between the Two Rivers*, pp. 25–34.

3 Ibid., p. 30.

4 David Oates, 1990, 'Innovations in mud-brick: decorative and structural techniques in ancient Mesopotamia', p. 388.

5 Troels Pank Arbøll et al., 2023, 'Revealing the secrets of a 2900-year-old clay brick, discovering a time capsule of ancient DNA'.

6 M. Stol, 2012, 'Bitumen in Ancient Mesopotamia', p. 48.

7 'Clay Bricks for the Ziggurat of Uruk (Iraq)', *Cultural Heritage News* (blog), 13 November 2018, https://www.culthernews.de/clay-bricks-for-the-ziggurat-of-uruk/

8 Following translation of Douglas Frayne, 1997, *Ur III Period (2112–2004 BC)*, p. 257.

9 Ibid., p. 256.

10 Tzvi Abusch and Daniel Schwemer, 2016, *Corpus of Mesopotamian Anti-Witchcraft Rituals*, vol. 2, p. 156.

11 As an example, a passage from a canonical series of incantations and rituals geared at protecting against Lamashtu's harm reads, 'Bitumen (*kupru*) from a boat, bitumen from the rudder, bitumen from an oar / bitumen from any other equipment of a boat, dirt from an embankment and a ford, / lard, fish train, hot bitumen (*qīru*), . . . donkey's hide, fullers paste, a soiled cloth, . . . lard from a white pig: (use as) ointment' (Walter Farber, 2014, *Lamaštu*, pp. 190–91). I am grateful to Dr Ulrike Steinert for this reference.

12 Tzvi Abusch and Daniel Schwemer, 2016, *Corpus of Mesopotamian Anti-Witchcraft Rituals*, vol. 2, p. 152.

13 Ibid., p. 265.

14 Although there is some debate among scholars over how to divide this period up according to subtle changes in the archaeological record, it is typically split into three time frames, with changes in pottery styles determining the dividing lines between the centuries: Early Dynastic I–II (2900–2700 BCE), Early Dynastic IIIa (2700–2500

BCE), and Early Dynastic IIIb (2500–2340 BCE). Previously, scholars included Early Dynastic II in this list, which has now been swallowed up in the period covered by Early Dynastic I because not enough difference seemed to separate the two to justify a label associated with a whole new era. A handful of scholars argue that the Early Dynastic period should be treated as a whole, while others continue to revise its internal chronological borders.

15 This is recorded for the year that Bur-Saggilê of Guzana was an official. The technical term for this type of list of officials, typical of the Assyrian empire, is an *eponym* list. It is mind-blowing to me that we can calculate the exact dates of such phenomena and map references in ancient texts onto them. Even more mind-blowing is that the methods used to make such calculations first appear in cuneiform sources of the first millennium BCE. We are, in essence, using ancient Mesopotamian methods to go back and date events from ancient Mesopotamia.

16 As a result of disagreement over dating, four possible chronologies are followed for these early periods: the High, Middle, Low, and Ultra-Low Chronology. The justifications for each pivot mainly on how to interpret early reports of astronomical phenomena recorded in non-astronomical texts, like omens. In this book, we use the 'Middle Chronology' following most Assyriologists. See T. de Jong, 2013, 'Astronomical Fine-Tuning of the Chronology of the Hammurabi Age', p. 147.

17 Or maybe not – many scholars disagree on where and when the wheel actually originated. On the potter's wheel in ancient Mesopotamia, see Johnny Baldi, 2021, 'How the Uruk Potters Used the Wheel'. On wheels and wheeled vehicles, see Maria Bondar, 2024, 'Prehistoric Innovations'.

18 See Stefan Burmeister et al., 2019, 'Some Notes on Pictograms Interpreted as Sledges and Wheeled Vehicles in the Archaic Texts from Uruk', p. 55.

19 See McGuire Gibson, 'The First Actual Stratigraphic Profile of the Y Trench', p. 78.

20 See, for example, Federico Zaina, 2015, 'Craft, administration, and power in Early Dynastic Mesopotamian public buildings'.

21 P.R.S. Moorey, 1978, *Kish Excavations, 1923–1933*, p. 59.

22 See P.R.S. Moorey, 1964, 'The "Plano-Convex Building" at Kish and Early Mesopotamian Palaces', p. 84. See also Irene J. Winter, 1993, '"Seat of Kingship"', pp. 28–29, and Stefano Anastasio, 2020, *Building between the Two Rivers*, p. 99.

23 Jason Ur, 2013, 'Patterns of Settlement in Sumer and Akkad', p. 131.

24 See recently Emily Hammer et al., 2022, 'The Structure and Hydrology of the Early Dynastic City of Lagash (Tell Al-Hiba) from Satellite and Aerial Images' and Emily Hammer, 2022, 'Multi-centric, Marsh-based Urbanism at the Early Mesopotamian City of Lagash (Tell al-Hiba, Iraq)'.

25 On Baghdad's architecture, see for example Rand Hazim Mahmood Agha, 2016, 'The role of intelligent systems in traditional courtyard houses in Baghdad, Iraq' : http://theses.ncl.ac.uk/jspui/handle/10443/4063

26 Mary Shepperson, 'Sunlight and Shade in the First Cities', *The Ancient Near East Today* (blog), August 2017. https://www.asor.org/anetoday/2017/08/sunlight-shade

27 Ibid.

28 C. Leonard Woolley and Max Mallowan, 1976, *Ur Excavations*, vol. 7, p. 22.

29 Simo Parpola, *Assyrian Prophecies*, Text 442.

30 See Simo Parpola, *The Correspondence of Sargon II*, Texts 236 and 235.

31 Douglas Frayne, *Sargonic and Gutian Periods*, pp. 121–2.

32 Christina Tsouparopoulou, 2021, 'Dogs and equids in war in third millennium BC Mesopotamia'.

33 Jeremy Black et al. (eds.), 1998–, 'Proverbs: collection 2+6', line 29, *The Electronic Text Corpus of Sumerian Literature*, https://etcsl.orinst.ox.ac.uk/proverbs/t.6.1.02.html; Jeremy Black et al. (eds.), 1998–, 'Proverbs: collection 5', lines 81–82 and line 110, *The Electronic Text Corpus of Sumerian Literature*, https://etcsl.orinst.ox.ac.uk/proverbs/t.6.1.05.html

34 The clay brick from the ziggurat of Ur-Nammu is now held in the collections of the British Museum with the identifier BM 137495. See Christina Tsouparopoulou, 2016, 'Deconstructing Textuality, Reconstructing Materiality', p. 270.

35 This brick names Ur-Nammu in the stamped inscription and is now held in the collections of the Penn Museum with the identifier CBS 16461.

4: The Statue of King Shulgi

1 See Changyu Liu, 2021, *The Ur III Administrative Texts of Puzrish-Dagan*; see also Martin Sauvage, 'Mathematical Computations in the Management of Public Construction Work in Mesopotamia', p. 203.
2 See Douglas Frayne, 1997, *Ur III Period (2112–2004 BC)*, pp. 92–110.
3 See P. Michalowski, 2012, 'The Mortal Kings of Ur', pp. 33–45.
4 Jeremy A. Black et al. (eds.), 1998–, 'A Praise Poem of Shulgi (Shulgi A): translation', *The Electronic Text Corpus of Sumerian Literature*, https://etcsl.orinst.ox.ac.uk/section2/tr24201.htm
5 Sam Mirelman, 'The gala musician Dada and the si-im instrument', pp. 40–41.
6 *Descent of Ishtar*, lines 4, and 8–9. For an open access translation, see 'CDLI Literary Descent of Ishtar (Composite) Artifact Entry', *Cuneiform Digital Library Initiative (CDLI)*, 2016. https://cdli.ucla.edu/P497322
7 'You will love him like a wife, caressing and embracing him', Gilgamesh's mother proclaims, and conversely, when Enkidu dies, Gilgamesh veils his face 'like a bride' (for these translations, see Andrew George, 2003, *The Babylonian Gilgamesh Epic*, p. 555 and p. 655). See Susan Ackerman, 2005, *When Heroes Love*.
8 *Star Trek: The Next Generation*, season 5, episode 2, 'Darmok', written by Joe Menosky and Philip LaZebnik, 30 September 1991.
9 All translations come from Andrew George, 2003, *The Babylonian Gilgamesh Epic*, pp. 702–25, especially pp. 707 and 709.
10 His name in this older version of the Flood story is Atra-hasis. See W.G. Lambert and Alan R. Millard, 1969, *Atra-hasis*, p. 93.
11 There are other ways kings may have tapped into this history. From other documents from the Early Dynastic period, we know that a number of city-states fell under the rulership of separate kings or governors, who all co-existed. But in the Sumerian King List, history

is presented in a very different way, as if the region had always been unified under one king. This fictional ideal that a single king ruled the region at any given time from a single city may have helped kings shore up their own legitimacy. 'If there has always ever only been a single king,' goes the logic, 'and I am king, then I must be legitimate.' That legitimacy tied into their own self-presentation and their compliance with the ideology of a good king. See for example Gianni Marchesi, 2010, 'The Sumerian King List and the Early History of Mesopotamia'.

12 Gianni Marchesi, 2010, 'The Sumerian King List and the Early History of Mesopotamia', p. 234.

13 The 5,000-year-old tablet excavated in Uruk is now in the Ashmolean Museum with the identifier Ashm 1926–583. See Robert K. Englund et al., 1991, *The Proto-Cuneiform Texts from Jemdet Nasr*, Text 2. I am grateful to Dr Jacob L. Dahl for explaining this difficult text to me. Any mistakes or misunderstandings are my own. See also Robert K. Englund, 1998, 'Texts from the Late Uruk Period'.

14 On the idea of kingship as the final step in the evolution of leaders as consorts of the goddesses who once dominated the pantheon, see Piotr Steinkeller, 1999, 'On Rulers, Priests, and Sacred Marriage'. For more general overviews of possible explanations for the rise of the idea of the king and of divine kingship, see Nicole Brisch, 2006, 'The Priestess and the King', pp. 161–164, and Piotr Michalowski, 2008, 'The Mortal Kings of Ur', pp. 33–34.

15 On the chronological range of burials, see recently Luca Volpi, 2020, 'The Royal Cemetery at Ur During the Second Half of the Third Millennium B.C.'.

16 In fact, the identity of many of the people buried in these sixteen graves remains an open question, but the label continues to be used.

17 For a relatively recent look at the Great Death Pit, the identity of the people buried in it, and the possible role of music in Sumerian funerary rituals, see Massimo Vidale, 2011, 'PG 1237, Royal Cemetery of Ur'.

18 Aubrey Baadsgaard et al., 2011, 'Human sacrifice and intentional corpse preservation in the Royal Cemetery of Ur', pp. 36–38.

19 Cited in William B. Hafford, 2015, 'Magnificent with Jewels', p. 88.

20 Ibid., pp. 97-99.

21 C. Leonard Woolley, 1934, *Ur Excavations*, vol. 2, p. 87.

22 Or Ku-Baba in some modern readings of her name.

23 Glenn Schwarz et al., 2006, 'A Third Millennium B.C. Elite Mortuary Complex at Umm el-Marra, Syria', p. 620 and p. 631 n115.

24 Herodotus, *The Histories*, translated by A.D. Godley, I.184.1.

25 See Jan Stronk, 2017, *Semiramis' Legacy*.

26 Saana Svärd, 2016, 'Neo-Assyrian Elite Women', p. 127.

27 The feat is recorded in a foot-tall stone obelisk. Shaped like a long, narrow tombstone, the grey stone is almost entirely covered in large cuneiform characters that describe the battle in brief. According to the narrative, Ushpilulume, king of the Kummuhites, 'caused Adad-nirari, king of Assyria, and Sammu-rāmat, the woman of the palace to cross the Euphrates'. The text then details the battle before describing that both mother and son erected the boundary stone to mark the victory. The wording suggests equal status between the two royal victors. As one of very few known examples of royal women associated with military action, the record is also unique. See A. Kirk Grayson, *Assyrian Rulers of the Early First Millennium BC (1114–859 BC)*, pp. 204–5.

28 Erle Leichty, 2011, *The Royal Inscriptions of Esarhaddon, King of Assyria (680–669 BC)*, p. 316.

29 Simo Parpola, *Letters from Assyrian and Babylonian Scholars*, Text 244. See Eckart Frahm, 2023, *Assyria*, pp. 237–240.

30 Martha T. Roth, 1997, *Law Collections from Mesopotamia and Asia Minor*, p. 16.

31 This figure comes from Zólyomi et al., 2008–, 'The Electronic Text Corpus of Sumerian Royal Inscriptions', which is part of the *Online Richly Annotated Cuneiform Corpus*, https://oracc.museum.upenn. edu//etcsri/index.html

32 Piotr Michalowski, 2008, 'The Mortal Kings of Ur'.

33 Douglas Frayne, 1997, *Ur III Period (2112–2004 BC)*, p. 141.

34 A. Kirk Grayson and Jamie Novotny, 2012, *The Royal Inscriptions of Sennacherib, King of Assyria (704–681 BC)*, pp. 48–55.

35 See Joshua Jeffers and Jamie Novotny, 2023, *The Royal Inscriptions of Ashurbanipal (668–631 BC), Aššur-Etel-Ilāni (630–627 BC), and Sîn -Šarra-Iškun (626–612 BC), Kings of Assyria, Part 2*, p. 323.

36 Eckart Frahm, 2011, 'Keeping Company with Men of Learning', pp. 508–32.

37 See Eleanor Robson, 2019, *Ancient Knowledge Networks*, pp. 12–23.

38 Grant Frame and Andrew George, 2005, 'The Royal Libraries of Nineveh', p. 269.

39 Andrew George, 2003, *The Babylonian Gilgamesh Epic*, pp. 526–7.

5: The School Tablets

1 Jeremy A. Black et al. (eds.), 1998–, 'Proverbs: collection 2+6', *The Electronic Text Corpus of Sumerian Literature*.

2 Ibid.

3 C. Leonard Woolley, 1929, *Ur of the Chaldees*, p. 202. Note that Woolley's initial excavation report published in 1925 in the *Antiquaries Journal* describes these tablets as being found in rooms 'ES 1' and 'ES 4', rather than a single room (C. Leonard Woolley, 1925, 'The Excavations at Ur, 1924–1925', p. 383). According to the much later final excavation reports, the tablets appeared in ES 3 (C. Leonard Woolley, 1962, *Ur Excavations*, vol. 9, p. 17). Whichever precise room in the palace made for their final resting place, Woolley came to associate them with the collection of antiquities and overall character of Ennigaldi-Nanna's dwelling.

4 C. Leonard Woolley, 1929, *Ur of the Chaldees*, p. 202.

5 C. Leonard Woolley, 1962, *Ur Excavations*, vol. 9, p. 17.

6 Although the card notes that the tablet was found in ES 7, its content is the only one that I can find that matches up to what is described in Woolley's memoir. Once again, we must contend with the understandable limits of his recall and the shortcomings of my archival skills. The excavation number for this fragment is U. 2815. See also Petra Gesche, 2000, *Schulunterricht in Babylonien im ersten Jahrtausend v. Chr.*, p. 666.

7 A. Guinan and E. Leichty, 2010, 'Tasteless Tablet'.

8 On the Amorites, see Aaron A. Burke, 2020, *The Amorites and the Bronze Age Near East*.

9 Unlike the name Hammu-rabi, which requires quite a bit of mental gymnastics to translate, the name 'Ammu-rapi has a clear meaning

with dynastic import given the king's Amorite origins. Among other things, the Amorites had a cult of dead ancestors, and Hammurapi's name reflects the importance of the past in furnishing the living with tools of legitimation. See Seth L. Sanders, 'Hammurabi, King of the Dead', *sethlsanders* (blog), 14 November 2019, https://sethlsanders. wordpress.com/2019/11/14/hammurapi-king-of-the-dead/

10 'CDLI Literary 000754 (Edubba A) Composite Artifact Entry', 2014, *Cuneiform Digital Library Initiative (CDLI)*, https://cdli.ucla. edu/P464238

11 A. Gadotti and A. Kleinerman, 2017, 'The Rules of the School'.

12 For a summary of the site, see Richard L. Zettler, 1997, 'Nippur'. See also Bernard Schneider, 2022, 'Nippur'.

13 Donald McCown, 1951, 'Nippur', p. 14.

14 Eleanor Robson, 2001, 'The Tablet House'.

15 See Eleanor Robson, 2008, *Mathematics in Ancient Iraq*, pp. 65–6 and pp. 110–15.

16 See also John P. Britton et al., 2011, 'Plimpton 322'.

17 Sophus Helle, 2023, *Enheduana*, p. ix.

18 Ibid, p. x.

19 See Rivkah Harris, 1962, 'Biographical Notes on the nadītu Women of Sippar', pp. 1–2.

20 See Brigitte Lion, 2001, 'Dame Inanna-ama-mu, scribe à Sippar'.

21 Victor Avigdor Hurowitz, 2000, 'Literary Observations on "In Praise of the Scribal Art"', p. 56.

22 Eventually, I sought help once again from Dr Jacob Dahl, who kindly walked me through every single syllable and endured listening to me practise my pronunciation over and over again.

23 The museum opted to air the latter.

24 Unless otherwise cited, all proverbs in this section come from Jeremy Black et al. (eds.), 1998–, *The Electronic Text Corpus of Sumerian Literature*, https://etcsl.orinst.ox.ac.uk/catalogue/catalogue6.htm

25 This bilingual proverb in Akkadian and Sumerian comes from the Library of Ashurbanipal. Jeremiah Peterson (ed.), 2014–, 'Bilinguals in Late Mesopotamian Scholarship: K. 5688', *The Open Richly Annotated Cuneiform Corpus*, http://oracc.org/blms/P396094

26 Irving L. Finkel and Jonathan Taylor, 2015, *Cuneiform*, figure 12.

27 Irving L. Finkel, 'Bettany Hughes and Irving Finkel discuss "The First Ghosts"', *YouTube*, 28 October 2021.

28 Ibid.

29 Jean-Pierre Grégoire, 1996, *Archives Administratives et Inscriptions Cunéiformes Ashmolean Museum*, vol. 1/1, plate 70.

6: The Cone of Kudur-Mabuk

1 Frauke Weiershäuser and Jamie Novotny, 2020, *The Royal Inscriptions of Amēl-Marduk (561–560 BC), Neriglissar (559–556 BC), and Nabonidus (555–539 BC), Kings of Babylon*, pp. 165–9.

2 Ibid.

3 Ibid., pp. 106–10.

4 Christina Tsouparopoulou, 2014, 'Hidden messages under the temple'.

5 See, for example, Seraina Nett, 2023, 'The Office and Responsibilities of the En Priestess of Nanna', pp. 112–14, and Penelope Weadock, 1958, *The Giparu at Ur*, pp. 8–10.

6 Frauke Weiershäuser and Jamie Novotny, 2020, *The Royal Inscriptions of Amēl-Marduk (561–560 BC), Neriglissar (559–556 BC), and Nabonidus (555–539 BC), Kings of Babylon*, p. 168.

7 Baptiste Fiette, 2020, '"King" Kudur-Mabuk'.

8 Douglas Frayne, 1990, *The Old Babylonian Period (2003–1595 BC)*, pp. 209–10.

9 Some clues suggest they came from the Zagros Mountains to the east, such as elements in the military titles they used that are referenced in cuneiform sources. The 'head of the cattle pen' was in charge of charioteers, the troops who rode horse-drawn chariots into battle, and they are mentioned alongside the 'kings of Kassite troops', another military title that indicated the highest level of authority. Based on a literal understanding of 'head of the cattle pen', it's possible that the charioteers were organised into units that travelled with herds (some were actually paid in sheep). The link between cattle and chariotry may suggest a way of life based on herding prior to settling in Babylonia or at a military structure shaped by the ecology of the grasslands of the Zagros Mountains. See Helen Malko, 2020, 'The Kassites of Babylonia', p. 183.

10 Everyday documents, like receipts or military records, make the same distinction, by designating certain individuals or troops as hailing from the land of the Kassites. See, for example, Takayoshi Oshima, 2012, 'Another Attempt at Two Kassite Royal Inscriptions', p. 242. See also Helen Malko, 2020, 'The Kassites of Babylonia', p. 183.

11 The Amarna archive also included educational texts, like the ones surveyed in the previous chapter. Lists of signs and words, bilingual dictionaries of words in Akkadian and Egyptian, and epic poems confirm that Egyptian scribes had mastered the diplomatic *lingua franca* of Akkadian and its script, cuneiform. See Izre'el Shlomo, 1997, *The Amarna Scholarly Tablets*.

12 Anson F. Rainey, 2015, *The El-Amarna Correspondence*, pp. 69–71. (The letter is known by the identifier 'EA 3'.)

13 Ibid., pp. 72–5. (The letter is known by the identifier 'EA 4'.)

14 Nils P. Heeßel, 2009, 'The Babylonian Physician Rabâ-ša-Marduk'.

15 See ibid.

16 See Izre'el Shlomo, 1997, *The Amarna Scholarly Tablets*. See also Matthew T. Rutz, 2016, 'Astral Knowledge in an International Age'.

17 For example, first-millennium BCE scholars often hark back to ancestry with Kassite names, and colophons – or signature sections – of scholarly works from the first millennium BCE invoke Kassite -period scholars. In letters to the king, later astronomers occasionally cite scholars from this era, such as a lengthy report from one named Akkullanu, who served two Neo-Assyrian kings, Esarhaddon and Ashurbanipal. Defending an interpretation of scanty rain that year as a sign of good health for the king, he cites a report written by an astronomer named Ea-mushallim, who lived at the end of the second millennium BCE and served under king Marduk-nadin-ahhe (Simo Parpola, *Letters from Assyrian and Babylonian Scholars*, Text 100). The evidence for an explosion of scholarly activity in the last half of the second millennium BCE is scattered but strong. See also Alan Lenzi, 2015, 'Mesopotamian Scholarship'.

18 Benjamin R. Foster, 2005, *Before the Muses*, vol. 1, p. 353.

19 Sally Freedman, 2017, *If a City Is Set on a Height*, vol. 3, p. 44.

20 For an overview of other omen compendia that deal with related

terrestrial and physiognomic observations, see Ulla Susanne Koch, 2015, *Mesopotamian Divination Texts.*

21 Jeremy A. Black et al., 1998–, 'Iddin-Dagan A', *The Electronic Text Corpus of Sumerian Literature*, https://etcsl.orinst.ox.ac.uk/section2/tr2531.htm

22 Simo Parpola, 1993, *Letters from Assyrian and Babylonian Scholars*, Text 51.

23 Ibid.

24 Nils P. Heeßel, 2018, 'Dating EAE', p. 254.

25 Erica Reiner and David Pingree, 1998, *Babylonian Planetary Omens*, p. 95.

26 Venus's 'crown' in planetary omens can actually have several interpretations depending on how it is used. See, for example, Erica Reiner and David Pingree, 1998, *Babylonian Planetary Omens*, p. 11.

27 Hermann Hunger, 1992, *Astrological Reports to Assyrian Kings*, Text 73.

28 Simo Parpola, 1993, *Letters from Assyrian and Babylonian Scholars*, Text 72.

29 Erica Reiner and David Pingree, 1998, *Babylonian Planetary Omens*, p. 47.

30 Ibid., p. 93.

31 See, for example, Lis Brack-Bernsen and John M. Steele, 2005, 'Eclipse Prediction and the Length of the Saros Cycle in Babylonian Astronomy'.

32 John Steele, 2011, 'Making Sense of Time'.

33 Benjamin Foster, 2005, *Before the Muses*, vol. 1, pp. 377–8.

34 On the development of the zodiac, see John M. Steele, 2018, 'The Development of the Babylonian Zodiac'.

35 See John Steele, 2019, 'The Early History of the Astronomical Diaries'.

36 Abraham J. Sachs and Hermann Hunger, 1996, *Astronomical Diaries and Related Texts from Babylonia*, vol. 3, No. 158.

37 Ibid., pp. 10–17.

38 Abraham J. Sachs and Hermann Hunger (ed.), 1988, *Astronomical Diaries and Related Texts from Babylonia*, vol. 1, Nos. 567 and 368.

39 Ibid., No. 322B. See Christopher Tuplin, 2019, 'Logging History in Achaemenid, Hellenistic and Parthian Babylonia', p. 81.

40 On the provenance of Late Babylonian scholarly texts, see Christine Proust and John Steele, 2019, 'Introduction', pp. 2–3.

41 Megan Gannon and Livescience, 'Babylonians Tracked Jupiter with Fancy Math, Tablet Reveals', *Scientific American*, 1 February 2016.

42 Douglas Frayne, 1990, *Old Babylonian Period (2003–1595 BC)*, pp. 209–10.

43 Ulla Koch-Westenholz, 2000, *Babylonian Liver Omens*, p. 440.

44 Ibid., p. 423.

45 Ulla Koch-Westenholz, 2002, 'Old Babylonian Extispicy Reports', pp. 134–5.

46 Seth Richardson, 2002, 'Ewe Should Be So Lucky', p. 237.

47 Simo Parpola, 1993, *Letters from Assyrian and Babylonian Scholars*, Text 179. See also Eckart Frahm, 2023, *Assyria*, pp. 265–6.

48 Jack M. Sasson, 2015, *From the Mari Archives*, p. 273.

49 For this particular example, see Daniel C. Snell, 1974, 'The Mari Livers and the Omen Tradition', p. 119.

7: The Boundary Stone

1 See S. Paulus, 2014, *Die babylonischen Kudurru-Inschriften*, pp. 325–34.

2 See Cyril J. Gadd and Léon Legrain, *Royal Inscriptions*, pp. 50–51 (Text 165). See also Kathryn E. Slanski, 2003, *The Babylonian Entitlement* narûs (kudurrus), p. 306.

3 David Prest, 'Royal Archive documents revealed at Windsor Castle', *BBC News*, 16 May 2014.

4 Kathryn E. Slanski, 2003, *The Babylonian Entitlement* narûs (kudurrus), pp. 75–9.

5 Ibid., pp. 48–53.

6 Marten Stol, 2000, *Birth in Babylonia and the Bible*, p. 28. The letter is now in the collections of the Iraq Museum with the identifier IM 5641.

7 Robert K. Englund, 2009, 'The Smell of the Cage', Sections §3.4 and §3.6.2.

8 See the Appendix of Robert K. Englund, 2009, 'The Smell of the Cage'.

NOTES

9 J.N. Reid, 2015, 'Runaways and Fugitive-Catchers during the Third Dynasty of Ur', p. 576.

10 J.N. Reid, 2014, 'Slavery in Early Mesopotamia from Late Uruk until the Fall of Babylon in the *Longue Durée*', p. 18.

11 Heather D. Baker, 2001, 'Degrees of Freedom', p. 23.

12 For example, in 532 BCE, one slave was apprenticed to another for seven months to learn how to become a baker. Another was apprenticed for four years to a seal-cutter of the crown prince Cambyses. Both examples are cited in Heather D. Baker, 2001, 'Degrees of Freedom', p. 23.

13 See Gauthier Tolini, 2013, 'The Economic Activities of Isḫunnatu'. See also Sophie Démare-Lafont, 2016, 'Women at Work in Mesopotamia', p. 318 n44.

14 Jerrold S. Cooper, 2016, 'The Job of Sex', p. 218.

15 J.N. Reid, 2014, 'Slavery in Early Mesopotamia from Late Uruk until the Fall of Babylon in the *Longue Durée*', p. 97.

16 J.N. Reid, 2020, 'Prisoners of War'.

17 Cited and translated in Raymond Westbrook, 1995, 'Slave and Master in Ancient Near Eastern Law', p. 1642. The tablet is in the collections of the Vorderasiatisches Museum in Berlin with the identifier VAT 7548.

18 Various readings of the names in earlier articles may cause some confusion. See Yoram Cohen, 2005, 'Feet of Clay at Emar', pp. 165–6.

19 Yoram Cohen, 2005, 'Feet of Clay at Emar', p. 165 n6.

20 See also Carlo Zaccagnini, 1994, 'Feet of Clay at Emar and Elsewhere'.

21 Or, to revisit the words of Dr J. Nicholas Reid, 'lower-stratum workers and households are left without a voice, except the voice that was provided for them by the elite' (J.N. Reid, 2015, 'Runaways and Fugitive-Catchers during the Third Dynasty of Ur', pp. 579–80).

22 Laws of Hammurabi §15–16, translated in Martha T. Roth, 1997, *Law Collections from Mesopotamia and Asia Minor*, p. 84. Those who return a runaway receive a reward of 2 shekels of silver (Laws of Hammurabi §17, Martha T. Roth, 1997, *Law Collections from Mesopotamia and Asia Minor*, p. 84).

23 Laws of Hammurabi §19, translated in Martha T. Roth, 1997, *Law Collections from Mesopotamia and Asia Minor*, p. 85.

24 J.N. Reid, 2014, 'Slavery in Early Mesopotamia from Late Uruk until the Fall of Babylon in the *Longue Durée*', p. 152.

25 Ibid., p. 169. The text is currently in the British Museum with the identifier BM 23165.

26 Unfortunately, the text does not preserve the person's name. See M. Molina and M. Such-Gutiérrez, 2004. 'On Terms for Cutting Plants and Noses in Ancient Sumer', p. 7.

27 This may alternatively have served as a metaphor for 'detain' without any literal nose piercing. See J.N. Reid, 2014, 'Slavery in Early Mesopotamia from Late Uruk until the Fall of Babylon in the *Longue Durée*', p. 168. See also Manuel Molina and Marcos Such-Gutiérrez, 'On Terms for Cutting Plants and Noses in Ancient Sumer', pp. 7–9.

28 The text is currently in the John Rylands Library with the identifier JRL 541, and is translated in J.N. Reid, 2014, 'Slavery in Early Mesopotamia from Late Uruk until the Fall of Babylon in the *Longue Durée*', p. 117.

29 For the available documentation related to La-Tubashinni, see Shalom E. Holtz, 2014, *Neo-Babylonian Trial Records*, pp. 182–197. See also Cornelia Wunsch, 1997/98, 'Und die Richter berieten', pp. 62–7, and Heather D. Baker, 2001, 'Degrees of Freedom', p. 21.

30 Lynn-Salammbô Zimmerman, 2023, 'Wooden Wax-Covered Writing Boards as Vorlage for *kudurru* Inscriptions in the Middle Babylonian Period', pp. 56–7.

31 William B. Hafford, 2019, 'The Royal Cemetery of Ur', p. 204.

32 Ibid.

33 C. Leonard Woolley, 1929, *Ur of the Chaldees*, p. 53.

34 Or perhaps someone else, as the connection of this room to Puabi's tomb remains unclear. See Richard Zettler and Paul C. Zimmerman, 2021, 'Two Tombs or Three?'

35 Ibid., pp. 285–6.

36 This grave is known as 'PG 1237'. For a discussion of the people buried there, see Massimo Vidale, 2011, 'PG 1237, Royal Cemetery of Ur'.

37 Palmiro Notizia, 2020, 'Wealth and Status in 3rd Millennium Babylonia', pp. 85–6.

38 Ibid., p. 88.

39 For a translation of this tablet, see Palmiro Notizia, 2020, 'Wealth and Status in 3rd Millennium Babylonia', pp. 100–102.

40 Palmiro Notizia, 2020, 'Wealth and Status in 3rd Millennium Babylonia', p. 93.

41 All excerpts are from Jacob Lauinger, 2020, 'The Electronic Idrimi', *The Open Richly Annotated Cuneiform Corpus*.

42 See Hélène Maloigne, 2017, 'How Idrimi came to London', pp. 203–4.

43 Morgens Trolle Larsen, 2015, *Ancient Kanesh*, pp. 169–240.

44 See Anita Fattori, 2021, 'Anatolian Women'.

45 Morgens Trolle Larsen, 1988, 'Old Assyrian Texts', p. 93.

46 Mathilde Touillon-Ricci, 2018, 'Trade and Contraband in Ancient Assyria', *The British Museum Blog* (blog), 2 April 2018.

47 Ibid.

48 Ibid.

49 The tablet is currently in the British Museum collections with the identifier BM 091022.

50 See Irving L. Finkel and Alexandra Fletcher, 2016, 'Thinking Outside the Box', p. 245.

51 Kathryn E. Slanski, 2003, *The Babylonian Entitlement* narûs *(kudur-rus)*, pp. 48–50.

52 Ibid., pp. 44–5.

53 Ibid., pp. 115–16.

8: The Mace Head

1 Dunya Mikhail, 2013, 'The Iraqi Nights'.

2 Andrew George, *The Babylonian Gilgamesh Epic*, vol. 1, p. 637.

3 Jeremy A. Black and Anthony Green, 2004, *Gods, Demons, and Symbols of Ancient Mesopotamia*, pp. 35–6.

4 Jeremy A. Black et al., 1998–, 'The Exploits of Ninurta', *The Electronic Text Corpus of Sumerian Literature*, https://etcsl.orinst.ox.ac.uk/section1/tr162.htm

5 C. Leonard Woolley, 1934, *Ur Excavations, vol 2*, p. 49.

6 Jeremy Black et al. (eds.), 1998–, 'The Death of Ur-Namma (Ur-Namma A): a version from Nippur', *The Electronic Text Corpus of Sumerian Literature*, https://etcsl.orinst.ox.ac.uk/section2/tr2411.htm. I note that Ur-Namma is an alternative spelling for the king's name, but we will stick with Ur-Nammu in this book.

7 Tzvi Abusch and Daniel Schwemer, 2016, *Corpus of Mesopotamian Anti-Witchcraft Rituals*, vol. 2, p. 256.

8 Marham J. Geller, 2016, *Healing Magic and Evil Demons*, pp. 268–9.

9 Douglas Frayne, 2008, *Presargonic Period*, p. 131.

10 Ibid., pp. 194–9. Quite a number of sources from this era memorialise this conflict, from boundary stones and stelae to cones and jars, across the reigns of several kings. For a reconstruction of the events based on such primary sources, see Jerrold S. Cooper, 2002, *Reconstructing History from Ancient Inscriptions*. For a recent archaeological analysis, see Carrie Hritz, 2021, 'The Umma-Lagash Border Conflict'.

11 A. Kirk Grayson, 1987, *Assyrian Rulers of the Third and Second Millennia BC (to 1115 BC)*, p. 234.

12 A. Kirk Grayson, 1991, *Assyrian Rulers of the Early First Millennium BC (1114–859 BC)*, p. 14.

13 Anne Porter et al., 2021, '"Their corpses will reach the base of heaven"'.

14 Augusta McMahon et al., 2011, 'Late Chalcolithic mass graves at Tell Brak, Syria', p. 203.

15 This structure actually turned out to be a large administrative building rather than a royal palace. See David Oates and Joan Oates, 1989, 'Akkadian Buildings at Tell Brak', p. 193.

16 Augusta McMahon, 'Tell Brak', p. 79.

17 Ibid., p. 80.

18 Anne Porter et al., 2021, '"Their corpses will reach the base of heaven"', p. 915.

19 Steven Garfinkle, 2020, 'Violence and State Power in Early Mesopotamia', p. 223.

20 Simo Parpola, 1987, *The Correspondence of Sargon II, Part I*, Text 193.

21 Far from a clean break with previous periods, the kings of this era sought to connect themselves with their forebears by taking throne

names – the name a king gets upon ascending the throne – and royal titles of earlier rulers. Some even called themselves 'king of the world' in an attempt to copy the self-presentation of their ancestors, a title that would not be too far from reality within a few generations (Eckart Frahm, 2023, *Assyria*, p. 92). The empire's capital during the second millennium BCE was Assur, named for their supreme god (pronounced Ashur). The king in ancient Assyria had to comply with all the usual expectations of a king in ancient Mesopotamia, but unlike earlier rulers, he was also the highest priest to the god Assur with some added pressures. On elements of Assyrian royal ideology, see Shana Zaia, 'Divine Foundations', pp. 115–17.

22 Jamie Novotny and Joshua Jeffers, 2018, *The Royal Inscriptions of Ashurbanipal (668–631 BC), Aššur-Etel-Ilāni (630–627 BC), and Sîn-Šarra-Iškun (626–612 BC), Kings of Assyria, Part 1*, pp. 347–9.

23 For the star planisphere, see M. Willis Monroe, 2022, 'Astronomical and astrological diagrams from cuneiform sources', pp. 346–8. For examples of medical texts, see 'The Nineveh Medical Project', *The Open Richly Annotated Cuneiform Corpus*. The letters referenced are from Simo Parpola, 1993, *Letters from Assyrian and Babylonian Scholars*, Text 187, and M. Luukko and G. Van Buylaere, 2002, *The Political Correspondence of Esarhaddon*, Text 28.

24 Thousands of administrative texts show that the ruler was supported by a vast network of personnel stationed throughout the immense territory. The empire was divided into provinces and run by about 100–120 governors and delegates known as *rabbûte*, literally the 'Great Ones' of Assyria – usually translated with the English word 'magnates'. The king also relied heavily on the Palace Scribe and the commander-in-chief of the army. See Raija Mattila, 2000, *The King's Magnates*, and Karen Radner, 2011, 'Royal decision-making'.

25 See Karen Radner, 2014, 'An Imperial Communication Network'.

26 Unearthed in nearby Egypt, a tattered leaf of brown papyrus preserves in black ink a form of writing known as Demotic, a cursive version of Egyptian hieroglyphs. Interrupted only by the occasional tear, the story inked on the papyrus tells how several parties travelled to Babylon to convince Shamash-shumu-ukin to return to Nineveh and make peace with his brother, Ashurbanipal, but to no avail.

Instead, Shamash-shumu-ukin built a dwelling made of sticks, tar, and bitumen that he proceeded to set alight. He died in the fire he started, and the text ends with Ashurbanipal's grief after begging for his brother's life. 'Let them slay Babylon,' he had apparently told his general, 'but spare my brother!' Interestingly, both Ashurbanipal's (admittedly vague but contemporary) royal inscriptions and the later papyrus record mention death by fire, but the episode remains shrouded in mystery. See Shana Zaia, 2019, 'My Brother's Keeper: Assurbanipal versus Šamaš-šuma-ukīn'.

27 See, for example, Jamie Novotny and Joshua Jeffers, 2018, *The Royal Inscriptions of Ashurbanipal (668–631 BC), Aššur-Etel-Ilāni (630–627 BC), and Sîn-Šarra-Iškun (626–612 BC), Kings of Assyria, Part 1*, p. 158.

28 Eckart Frahm, 2023, *Assyria*, p. 279.

29 Eckart Frahm, 2019, 'The Neo-Assyrian Royal Inscriptions as Text', p. 139.

30 Lori Hinnant, 'Turning Iraq history into rubble, leaving the mess to looters', *AP News*, 31 December 2016.

31 Jonathan Jones, '"Some of the most appalling images ever created" – I Am Ashurbanipal review', *Guardian*, 6 November 2018.

32 Zainab Bahrani, 2004, 'The King's Head', p. 115.

33 John Malcom Russell, 1999, *The Writing on the Wall*, pp. 170–71.

34 Augusta McMahon et al., 2011, 'Late Chalcolithic mass graves at Tell Brak, Syria', p. 202.

35 Diana Pickworth, 2005, 'Excavations at Nineveh', p. 310.

36 Yosef Garfinkel et al., 2019, 'Lachish Fortifications and State Formation'.

37 For more details on logistics, weaponry, and personnel, see Stephanie Dalley, 2017, 'Assyrian Warfare'.

38 Manfried Dietrich, 2003, *The Babylonian Correspondence of Sargon and Sennacherib*, Text 152.

39 For example, Sargon II ordered the governor of the Ṣupat province to provide bread and food for chariot troops, including of course their horses, and in one case, far more grain than seems to have been agreed upon was taken from a silo without his permission. Simo Parpola, 1987, *The Correspondence of Sargon II*, Text 181.

40 Simo Parpola, 1987, *The Correspondence of Sargon II*, Text 175.

9: *Ennigaldi-Nanna*

1 See '#0040470', '#0040148', '#0040508', and '#0040156', *Online Corpus of the Inscriptions of Ancient North Arabia.*

2 See '#40238', ibid. See also '#0040508', ibid.

3 He holds a staff and, this time, he faces four divine symbols rather than three, including the usual suspects from other stelae (Sîn, Ishtar, and Shamash) plus an image of a snake-like loop that may have been connected to contemporary local deities. A badly damaged cuneiform inscription runs for 20 lines that include, about halfway through, the words 'Nabonidus, king of Babylon'. See Arnulf Hausleiter and Hanspeter Schaudig, 2016, 'Rock Relief and Cuneiform Inscription of Nabonidus'.

4 For a relatively recent collection of studies on the Cyrus Cylinder, as well as an edition of the cuneiform text, see Irving Finkel (ed.), 2013, *The Cyrus Cylinder.*

5 Frauke Weiershäuser and Jamie Novotny, 2020, *The Royal Inscriptions of Amēl-Marduk (561–560 BC), Neriglissar (559–556 BC), and Nabonidus (555–539 BC), Kings of Babylon*, p. 27.

6 Ibid., pp. 167–8.

7 Paul-Alain Beaulieu, 1989, *The Reign of Nabonidus*, p. 119. For the reasoning behind identifying 'king's daughter' with Ennigaldi-Nanna, see also Paul-Alain Beaulieu, 2021, 'The City of Ur and the Neo-Babylonian Empire', p. 162.

8 Paul-Alain Beaulieu, 2021, 'The City of Ur and the Neo-Babylonian Empire', p. 162.

9 Ibid., pp. 163–4.

10 The earliest possible physical remains of an *en*-priestess, however, may come from a death pit in the Royal Cemetery of Ur. See William B. Hafford, 2019, 'The Royal Cemetery of Ur', p. 218. For Ninmetabbari, see Penelope Weadock, 1975, 'The Giparu at Ur', p. 105 n40.

11 Alhena Gadotti, 'Mesopotamian Women's Cultic Roles', *Women in Antiquity*, p. 68. The omen and subsequent appointment of the priestess carried such importance that kings sometimes named the relevant year or years of their rule after these events. The fifteenth

year of the reign of King Shulgi, for example, gets its name from his daughter, En-nirza-ana, being 'chosen by extispicy', and the seventeenth year was the year that she 'was installed' as the high priestess. These year names appear on administrative texts from the Ur III period as part of date formulae, as part of the dates themselves. See also Seraina Nett, 2023, 'The Office and Responsibilities of the En Priestess of Nanna'.

12 Cited in Alhena Gadotti, 2016, 'Mesopotamian Women's Cultic Roles', p. 69.

13 Joan Goodnick Westenholz, 1989, 'Enheduanna, En-Priestess, Hen of Nanna, Spouse of Nanna', p. 554.

14 Douglas Frayne, 1993, *Sargonic and Gutian Periods (2334–2113 BC)*, pp. 35–6.

15 Irene J. Winter, 2010, *On Art in the Ancient Near East*, vol. 2, pp. 68–9.

16 Douglas Frayne, 1990, *Old Babylonian Period ((2003–1595 BC)*, pp. 300–301.

17 Jeremiah Peterson, 2016, 'The Literary Corpus of the Old Babylonian Larsa Dynasties', pp. 34–8.

18 Another possible interpretation is that the priestess was an earthly embodiment of the moon god's wife, Ningal. Either way, this role carried responsibilities towards Ningal herself as well as towards the moon god.

19 Penelope N. Weadock, 1958, *The Giparu at Ur*, pp. 83–4.

20 Ibid.

21 Douglas Frayne, 1990, *Old Babylonian Period ((2003–1595 BC)*, p. 229.

22 Cited in Joan Goodnick Westenholz, 1989, 'Enheduanna, En-Priestess, Hen of Nanna, Spouse of Nanna', p. 548.

23 Penelope N. Weadock, 1958, *The Giparu at Ur*, p. 4.

24 See Douglas Frayne, 1990, *Old Babylonian Period (2003–1595 BC)*, pp. 224–31.

25 Frauke Weiershäuser and Jamie Novotny, 2020, *The Royal Inscriptions of Amēl-Marduk (561–560 BC), Neriglissar (559–556 BC), and Nabonidus (555–539 BC), Kings of Babylon*, p. 168.

26 See Stephanie Dalley et al., 1976, *The Old Babylonian Tablets from Tell Al Rimah*.

27 Cited in Cécile Michel, 2020, 'Wool Trade in Upper Mesopotamia and Syria According to Old Babylonian and Old Assyrian Texts', p. 250 n152.

28 See Jack M. Sasson, 2015, *From the Mari Archives*, p. 283, p. 153 n89, and p. 331.

29 See J.J. Finkelstein, 1976, 'Šilip rēmim and Related Matters', pp. 190–191.

30 Howard Farber, 2021, *An Examination of Prices and Wages in Babylonia*, p. 152.

31 The relevant law reads, 'If a man gives his child for suckling and for rearing but does not give the food, oil, and clothing rations (to the caregiver) for 3 years, he shall weigh and deliver 10 shekels of silver for the cost of the rearing of his child, and he shall take away his child.' Laws of Eshnunna §32, translated in Martha T. Roth, 1997, *Law Collections from Mesopotamia and Asia Minor*, p. 64. Law collections like this one also give details about the rations and pay owed to a wet-nurse. On wet-nurses, see Sophie Démare-Lafont, 'Women at Work in Mesopotamia', pp. 319–23.

32 Rivkah Harris, 1975, *Ancient Sippar*, p. 30.

33 Ibid., p. 311.

34 See Howard Farber, 2021, *An Examination of Prices and Wages in Babylonia*, p. 136, in which he also notes that over half of the surviving cuneiform contracts for the rental of houses in Sippar show a *naditum* as lessor. They also appear as buyers in over half of the surviving cuneiform contracts that record the sale of houses in the city (Rivkah Harris, 1975, *Ancient Sippar*, p. 311).

35 Rivkah Harris, 1963, 'The Organization and Administration of the Cloister in Ancient Babylonia', p. 139.

36 Bertrand Lafont, 2016, 'Women at Work and Women in Economy and Society during the Neo-Sumerian Period'.

37 On average, women were given 30–40 litres per month, whereas men started at 60 litres and were paid up to 300. See Bertrand Lafont, 2016, 'Women at Work and Women in Economy and Society during the Neo-Sumerian Period', p. 163. See also Marc Van De Mieroop, 1989, 'Women in the Economy of Sumer', p. 64.

38 Cécile Michel, 2020, *Women of Assur and Kanesh*, p. 268 (Letter 165).

39 Ibid., pp. 268–70 (Letter 166).

40 Ibid., pp. 239–40 (Letter 147).

41 Cécile Michel, 2016, 'Estimating an Old Assyrian Household Textile Production'.

42 Cécile Michel, 2020, *Women of Assur and Kanesh*, pp. 274–5 (Letter 170).

43 Ibid., pp. 298–9 (Letter 196).

44 Ibid., pp. 299–300 (Letter 197).

45 See Cornelia Wunsch, 2003, 'Women's Property and Law of Inheritance in the Neo-Babylonian Period', p. 1 n1.

46 Discussed in Yoko Watai, 2016, 'Economic Activities of Women in 1st Millennium Babylonia', p. 499.

47 JoAnn Scurlock, 2014, *Sourcebook for Ancient Mesopotamian Medicine*, pp. 602–3.

48 All references in this paragraph come from Natalie Naomi May, 2018, 'Female Scholars in Mesopotamia?', pp. 152–4.

49 Blind musicians, some designated as male and some as female, appear in numerous records, including ration lists from the southern Mesopotamian cities of Umma and Girsu, so we at least know that Shinunutum was not unique in her pursuit, voluntary or otherwise, of a career in music. See Eric J. Harvey, 'The Songbird', *All of Us* (blog), 11 May 2020, https://allofusdha.org/research/the-songbird-linking-music-and-blindness-in-ancient-babylonia/

50 Ibid.

51 Ibid.

Epilogue: Between Us and Them

1 John Steele and Srishti Ganguli, 'Babylonian records of transient astronomical phenomena', Section 5.9.

2 Ibid.

Index